Bone Builders™

Over 150 Lowfat Calcium-Rich Recipes

Plus Important New Information

- How calcium can save your life.
- What foods interfere with calcium absorption.
- How to get enough calcium even with milk allergies.
- Why your teen needs extra calcium.
- How to make sure your baby gets a good calcium start.
- How to pick the right calcium supplement.
- Why osteoporosis is the #4 cause of death among women.
- Why a broken bone can kill you.
- If your family history is working for or against you.
- How calcium may lower your blood pressure.
- How calcium may reduce your risk for colon cancer.
- When to get a bone density test.
- How estrogen can help replace lost bone.
- How to gain the calcium and lose the fat.
- How a visit to the dentist could save your life.
- What exercises can build up your bone mass.
- How to be a vegetarian and still get loads of calcium.
- What common medications block calcium.
- What favorite snacks are calcium robbers . . . and more!

Other Books
by
Edita M. Kaye

My Little Fountain of Youth Book

*Everything You Wanted To Know About PVD
And Didn't Know Who To Ask*

Medicare Money

Managing & Marketing Your Refractive Surgery Practice

Healthcare Joint Ventures

Bone Builders™

The Complete Lowfat Cookbook
Plus Calcium Health Guide

REVISED EDITION

Edita M. Kaye

WARNER BOOKS

A Time Warner Company

Important: Please Read Carefully

The information, ideas, suggestions and answers to questions in this book are not intended to substitute for the services of a physician. You should only undertake a health and wellness modification program in conjunction with the services of a qualified health professional. This book is intended as a reference guide only, not as a manual for self-treatment. If you suspect you have a medical problem or have questions, please talk to your health care professional. All the information here is based on research available at the time of this printing.

Warner Books Edition
© 1995 by Fountain of Youth Group, Inc.
All rights reserved.
No part of this book may be reproduced or utilized in any form or by any means, electronic or mechanical, including photocopying, recording, or any information storage or retrieval system, without permission in writing from the Publisher.

This Warner Books edition is published by arrangement with the Author.
Warner Books, Inc. 1271 Avenue of the Americas, New York, NY 10020

W A Time Warner Company

Printed in the United States of America

First Warner Books Printing: June 1996
1 2 3 4 5 6 7 8 9 10

Library of Congress Cataloging-In-Publication Data
Kaye, Edita M.
        Bone Builders: the complete lowfat cookbook plus calcium health guide.
Edita M. Kaye–(Rev. Ed.)
        p. Cm.
        Originally published under the title: Bone builders cookbook.
        ISBN 0-446-67247-5
        1. High-calcium diet–Recipes. 2. Low-fat diet–Recipes.
I. Kaye, Edita M. Bone builders cookbook. II. Title.
RM237.56.K39 1996   95–52716
613. 2 8–dc20   CIP

Bone Builders™
is dedicated to
all women
in the hope that
we can live longer, healthier lives.

I Want To Hear From You

I wrote this book for myself, my family and most of all, for all of you. Please let me know if you have any questions, comments or suggestions and I will do my best to answer and with your help, keep improving *Bone Builders*™ so that it is the very best it can be.

Write to me
Edita Kaye,
c/o Bone Builders™
830-13 A1A North, Suite 313,
Ponte Vedra Beach, Florida 32082

Thank You Page

Nobody can ever complete a massive project such as this without the help, support, encouragement, love and prayers of a lot of very special people. I would like to take this space to thank those who were there for me and to say that without their help, prayers, and love this book would not have been such a joy and adventure to write.

Thanks to **Hugh Barber, M.D.** for taking the time and interest to review the manuscript for *Bone Builders*™ and make valuable suggestions and comments and for believing in the project enough to contribute a thoughtful and positive preface.

My thanks go to **Gerry Scanlon**, my favorite Irishman, for the good times.

Thanks to **Pam Mycoskie,** author of ***Butter Busters The Cookbook,*** and ***I'm Listening*** for her generosity, enthusiasm, and moral support. Pam was there for me more times than I can count, with a supportive phone call or a wonderful prayer which got me through many difficult times. Pam was also the pioneer in whose footsteps I followed. She gave me the courage to publish *BONE BUILDERS*™ myself. And then it was Pam who introduced me to the wonderful people at Warner Books who made this edition possible. God Bless You, Pam!

I also want to thank another remakable woman and friend, **Bonnie Johnson.** Bonnie was my very first customer and bought 11 copies of *Bone Builders*™. She was with me during the early excitement of interviews, booksignings and talk shows. Bonnie helped me cook in hotel rooms, in cramped bathrooms and once, even in a train. She never failed to smile, to encourage and to inspire. It was her talent in decorating a humble booth at a major trade show that helped bring *Bone Builders*™ to the attention of many distinguished publishers and ultimately to Warner's. I feel truly blessed having Bonnie in my life.

Thanks to **Mark**, a son to be proud of and a good friend besides.

Thanks to my sister, **Marg**, who will always be #1 with me.

I would also like to thank my wonderful friends and spiritual leaders at the Sawgrass Chapel. The sunrise services overlooking the ocean, the smiles, the hugs, the messages of inspiration filled me with faith and love. I hope that some of this love has written itself into the pages of this book.

Thanks to the wonderful library system of St. John's county and the very special people at the Ponte Vedra Beach branch. My grateful appreciation to **Mary Jane Little, Doug Cisney, Cheryl Hirschi, Marilyn Alberti, and Ellen Davis.**

I would like to thank **Mel Parker** and **Susan Suffes** at Warner Books. Their generosity, talent, committment and enthusiam has made my work on this, the Warner edition, a particular joy. It is very rewarding for an author to be associated with such stellar professionals and to be able to count them as friends.

I would be very remiss if I didn't extend my most heartfelt thanks to my attorney, **Mark Lawless,** who never failed to offer me excellent advice and encouragement.

Thanks also to **David MacDonald** and **Jeff Mayzurk** of Arion Software and MasterCook Mac. These remarkable folks developed the nutritional analysis program and reviewed every recipe.

And a special thanks to all the companies that shared their lowfat calcium-rich recipes and helped me share them with you. They are good folks.

Table of Contents

The Calcium Part

What You Should Know About Calcium

Osteoporosis

Is There Anything On The Downside?

Calcium Robbers

Your Children & Calcium

Pregnancy & Calcium

Menopause & Calcium

Men & Calcium

Nutrients & Calcium

Calcium Supplements

Lactose Intolerance & Milk Allergy

Vegetarians

Calcium & Exercise

The Nutrition Part

Dairy Foods

Soybeans & Tofu

The Food Adventure

The Cookbook Part

Calcium-Rich Breakfasts

Appetizers

Soups

Salads

Side Dishes

Main Courses

Desserts

Snacks

Drinks

The Resources Part

How To Use This Book

Welcome to ***Bone Builders***™! I have tried to make this book as practical, informative, and easy-to-use as I could. There is something in these pages for everyone, whether you are looking for information about calcium, whether you want a reference guide that can answer many of your calcium questions, or whether you want to start whipping up the over 150 tasty recipes and start getting loads more calcium in a healthy, lowfat way.

The book is divided into several parts:

<u>The Calcium Part</u> gives you up-to-date information about calcium and your health.This is a must-read if you want to learn how to fight osteoporosis, cancer, heart disease, high-blood pressure and other threats to your health and the health of your loved ones and family.

<u>The Nutrition Part</u> gives you tips on how to shop, eat-out, and select lowfat, high-calcium foods whether you are lactose intolerant, a vegetarian or a meat and potatoes person. Plus there are dozens of hints and tips on how to make calcium a daily nutritional choice.

<u>The Cookbook Part</u> gives you over 150 yummy, nutritious, recipes that are high in calcium and low in fat. There are new recipes to try out, and old favorites made calcium-richer. You and your family will love them. And as an added bonus they are easy to make—a big plus for busy cooks.

<u>The Resources Part</u> tells you where to get more information, gives you your own personal calcium counter and also gives you detailed nutritional analyses of each recipe in the cookbook.

I hope you have as much pleasure from reading this book, using it, and enjoying the recipes as I have had in putting it all together for you.

To your good health!

A Woman's Prayer

Our deepest fear is not that we are inadequate.

Our deepest fear is that we are powerful beyond measure.

It is our light, not our darkness, that frightens us.

We ask ourselves, who am I to be brilliant, gorgeous, talented and fabulous?

Actually, who are you <u>not</u> to be?

You are a child of God.

Anonymous

Preface
by
Hugh R. K. Barber, M.D.

Professor of Clinical Obstetrics & Gynecology at Cornell University
Medical College, New York
Director, Department of Obstetrics & Gynecology at Lenox Hill Hospital,
New York
Editor, Female Patient Journal

This book is truly the ABC of the many contributions that calcium makes to a variety of organs and to maintaining a lifestyle that is marked by good health and longevity.

It is a book that should be read in its entirety. There may be a tendency to skip over the first part to get to the outstanding number of lowfat, calcium-rich recipes but this would deny the reader an extensive understanding of the metabolic and physiologic mechanisms of calcium. This is more–namely, it is a reference book to which a physician or health care provider can turn as he or she searches for an answer about calcium.

It is not an overstatement to say that it is a book that supplies all you need to know about calcium. The purpose of this book is not to take the place of standard textbooks but to serve as an extension of the material found in those textbooks. It covers the many facets of calcium without diluting the individual topic. It is structured so that the busy clinician, who shares the major burden of patient care, can keep abreast of the wide applications of calcium therapy for improving the health care of patients. The aim of the book is to present the basic and practical aspects of calcium in a readable format.

Edita M. Kaye has made the material in the book concise without being superficial and it will serve as an overall framework in which new knowledge will be placed and then used in the delivery of health care to women.

The author has borrowed freely from the literature and has included outstanding research and a credible bibliography. In addition, she has achieved simplicity of style, brevity, and clarity.

The author discusses the role of osteoporosis and cancer in the health care of women and does emphasize that the role of calcium affects all disciplines of medicine. She repeatedly states with documentation that calcium should be added as a supplement very early in life. It protects against many diseases and by doing

this can bring the person into menopause with an excellent bone mass, providing protection against those conditions that can be a bone robber.

The different parts of the book are well arranged and it leads from the beginning, getting to know calcium, on up through how new calcium research can help, provides ways of telling whether you are getting enough calcium and the signs and symptoms if there is a calcium deficiency. From time to time, the author presents a quiz that is well designed and adds a new dimension to the presentation.

In a very concise but accurate way, the author presents diagnostic wonders and what can be done immediately to correct bone loss. With courage, she even takes a peek into the future and does this in a very easy but readable, manner.

She constantly points out what food substances can block the absorption of calcium and often provides ways to circumvent this. She accurately presents material on the fetus and calcium, what the requirements are, and how they can best be obtained.

Edita M. Kaye has presented material supporting the use of nutrients as a supplement to calcium therapy. There are many surprises for the health care provider in the presentation when she discusses potassium, magnesium, zinc, vitamin D, vitamin C and other supplements with charts giving the recommended daily allowances.

When she discusses calcium supplements, she accurately reports that the faster they dissolve the better the body absorbs them and she says that to test your own supplement all that is necessary is to drop one of the supplements into a glass of vinegar. If it hasn't dissolved after 30 minutes, it isn't being absorbed fast enough.

When discussing exercise, she has a pithy heading which says, "Use It Or Lose It."

Her material on lactose intolerance and allergies is well presented.

The part of the book called "The Nutrition Part" is excellent. She discusses the calcium in foods and presents it in a readable format. She has tips for identifying the value of milk, storing and handling it, as well as ways to structure breakfast, lunch, dinner and snacks so as to provide the best possible lifestyle. There is one section entititled "Add A Little Yogurt To Your Life," and she outlines how to do this. She also states and gives the reference that yogurt eaters have 25% fewer colds and that yogurt may boost the immune system by aiding in the production of gamma interferon.

Constantly there are one-liners that are truly medical pearls and add to the joy of reading this interesting presentation.

The last part is entitled "The Cookbook." It is fascinating that there are more than 150 lowfat, calcium-rich recipes, and many of them have a little editorial pearl at the end of the recipe. For example, in the recipe "Pineapple Carrot Raisin Muffins" there is a pearl that states that "Studies show that calcium is an antioxidant. Add the 20,000 IU of betacarotene from carrots in this recipe and you have major protection from premature aging and disease." At the end of one recipe she states that the two minerals most deficient in American women's diets are calcium and iron. At the end of another, she states that calcium boosts brain power. This whole section is enriched by medical pearls. Having read through all of the recipes, one's appetite is stirred to the point where plans are made to try them one after another.

The book should be of interest to all health care workers, including medical students, residents, postgraduate fellows, physicians in practice and the general public which has so much interest in subjects relating to medicine. The lay public will find that it has brought the science of calcium together in one book for the benefit of the patient and at the same time it has been able to lighten the work of the busy physician.

The book qualifies as an outline for each physician's continuing medical education. Every aspect of the book is a plus and the only negative may be that it should have been written at least 15 years ago.

Hugh R. K. Barber, M.D.

Introduction

My name is Edita Kaye and I would like to tell you why I wrote this book.

I grew up during a time, not so very long ago, when few of us thought about the relationship between what we ate and how we felt. We were always devastated when we heard that someone had a heart attack, or developed cancer, or had a stroke. . .but we really didn't make the leap between those deadly diseases and the good times that in my family were breakfast, lunch and dinner. Our kitchen was where I grew up, and food was the glue that bound our family and friends together.

This was also the time when my mother and her friends would sit around a table drinking coffee and smoking cigarettes in that quiet afternoon hour before the kids came home from school. They would talk and tell each other how women outlived men because they were "stronger" and had some sort of divine protection. Women, it was widely believed, didn't get heart attacks. Cancer was some random toss of the dice. And nobody had even heard of osteoporosis, much less worried about it over a third cup of coffee and another cigarette. If some life-threatening problem hit, it was chalked up to fate, or genes. It was shrugged off, and then the school bus pulled in, the kids spilled out, and it was time to start the meat, potatoes, cooked vegetables and pie that was supper.

It wasn't until much later, at a neighborhood reunion, that I discovered to my horror that my mother's coffee klatch had been decimated by heart disease, cancer, stroke and osteoporosis–the one disease they hadn't heard about, couldn't pronounce and certainly never believed was killing them even then when they were twenty, and thirty, and sipping their fourth or fifth cup of coffee of the day.

It was my slim, tiny mother who ended up with the bone-breaking risk of osteoporosis and my four sisters who share it with me.

That's why I wrote this book. I have been a medical journalist for most of my life. I want to share what I have learned with others–especially women. After all we are the gatekeepers of our own and our family's health and as we live longer we can no longer count on the biological protection that blessed us for so long. Most of all I want to know how to grow older with grace, dignity, and glowing good health, don't you?

The Calcium Part

Calcium Counts

1. None of us gets enough calcium. Almost 90% of women get less than half the calcium we need every day. In fact, calcium along with iron are the two most deficient minerals in a woman's diet.

2. Calcium is the most abundant mineral in our bodies. Ninety-eight percent of our calcium is stored in our bones, the other two percent is in our teeth, blood and soft tissues, keeping us healthy and young.

3. Almost all of us make big withdrawals of calcium from our bone bank but don't make deposits. The result? The lack of calcium affects our total health and puts us at serious risk for osteoporosis, the fourth leading cause of death of women.

4. The situation isn't hopeless. It is never too late to start adding calcium to our diets and it is never too soon to worry about calcium deficiency.

****

**Calcium was first isolated in 1808 by Sir Humphrey Day,
the inventor of the miner's safety lamp.
Calcium is almost 200 years old!**

Calcium vs. The Big Four

Practically everyone has heard about the importance of calcium in the fight against osteoporosis. But exciting new research shows that calcium is a mighty warrior in the fight against heart disease, cancer and hypertension as well.

√ Calcium protects us from osteoporosis, the fourth leading cause of death among women.

√ Calcium offers protection against colon cancer, the second deadliest form of cancer, after lung cancer. Some studies show that calcium may even reverse the course of deadly colon cancer after it has begun.

√ Calcium has been shown to lower blood pressure.

√ Calcium studies show that this mineral has the ability to lower overall cholesterol. It also can lower the amount of "bad" cholesterol and raise the amounts of "good cholesterol" and reduce the risk of heart disease.

****

The Calcium Crusader Fights
Heart Disease
High Blood Pressure
Cancer
Osteoporosis

Calcium Keeps Us Young & Active

Calcium research shows how this mineral helps us to enjoy our lives and to extend them in lots of ways that science is just now beginning to understand.

√ Calcium is being studied as a "brain booster."

√ In the circulatory system, strands of a protein called fibrin combine with calcium to thicken blood and form healing clots when an injury occurs.

√ Calcium triggers the flow of impulses from one cell to the next, regulating signals that cause muscles, including the heart, to contract and relax.

√ Calcium stimulates production of fat-digesting enzymes.

√ Studies show a link between nearsightedness and chromium and calcium.

√ Calcium helps menstrual symptoms, bloating, cramps and monthly "blues."

√ New research finds calcium can boost energy and reduce fatigue.

√ Scientists have found that cheddar cheese, high in calcium, can reduce the risk of cavities by over 50%.

√ Johns Hopkins University finds that milk drinking smokers are less likely to develop bronchitis than smokers who get less calcium.

√ Calcium helps protect our stomach lining from ulcer-causing acid and pollutants.

√ Calcium can protect against colds, allergies and hayfever.

Getting To Know Calcium

There is a great deal more to calcium than strong bones and milk. Calcium is a lifesaver and life-extender in more ways than one, and scientists around the country and around the world are just now beginning to discover many of the health benefits of calcium, and the serious health risks of calcium deficiency.

1. The first thing to know about calcium is that most of us don't get enough. Research shows that calcium and iron are the two most common nutritional deficiencies for women. And not getting enough is a problem that compounds itself, getting worse and worse every day, every month every year.

2. The second thing to know about calcium is that it is the most abundant mineral in our bodies. Ninety-eight percent of the calcium we have is in our bones. The other 2% is in our teeth, blood, and soft tissues.

Even though only a tiny fraction of the calcium we have circulates around, this teensie bit is critical to our health. Calcium is so important that if we don't get enough from our diet, if we can't absorb enough through our intestines, if we excrete too much through our kidneys, our body "steals" what it needs from our bones, where it is stored.

That's why it is so important to build up calcium reserves in our bones, against those days when we forget to drink our milk, don't have time to stop for a quick cheese sandwich, lose our supplements with our luggage, or spend a couple of weeks in bed with the flu, those days when our body simply goes into our bones and takes what it needs.

Countless studies show that the calcium reserves we build early in life (and it's never too soon or too late to start) can offer real protection against not only the development of osteoporosis, but can also help our aging bodies reduce high blood pressure, fight off the all too common threat of colon cancer and keep us young and active.

✳✳✳✳✳✳✳✳✳✳

The Rule Of 700

700 mg of calcium, the amount in about two cups of milk, enters and leaves our bones every single day.

Are You Getting Enough Calcium?

The situation is reaching critical. Most Americans (and women are worse off than men) don't get enough calcium from their daily diet, and haven't been getting enough since the age of about 11.

The U.S. Department of Agriculture reports the results of a ten-year study of 35,000 Americans that showed 68% of the total population does not meet the recommended dietary allowance (RDA) for calcium.

It gets worse. The ones who need it the most are even worse off in meeting the RDAs.

Young girls between the ages of 15 and 18 are 87% deficient in calcium–just at the time of their lives when they need to be building up reserves. Instead our pre-teen, teen and young adult daughters are sucking down sodas, skipping meals, and starting on a lifetime of yo-yo dieting to look "cool."

And women (moms, grandmothers, aunts and cousins) 35 to 50, in the critical child-bearing and premenopausal years, are 84% deficient. Again, a lifetime of weight loss-weight gain, not enough time to eat right, too much stress, and too much fast food slowly take their toll, a little bit every day.

Finally, post-menopausal women, women past the age of 51, who have a lifetime of poor or inadequate nutrition behind them face a bleak health future with insufficient amounts of calcium stored in their bone banks against the days when falling estrogen levels, poor diet and lack of exercise deplete reserves and cause injury and death.

And men are not exempt. While fathers, sons, brothers and uncles have a better lifelong history of getting enough calcium, they are also at risk for osteoporosis as well as the other major diseases, which shorten life and which can be warded off with a diet rich in this marvelous mineral.

****

Are You A 500?

Statistics verify that the national average for calcium intake for women is below 500 mg per day–half of what is needed for strong bones and general good health.

Signs & Symptoms Of Calcium Deficiency

If you are a woman between the ages of 15 and 60 you don't even need to bother checking–you probably aren't getting nearly enough calcium every day. And unfortunately the problem with calcium deficiency is that by the time you begin to notice these symptoms it is too late–you have a lot less bone than you think.

Ask yourself if you have any of these signs and symptoms.

- More cavities than usual.
- Periodontal disease.
- Irregular heartbeat.
- Muscle spasms.
- Convulsions.
- Rickets (in children) .
- Osteomalacia (adult rickets).
- Frequent fractures.
- Muscle cramps.
- Lower backache.
- Minor irritability.
- The beginnings of a hump.

****

Caveperson Calcium

Did you know that our early ancestors got almost 10 times the amount of calcium we get today. They averaged between 3,000 and 5,000 mg a day!

The Calcium Quiz

Still not convinced? Still think you're getting enough calcium?
Before you say YES too fast, take this quiz and find out.

1. I hate milk.	Yes	No
2. I drink more than three cups of coffee per day.	Yes	No
3. I get pains in my stomach and gas whenever I drink milk or eat dairy products.	Yes	No
4. I'm under so much stress that my stomach is always upset and I take a lot of antacids.	Yes	No
5. I eat many of my meals on the run, mostly in fast-food places.	Yes	No
6. I hardly ever cook at home.	Yes	No
7. There's always an open can of soda on my desk or wherever I happen to be.	Yes	No
8. I'm a real meat & potatoes person.	Yes	No
9. I'm often constipated and take extra fiber to regulate me.	Yes	No
10. I love my salt shaker.	Yes	No
11. I often forget to take my regular multivitamin.	Yes	No
12. I don't take any special calcium supplements.	Yes	No

Scoring: If you answered **YES** to even one of these questions, you run a serious risk of not getting sufficient calcium from your daily diet. This can lead to bone loss and loss of potential protection against high blood pressure and colon cancer.

The Great American Calcium Gap

Despite the importance of calcium, most of us find it really difficult to meet our minimum needs. Why? Because it isn't enough to concentrate on how to get more calcium through food and supplements, it is just as important to focus on things in our diet and lifestyle that block the calcium we are taking in from being absorbed and put to use.

1. Poor Food Choices

Check out this typical food day for most of us. Breakfast is a cup of coffee and a roll gulped on the run. Lunch is a hamburger or tuna salad sandwich, a handful of french fries and a soda. A midafternoon snack is a bag of potato chips or a chocolate bar and another soda. And even if dinner is chicken, a baked potato, salad, and just the tiniest slice of apple pie–all that adds up to less than 400 mg of calcium a day.

2. Yo-Yo Dieting

How many times have we all passed up milk for a diet soda? Cheese for a carrot stick? That slice of pizza for the plain grilled hamburger patty? All these seem like great diet choices. But they aren't. The diet soda contains phosphate which blocks the absorption of calcium, the carrot stick is high in beta carotene but has no calcium to speak of, and the meat patty has too much protein, which also blocks the absorption of calcium. See? You really need to know what you are doing when you diet. It is possible to live a lowfat life, and still get loads of calcium. The idea is to stop yo-yo dieting and start a sensible eating plan that offers balance and good nutrition.

3. Dairy Product Allergies

Many of us stay away from dairy products because they give us cramps, gas, bloating, and diarrhea. Whether we are truly lactose intolerant or suffering from real or imagined dairy food allergies, these symptoms will prevent us from getting the calcium we need through the most common and plentiful sources–dairy products.

4. Lifestyle Abuse

Cigarettes, alcohol, and even certain medications all block the absorption of dietary calcium by our system and speed up the erosion of calcium reserves in our bones.

Calcium Crusaders Meet

Over ten years ago, in 1984, the first Consensus Development Conference on Osteoporosis first suggested that increasing the amount of calcium in our diet may help prevent osteoporosis.

Ten years later, during a wonderful couple of spring days in June 1994, an impressive group of scientists and health professionals met in Washington to take a look at the massive amount of research being done on calcium and its impact on the various killer diseases that shorten our lives, and to recommend optimum amounts of calcium to keep us healthy.

The Conference, called the Concensus Development Conference on Optimal Calcium Intake, included the who's who of American healthcare. Under the wide banner of the National Institutes of Health, the conference was cosponsored by the Office of Research on Women's Health, the National Institute on Aging, the National Institute of Child Health and Human Development, the National Cancer Institute, the National Institute of Diabetes and Digestive and Kidney Diseases, the National Heart, Lung, and Blood Institute and dozens of experts in every field of health and medicine.

These experts met to answer six vital calcium questions:

1. What is the ideal amount of calcium we should be taking every day?

2. What other factors are necessary for calcium to do its job?

3. What health risks do we run if we take more calcium?

4. What are the very best ways to get the ideal amount of calcium every day?

5. What should be done to make sure everyone gets the calcium message?

6. What does the crystal ball say about the future of calcium?

✳✳✳✳✳✳✳✳✳

**The National Institutes of Health held a conference in June 1994
to determine how much calcium we need to fight
osteoporosis, heart disease, colon cancer
and hypertension.**

Calcium Crusaders Answer Key Questions

When the two days were over, this remarkable NIH Conference had come to some far-reaching decisions to help us all get the calcium we need and to understand the role calcium plays at every stage of our development.

Here's how the folks at the NIH meeting answered the questions they had set out for themselves and for us.

1. What is the ideal amount of calcium we should be taking every day?

The ideal amount of calcium is the amount we need to grow as much bone as possible by the time we are adults, to keep as much bone mass as possible, and to lose as little as we can as we get older. This means that we need different amounts of calcium throughout our lives and at each stage of our development. The recommended dietary allowances (RDAs) for calcium should be used just as guidelines, because they are too low for a lifetime of calcium health.

2. What other factors are necessary for calcium to do its job?

There are lots of factors that determine just how much calcium we actually absorb. Our age, ethnic background, diet, hormone level, medications, the amount of exercise we get, diseases, all affect the amount of calcium we retain.

Vitamin D is critical because it helps calcium become absorbed from our digestive tract. We need between 600 and 800 IU of vitamin D every day either from supplements, sunlight, fortified dairy products, cod liver oil and fatty fish.

Exercise is vital at every age level to help our system absorb calcium.

3. What health risks do we run if we take more calcium?

Studies show that taking up to 1500 mg of calcium per day should not cause any adverse side-effects. However, before you increase the amount of calcium you take you should discuss your unique health profile with your physician.

There is a chance that taking excessive amounts of calcium may increase the risk of kidney stones (although some studies show that increasing calcium actually may reduce the risk of kidney stones in some men). Finally it is possible that taking too much calcium may interfere with the absorption of other nutrients such as iron or with the absorption of certain medications such as tetracyline. Some people who take too much calcium may become constipated or suffer acid stomach.

****

1500 mg of calcium per day is considered a safe and healthy amount.

Calcium Crusaders Answer
More Key Questions

4. What are the best ways to get the ideal amount of calcium every day?

The very best way to get the calcium we need every day is through our diet, experts agree. Dairy foods, always the lowfat variety, ranked number one as sources of calcium. Next came green vegetables, canned fish, seeds, nuts and breads. The next best way to get sufficient calcium is through supplements. Since we often don't eat right, a combination of food and supplements is probably the best way for most of us to get sufficient calcium every day.

5. What should be done to make sure everyone gets the calcium message?

The problem is severe. Recent studies show that children between the ages of 6 to 11 are getting less calcium than ever. And kids aren't the only ones. The majority of Americans, both men and women, get less calcium than needed to maintain health and vigor.

The NIH suggested that we all become calcium crusaders. We should learn as much as we can about calcium and teach others the importance of adequate daily calcium. We need to become partners with our health care professionals and get this vital calcium message out.

Manufacturers can continue to add calcium to our favorite foods. Restaurants, grocery stores, cookbooks could make calcium-rich foods more prominent and visible and could list the calcium content of foods.

6. What does the crystal ball say about the future of calcium?

Some of the most important new research that needs to be done is:
- To study the effects of calcium on youngsters and the amount of bone they develop by taking different amounts of calcium.
- To study the ideal amount of calcium women need to take in their forties, just before they reach menopause.
- To study the interaction between calcium supplements and other nutrients.
- To be able to identify people who are at risk for not getting enough calcium.
- To study the relationship between estrogen replacement therapy and calcium supplements.
- To educate everyone about the importance of a lifetime of calcium.

New National Institutes of Health Calcium Recommendations

Remember, we need different amounts of calcium at different stages of our lives.

Infants from birth to 6 months..400 mg/day

Infants from 6 months to 1 year...600 mg/day

Children from 1 to 5 years..800 mg/day

Children from 6 to 10 years...800 to 1200 mg/day

Adolescents from 11 to 24 years..1200 to 1500 mg/day

Pregnant Adolescents...2000 mg/day

Pregnant Women..1200 to 1500 mg/day

Premenopausal Women 25 to 50..1000 mg/day

Postmenopausal Women over 50 on estrogen..1500 mg/day

Postmenopausal Women not on estrogen...1000 mg/day

Men 25 to 65.. 1000 mg/day

Men 65 plus...1500 mg/day

****

**Always check with your doctor or health professional
<u>before</u> taking any supplements.
Everyone is unique and your doctor can tell you
exactly how much calcium is right for you.**

The Great Calcium Quest

Just by reading this copy of ***Bone Builders*™** you are well on your way to finding the best ways to get enough calcium every day.

Calcium is a food, not a drug. It is a nutrient. Calcium is in your kitchen. That's why ***Bone Builders*™** is also a cookbook and food guide.

Most Common Sources of Calcium

The most common sources of calcium are dairy products like milk, cheese, yogurt, ice cream and frozen yogurt.

Non-Dairy Sources of Calcium

Other excellent sources are sardines and salmon (with bones), and vegetables like spinach, broccoli, greens and bokchoy. Oranges are good sources of calcium, as is tofu. And don't forget the nut family. Many nuts are loaded with calcium, too.

Products Reinforced With Calcium

Recognizing the importance of dietary calcium, many manufacturers have started to add calcium to their food products. Orange juice may be fortified with calcium and many cereals now have extra calcium to get you off to a good start in the morning.

But most of us don't always have the time to eat properly. We often eat on the run, eat under stress, don't eat at all, or eat too much. Sometimes we smoke too much and drink too much, blocking the precious calcium in our food.

Scientific studies show that we ate our way into calcium-rich bones from birth. But only about 25% of the calcium we take in every day, through food, is actually absorbed.

Calcium Supplements

Enter supplements. Whether we eat right or not, our body still needs a steady, measured supply. Because our diet may be unreliable, supplements can provide a vital back-up system to keep the calcium coming in a form and in the amounts that our bodies need.

****

And if you are one of the lucky ones who drink hard water regularly you could be getting as much as 375 mg of calcium per liter.

There's More To Calcium Than Just Bones

Our body is really smart. It needs the 2% of the calcium swimming around outside our bones to do lots of very important things for us.

o Regulates our heart, making sure it beats regularly.
o Helps our blood clot when we get an injury so we don't bleed to death.
o Moves nerve impulses along with important messages.
o Makes sure we are producing hormones properly.
o Keeps the "cement" that keeps our cells' shape and form intact.
o Stimulates fat burning enzymes to help us regulate our weight.
o Quiets the rapidly multiplying cells that cause colon cancer.
o Fights the high blood pressure that doesn't respond to a low salt diet.
o Fights the build-up of gummy plaque that often leads to heart disease.
o Increases the amount of "good cholesterol" and lowers the bad kind.
o Helps us get over the worst PMS symptoms.
o Fights debilitating migraine headaches.
o Stimulates the production of "feel good" hormones to stabilize our mood.

And the list goes on, with new benefits being added with every study. A lot of health from one nutrient.

Because our body performs so many important functions with relatively little calcium, it is very selfish about the calcium it needs. And when our body doesn't get fresh calcium every day from our diet, it does three things.

First, it makes sure that our kidneys don't excrete too much calcium.

Second, it makes sure that the amount of calcium we are absorbing goes up so there is less waste.

Third, and finally it goes into the bone bank, where calcium is stored and takes out the amount it needs and uses it. Then if it still isn't getting enough, it goes back and makes another withdrawal and so on.

****

PTH & CALCITRIOL: The Calcium Patrol

PTH is a hormone that stops calcium from being excreted and opens up the bone bank for withdrawals. Calcitriol is a form of vitamin D and boosts the absorption of calcium by as much as 45%.

Calcium vs. High Blood Pressure
Part I

Blood Pressure: Our Problem

High blood pressure or hypertension has been called the silent killer for good reason. Almost 60 million Americans suffer from hypertension and it is estimated that thousands more have it, but just don't know they do. Research shows that even slightly elevated blood pressure can increase your risk of heart attack and stroke.

How Our Blood Gets Pressurized

The circulatory system pumps 55 million gallons of blood in the course of a normal lifetime through 60,000 miles of blood vessels. It takes a drop of blood only one minute to be pumped through the heart, around the body, and back again.

Blood pressure is determined by the amount and rate of blood flow through our system and the capacity of our arteries to handle the amount of flow. The blood vessels that have the greatest effect on your blood pressure are not the largest ones, but the smallest ones. These are often surrounded by muscle fibers which, if they are constricted, can close off access to the narrower blood vessels. Think of these blood vessels like a garden hose–if you step on it, the flow of water slows to a trickle, and even stops altogether. The result? Higher pressure in the whole system. So, what keeps blood flowing normally and all the blood vessels wide open and relaxed? The same system that regulates your heart, kidneys, lungs and all the other autonomic functions your body performs to keep you alive and healthy.

Whoa! Too Much Pressure

However, there are many things that can throw this automatic monitoring and regulating system out of whack–too much alcohol, certain medications, stress, too much salt, too little exercise, too much cholesterol and fat, smoking, and certain medical conditions.

Like the rest of our bodily functions, blood pressure isn't static. It goes up. It goes down. When we are excited or nervous or afraid our blood pressure can rise.

****

Get Your Blood Pressure Checked At Least Once A Year

Calcium vs. High Blood Pressure
Part II

Normal Pressure

Most authorities agree that 120/80 blood pressure in an adult is in the normal range. Blood pressure measurements involve the heart muscle because the heart is the organ that pumps the blood through our arteries. The top number, the systolic, measures the pressure on the arteries every time the heart beats, pumping blood through the body. The bottom number, the diastolic, measures the pressure between heart beats when the heart muscle relaxes.

High Pressure

What is high blood pressure? When the readings of the systolic and diastolic pressure rise above normal and stay at a higher level, there is an indication of possible hypertension. Generally a reading of 140/90 is regarded as "borderline" while readings of 160/95 or higher are considered "definite" hypertension. Both require medical attention.

New Research On Blood Pressure & Calcium

New research has identified calcium as a player in the fight against high blood pressure and the data is impressive. Studies are showing two things about calcium and high blood pressure:

1. Calcium as a treatment may contribute to lowering high blood pressure.
2. Calcium as prevention may help to prevent high blood pressure.

****

Keeping A Lid On Your Pressure

Maintain your ideal weight, get plenty of exercise, stop smoking, moderate your drinking, cut down on salt and salty foods, learn some stress-fighting skills, and if you are on medication, keep taking it like your doctor says.

Calcium vs. High Blood Pressure
Part III

A Salty Story

Scientists and researchers have long pointed to sodium or salt as a contributing factor in the development of high blood pressure. Why? Our cells are filled on the inside with potassium and surrounded on the outside by sodium. Calcium and magnesium regulate the delicate balance. Exactly how calcium works is not yet clear. Calcium may be an effecive block against the harmful effects of too much salt and may decrease the muscle contraction in the walls of the blood vessels, making it easier for blood to flow through. Scientists are now discovering that too little calcium, magnesium and potassium may be just as big a factor in high blood pressure as too much salt.

Study #1

The Oregon University School of Medicine where a group of patients with high blood pressure were given 1000 mg of calcium supplements a day reported a drop in blood pressure after 8 weeks. Patients who were not given calcium supplements had no change in their blood pressure.

Study #2

A report in the New England Journal of Medicine suggests that pregnant women taking calcium supplements have a decreased risk of high blood pressure.

Study #3

Cornell University's Hypertension Research Center & the National Heart, Lung and Blood Institute showed that people who don't drink milk may be twice as likely to have high blood pressure as those who drink a quart of milk a day.

✳✳✳✳✳✳✳✳✳✳

New Study

A new study from the Albert Einstein College of Medicine and Cornell University Medical College found that men in a low salt group had a 25% greater number of heart attacks than men who ate 10 grams of salt per day, the U.S. Average. Scientists say too little salt produces extra renin, a hormone that narrows blood vessels. What should you do? The American Heart Association recommends no more than 7.5 grams of salt per day. Check with your doctor.

7 Things You Can Do
To Protect Yourself
Against High Blood Pressure

1. Get your blood pressure checked regularly by a trained medical professional.

2. Stop smoking.

3. Decrease the amount of salt in your diet.

4. Get regular aerobic exercise at least three times a week.

5. Learn how to manage your stress through stress management techniques.

6. Maintain your weight at a good level for your body frame.

7. Get your calcium daily.

Does This Describe You?

Here's what else scientists are discovering about the calcium & high blood pressure link...

     o People with high blood pressure tend to eat 25 to 40 percent fewer calcium-rich foods than people with normal blood pressure.

     o Women who have osteoporosis are twice as likely to develop high blood pressure as women of the same age who do not have osteoporosis.

     o Calcium deficiency can trigger high blood pressure, especially in people who are sensitive to salt.

Calcium vs. Colon Cancer

What is the second most deadly form of cancer? If you said colon cancer you would be right. Colon cancer has the dubious distinction of ranking second, right after lung cancer, as the deadliest cancer killer. Now, scientists are discovering that calcium may be a vital and effective weapon in the battle against colon cancer.

Calcium may protect against the development of colon cancer. Calcium may reverse already present cancer of the colon.

In a major 19-year large-scale population study tracking 1,954 middle-aged men who took between 200 and 1,200 mg of calcium per day, it was found that the risk of colorectal cancer was significantly lower for those men who had consumed the higher amounts of calcium and vitamin D.

Another study involving men of Japanese descent living in Hawaii and eating a diet low in calcium compared them to Japanese men living in Japan and eating a diet rich in fish-derived calcium and vitamin D. The researchers found that the men who got less calcium had four times the rate of colorectal cancer.

To determine whether or not calcium was a factor in the slowing down of cells that could become cancerous, individuals at risk were given 1,200 mg of calcium a day for 8 to 12 weeks. The results? The suspicious cells returned to normal.

How Does Calcium Protect Against Colon Cancer?

The jury is still out on exactly how calcium works. And there are many often confusing results in different studies. However, some researchers believe that calcium may detoxify the fatty acids and bile acids in the colon and "quiet" the growth of cancer cells in high risk people.

****

Milk vs. Colon Cancer
The University of California at San Diego did a study of 2,000 men over 20 years and found that those who drank 2 1/2 glasses of milk a day had 1/3 the rate of colon cancer as those who didn't.

Cancer Fighting Strategies

1. Know Your Cancer Profile

2. Get Regular Check-Ups

3. Reduce The Amount Of Fat In Your Diet
To No More Than 30% Of
Daily Calories–20% Is Even Better

4. Stop Smoking

5. Drink Alcohol Only In Moderation

****

Cancer-Fighting Calcium

In animal studies different types of calcium had different results
Calcium carbonate blocked tumors by up to 45%
Calcium gluconate blocked tumors by up to 40%
Calcium chloride blocked tumors by up to 35%

Calcium vs. Heart Disease

The Best-Kept Calcium Secret

Here is one of the best-kept secrets about calcium. This miracle mineral actually lowers cholesterol. Actually it does more. It lowers the "bad" cholesterol and raises the "good" cholesterol. When did this wonderful breakthrough first happen? Back in the1950s. Forty years ago scientists had already discovered that calcium lowers cholesterol and protects against heart disease!

Back To The Future

It is now over forty years later. A new study from the University of Texas Southwestern Medical Center at Dallas shows that dietary calcium and supplements may prevent saturated fat from being absorbed and turned into the gummy cholesterol that blocks blood vessels and is a major factor in heart disease. The result? LDL levels of cholesterol (the "bad" kind) dropped 11 percent. That is enough to reduce the risk of heart attack by an impressive 20 percent. Researchers stressed the importance of a lowfat diet and at least 1,000 mg of calcium per day. The calcium should be a combo between diet and supplements.

Especially Good News For Women

A new study from the University of Ghent in Belgium compared the effect of calcium on the serum lipids (fats) in both men and women. The results? Again, there was a positive relationship between the amount of calcium and fat. The more calcium, the less fat in the bloodstream. But the good news for women is that extra calcium not only lowered the cholesterol level but raised the level of HDL ("good" cholesterol) and lowered women's risk of heart disease–the number one killer of women.

✳✳✳✳✳✳✳✳✳✳

Scrubbing Out Cholesterol

Researchers recommend between 800 and 1200 mg of calcium per day from diet and supplements as a way of lowering cholesterol levels. But just calcium alone won't do it. Always combine calcium with a lowfat diet, exercise program and healthy lifestyle.

7 Ways To Have A Heart

1. Avoid obesity

2. Cut down on total fat intake

3. Eat more high-fiber foods

4. Eat foods rich in vitamins C and A

5. Eat cruciferous veggies like cabbage, broccoli & brussels sprouts

6. Use alcohol moderately

7. Cut down on salt-cured, smoked & nitrite-cured foods

American Cancer Society Guildelines

****

Quick Heart-Saving Tips

Go Lowfat
Get Steamed
Pop corn or pick pretzels
Beware the bacon
Cool it with the cocktails
Yogurt is yummy . . . give it a try

Calcium vs. Fat

New From The Fat Front

While it is a little too early to start rejoicing and throwing out all those huge clothes, there is some good news on the horizon in the fight against fat.

New findings from Oklahoma State University show that calcium may help reduce the amount of saturated fat the body actually absorbs. How does it work? Researchers think that calcium sticks to fat molecules and help to flush them through the intestines.

Helping Calcium Win The War Against Fat

The preliminary research is encouraging. Calcium may help fight fat and all the diseases associated with it such as cardiovascular disease and cancer. But calcium can't do the whole job alone, it needs help. Here are some ways you can do your part in fighting fat:

Calcium Fat Fighters

Make sure you get at least 1000 to 1500 mg of calcium per day from both food and supplements.

Always pick nonfat or lowfat dairy products such as milk, yogurt & cheese.

Make sure that some of your calcium comes from green vegetables, breads, calcium-fortified juices and cereals.

Get plenty of exercise such as walking every day.

Be careful of calcium-robbers such as sodas, caffeine, cigarettes and others that block calcium and don't let it do its job.

Diabetes & Calcium

The Good News

People with either insulin-dependent (type I) or non-insulin-dependent (type II) diabetes do not have more bone fractures than the rest of the population. This means that if you have diabetes you do not have any <u>extra</u> worries about the amount of calcium you need. You still need to make sure though, that you get the recommended amount for your age every day.

The Not So Good News

People with diabetes are at higher risk for heart disease and stroke. This means that if you have diabetes you need to be especially careful about the amount of cholesterol and fat you consume. The fat issue is particularly problematic for people with non-insulin-dependent diabetes who are often also fighting obesity.

That's were the problem lies in terms of dietary calcium.

Some of the best sources of calcium are hidden in foods that are high in both fat and cholesterol. Nuts, whole milk, cheeses and foods which contain these ingredients.

The Best News

If you have diabetes you can still get your required calcium by concentrating on those calcium-rich foods that are also low in fat and cholesterol. Nonfat milk, products made from nonfat milk, nonfat cheeses, green vegetables, legumes, breads, and foods reinforced with calcium.

✳✳✳✳✳✳✳✳✳

Beyond *Bone Builders*™

The American Diabetes Association Family Cookbook
The Microwave Diabetes Cookbook

PMS, Migraine & The Moody Blues

Scientists are beginning to take a closer look at the role calcium may play in making us feel good, especially during the PMS time of the month.

Researchers have already found a link between calcium levels and the levels of certain brain chemicals. Now they are exploring the relationship between calcium levels and seratonin levels. Sertonin is the "feel good" chemical in the brain which is a major factor in our mood.

In a recent study at Mount Sinai Medical Center in New York, women taking calcium supplements and physician-monitored vitamin D reported fewer menstrual symptoms, including migraine headaches.

A second study undertaken by the United States Department of Agriculture, Agricultural Research Service found that a diet of 600 mg of calcium per day and a supplement of 700 mg of calcium per day made a big difference.

How big?

70 % of the women reported fewer backaches;
70 % reported fewer cramps;
80 % retained less water and had less bloating;
and a whopping 90 % were less irritable and depressed during their periods.

Gum Disease: Early Warning Sign

Your Dentist Can Be Your Best Friend

Next time you go to your dentist think more than x-rays, cleanings and possibly the unpleasant news of a necessary root canal. Your dentist can be the first one to warn you of bone loss, possible osteoporosis, and a serious calcium deficiency.

Study # 1 – The Gums Are The Clue
In a study, ten patients with periodontal (gum) disease were each given 1000 mg of calcium per day for six months. The result? This calcium therapy reduced the amount of bleeding around the gums, strengthened teeth so they didn't feel loose, and improved or eliminated gingivitis (inflammation of the gums). And as an added bonus, the extra calicum actually improved the bone structure supporting teeth and even added new bone mass!

Study #2 – Watch Out For Falling Teeth
In another fascinating study, a patient with "loose" teeth couldn't figure out what was causing them to keep getting more and more unstable. This young man was only in his twenties and got plenty of calcium every day, at least 1200 mg.

After a careful examination of his diet, his dentist discovered that this young man drank 8 cans of soft drinks every day. Sodas are loaded with phosphates. What do phosphates do? Two things: Phosphates upset the calcium-phosphorus balance necessary to build calcium bone reserves and phosphates interfere with our body's ability to absorb vitamin D. And without vitamin D, calcium can't get into the bone bank.

✳✳✳✳✳✳✳✳✳

Fascinating Fact
Did you know that your jaw bone is the first bone to lose calcium?

Calcium Tooth Tips

To save the calcium in your teeth

- Don't brush too vigorously.
- Don't leave sugary and starchy foods on your teeth.
- Don't drink too many sodas.
- Don't brush with a hard toothbrush–opt for a soft one.
- Rinse your mouth after drinking fruit juice.
- Rinse your mouth after drinking carbonated beverages.
- Drink sweet drinks through a straw.

Add calcium to your saliva and from there to your teeth

Eat lowfat cheeses, especially cheddar, which reduces cavities.
Use a fluoride toothpaste.
Use a fluoride mouthwash.

Healthy Tooth Foods

o Lowfat cheese
o Lowfat or nonfat yogurt
o Skim milk
o Fresh fruit
o Leafy green veggies

Calcium-Robbing Tooth Foods

o Cookies, candy
o Sugary snacks
o Sodas
o Packaged snacks
o Fast foods

****

Hot Sauce For Healthy Teeth
Salsa lovers! Hot salsa and jalapeño peppers stimulate the production of saliva that neutralizes acid and helps clean your teeth.

Try This Tooth-Health Recipe
Mix equal portions of salsa and plain nonfat yogurt together. Use as a dip or topping for potatoes or veggies. Terrific!

Bone Basics

Bone-Eaters & Bone-Builders

Even though most of us associate bone with skeletons, bone is alive. It is living tissue, just like our skin, our hair, our internal organs. And because bone is alive, it changes all the time. It keeps breaking down, eroding, growing and repairing itself throughout our lives. And its ability to do that effectively and without damaging our health is due to calcium.

Here's how it works. There are bone-eating cells called osteoclasts which break down our bones and actually create holes in bones. Then along come bone-building cells called osteoblasts and fill up those holes with fresh new bone. This whole process is called resorption.

30 Is The Magic Number

Up until you reach thirty, the bone-building cells outnumber the bone-eating cells. But, when you turn thirty, suddenly the bone-eating cells become the majority. They still keep blasting out holes in your bones, but there just aren't enough bone-building cells to keep filling them. So what happens? Bigger and bigger bites are taken out of your bones, and there is less and less to fill them. Pretty soon your bones begin to look like Swiss cheese.

Meet Your Bones

If you are healthy, and around 30, an age when most of your bone mass has been acquired, 25% of your bone weight is water, 25% is a form of connective tissue called collagen, and 50% is calcium phosphate. By age 30 we have about 200 bones in total, and they represent about 15% of total body weight. These 200 bones fall into four general categories:

- long bones–femur or thighbone
- short bones–ankle bones
- flat bones–shoulder blades
- mixed bones–vertebrae

Your Bone Bank

Calcium is the most abundant mineral in your body. It is estimated that 98% of all the calcium is stored in bones, the other 2% is in the cells, blood and soft tissues. Bone is our calcium warehouse or bank account. That's where calcium is stored and saved. And that's where the body goes when it needs some to regulate growth, the nervous system, reproduction, muscle contractions and other vital body functions.

Until we are about 30 we have an opportunity to really build up our calcium reserves against the days when we won't be able to save as much calcium and will be using it up faster than it can be replaced. And those days will come to all of us as we get older.

Think of the bank again. Investment experts tell us that the more money we can save while we are young, letting it compound, the more we will have when we retire and our capacity for making money is not what it used to be.

Calcium and the bone bank work exactly the same way. So until we are about 30 we can build more calcium deposits than we use up. A positive situation. After the age of 30, and into our fifties, sixties and seventies, we use up more calcium than we can replace. A negative situation.

However, young or old, our body needs a certain amount of calcium every day, so it goes into the bone bank and makes regular withdrawals.

****

Bone Bank Buddies

Calcium can't get into the bone bank without a few buddies.
Vitamin D unlocks the door.
Magnesium gets the calcium into the bone.
Lactose (found in dairy products) gives them all a lift.

Warning: Breaking Bones Ahead

Broken bones are no picnic. In the United States over 1.5 million people over the age of 50 break a hip, a vertebra or a wrist each year at a cost of $10 billion!

Are You Walking Around With An Invisible Broken Bone?

Not all fractures are the result of a fall, or are even immediately noticeable. Sometimes a weakened bone will fracture just from picking up a bag of groceries, turning to look into the rearview mirror, reaching across the table for the ketchup, or even sneezing! In fact, you may already have broken a bone and don't even know it. Here are some of the more common ways to tell if you have a fracture.

The Fracture Test

- **A fall, bump, or sudden pain when you bend or twist**

- **Pain in a localized area that gets worse when you touch it**

- **The sound of a bone cracking**

- **Any swelling or bruising around a bone**

- **Inability to move any part of your body that was injured**

****

The Case Of The Disappearing Calcium

Most adults only absorb about 25% of the calcium they take in, and that number goes down even more the older we get.

You Are Not Too Young or Too Old To Think About Osteoporosis

"I'm too old to do anything about it, even if I do have osteoporosis. I'm too young even to think about osteoporosis. That's something my Mom or grandmother need to worry about."

I can't tell you how many times in the past months at booksignings, seminars, workshops and lectures I have heard these two statements from women. Understand this:

Three Laws To Live By

You Are Never Too Old To Do Something About Osteoporosis

You Are Never Too Young To Protect Yourself From Osteoporosis

Osteoporosis Can Kill You . . . And Will

****

The Tragedy Of Eva Gabor

On June 21, 1995, Eva Gabor entered the hospital. On July 4, 1995, she was dead. Cause of death? Respiratory distress and infection. Why did she go to the hospital in the first place? She broke her hip.

Test Your Osteoporosis I.Q.
For Women Of All Ages

1. I'm too young/too old to worry about osteoporosis.   **True**   **False**

<u>False</u>: Osteoporosis really begins to erode your bone mass at the rate of between 1% and 2% per year from the age of thirty. By the time you are 39 you may have 20% less bone mass. By the time you are 45 you may have lost another 12% and so on, until your bones become so weakened that they not only break, they shatter. The most vulnerable time for a woman is the in the first seven years after menopause (after 51) when the most bone loss occurs.

2. Osteoporosis is pretty rare.   **True**   **False**

<u>False</u>: This "silent crippler" may affect as many as eight out of ten American women. It is one of the four leading causes of death among women. It isn't rare at all; it's far too common.

3. Osteoporosis isn't fatal.   **True**   **False**

<u>False</u>: While it is true that you probably won't die from any bones you may break, over 30% of women with a fracture die within a year from complications. Another 50% are crippled and spend the rest of their lives in bed or in a wheelchair.

4. I don't have to worry about osteoporosis. I get plenty of calcium from my diet.   **True**   **False**

<u>False</u>: Calcium deficiency is the leading cause of osteoporosis. Eighty percent of American women are estimated to be calcium deficient, getting only 400 mg of calcium per day. With women's busy, hectic schedules and often erratic eating patterns it is almost impossible to get the recommended 1000 mg of calcium on a daily basis through diet alone without some form of supplementation.

Osteoporosis
The Silent & Deadly Thief

Osteoporosis is described as a "silent thief." Why? Because what's being stolen is vital calcium mass from your bones, little-by-little, until what's left are brittle, porous, and extremely fragile shells of the strong, healthy bones you once had. That's what osteoporosis means—"porous bones," derived from the Latin. Why? Osteoporosis has few, if any, symptoms. It sneaks up on you, quietly, day-after-day, week-after-week, month-after-month, until one day you break a bone. And your life will never be the same again.

The first symptom of osteoporosis may be your last – a sneeze, a twist of the ankle, a slip and suddenly your rib cracks, or your ankle or wrist or leg or hip break. If your silent thief has severely depleted your calcium stores, even lifting your baby grandchild, or a box of old clothes for the homeless drive, or doing something so slight that normally wouldn't cause a bruise or a strain can easily cause one or more bones to break.

The complications arising from osteoporosis are deadly. The National Institutes of Health lists osteoporosis fourth on the list of leading causes of death in women, right after heart disease, cancer, and stroke.

The facts are sobering. There are 25 million people at risk for osteoporosis in the United States today, most of them women. Some 1.3 million will fracture a bone—most commonly the spine or wrist—and 250,000 will break a hip. The risk of a hip fracture is equal to the combined risk of developing breast, ovarian, or uterine cancers.

Of those who have surgery to replace a hip, some 50,000 will die of complications from being bed-ridden, such as pneumonia and blood clots, within six months of surgery. Of those who live after surgery, half will not be able to walk on their own, about a third will become totally dependent on others, and one-fifth will spend the rest of their lives in a nursing home.

****

**Osteoporosis is the fourth leading cause of death
among American women**

Really Scary Stats

More women die of osteoporosis than die of breast cancer, cancer of the cervix and cancer of the uterus, combined!

Twenty-five to 35 million Americans have osteoporosis–that's more than double the populations of New York, Chicago and Los Angeles.

The National Health, Nutrition and Educational Survey reports that 20% of women between the ages of 25 and 34 have already lost bone mass in their pinkie–that is almost 25 years before menopause.

Between 6% and 10% of a woman's bone mass is lost in the first year following her last period.

By age 45 as many as 20% of women may have osteoporosis.

By age 50, 54% of women will have fractured a bone.

By age 65 as many as 80% of women may have osteoporosis.

Fractures of the vertebrae result in 5 million days of restricted activity for American women every year.

For women over 45, 161,000 office visits to the doctor are related to fractures of the vertebrae.

Twenty percent of patients with hip fractures are unable to walk one year later.

Twenty-four percent of all patients with hip fractures may die within 12 months.

Thirty percent of women die of complications from fractures within the first year.

Test Your Osteoporosis Risk

It seems that just being a woman puts you in a higher risk group for developing osteoporosis. However, some women are at even higher risk than others. Ask yourself these questions.

Are you a woman?	Yes	No
Did you have a surgical menopause before age 45?	Yes	No
Did you start natural menopause before age 45?	Yes	No
Do you have light skin and fair hair?	Yes	No
Do you have small bones and a slight build?	Yes	No
Do you smoke?	Yes	No
Are you of Latin or Asian heritage?	Yes	No
Do you eat meat?	Yes	No
Are you a yo-yo dieter?	Yes	No
Did you ever take oral steriods for more than six months?	Yes	No
Are you a couch potato?	Yes	No
Do you drink a lot of coffee or sodas?	Yes	No
Do you get highly strenuous exercise?	Yes	No
Have you ever exercised so much your periods stopped?	Yes	No
Are you on thyroid medication?	Yes	No
Do you rely only on diet for your total nutrition?	Yes	No
Did your mother or sister ever break a bone (serious accidents i.e. car accidents don't count)	Yes	No
Do you now, or did you ever routinely take diuretics, insulin, antiulcer, anticoagulant or anticonvulsant medication?	Yes	No

Scoring: Each **Yes** answer adds to your risk for developing osteoporosis and is yet another reason to start increasing your calcium intake.

Risks You Can't Help

Race

Some risk factors are unavoidable. If you are Caucasian (white) or Asian and have a small frame these risk factors are <u>genetic</u>. There is obviously nothing you can do to change these! African-American women have been found to have one-half the risk and Hispanic women one-third the risk of white and Asian women, because genetically they have a denser bone mass.

Family History

If you do not know whether your family has a history of osteoporosis, now is the time to find out. These questions might help:
- Do any of your relatives (mother, grandmother, aunt, sister), have a "dowager's hump"?
- Have any fallen and broken a bone?
- Has a doctor tested any of them for osteoporosis?

Onset of Menopause

Postmenopausal women are at greater risk for osteoporosis because of the decline in estrogen which regulates monthly periods. Menopause simply means a stopping of menses, or monthy periods. The average woman begins menopause when she has just passed her 51st birthday. During menopause bone is lost at a faster rate than at any other time throughout our lives. In general, older women are more likely to suffer from osteoporosis.

Early or surgically induced menopause means your periods have stopped before the average age of 51 years. <u>Early menopause</u>–before the age of 45–can run in families. <u>"Surgically induced menopause"</u> means your menopause is brought on because your ovaries have been removed by surgery. Ovaries may also stop working because of chemotherapy or radiation therapy given for diseases such as cancer.

Medications for other conditions

Sometimes medications you are taking for other diseases, such as asthma, arthritis, cancer, or seizures may contribute to a loss of bone. Check with your doctor about your risk for osteoporosis if you are taking a thyroid medication or an anti-inflammatory steroid known as a glucocorticoid for any of the above conditions. Your doctor can monitor your bone loss and recommend a treatment program if such loss is found.

Risks You Can Reduce

Diet & Nutrition

What is your diet like? Do you consume a lot of foods containing calcium, such as milk, cheese, eggs, and broccoli or other leafy green vegetables? A lifetime of low calcium intake–less than 1000 mg daily, or what's found in three 8 oz. glasses of skim milk–can contribute to osteoporosis. Drinking more than 2 alcoholic drinks a day blocks calcium absorption. Excessive amounts of caffeine, or about what's in 10 cups of coffee a day, interferes with calcium absorption. Don't forget the caffeine in sodas and tea. Drinking more than one or two sodas a day robs you of calcium. Phosphorous, in regular and diet sodas, absorbs calcium. Phosphorus is also found in red meats, processed foods, and fast foods.

Lactose Intolerance

If you are "lactose intolerant," meaning you have trouble digesting the enzyme lactase found in milk and milk products, you can buy lactase tablets to take with foods that contain lactose. You can also now buy milk that's been specially treated for the lactose intolerant, and the bonus is this lactaid milk is reinforced with extra calcium.

Vegetarianism

Reducing the amount of meat and fat from meat you eat is very healthy, but you should take extra care with your diet to make sure you are getting all the necessary nutrients, especially calcium.

Couch Potatoism

Be honest about your physical activity. Are you a "couch potato"? Do you consider walking to your car exercise? Do you have a desk job? Weight-bearing exercise, such as brisk walking, is one of the best ways to bulk up your bone mass. (Interestingly, too much exercise can cause periods to stop, having a negative effect on bones. This loss of periods is called amenorrhea.)

Smoking

Smoking cigarettes–even if you have now quit–can contribute to a decrease in bone mass by speeding up menopause.

Crash Diets

Crash diets can also limit your daily intake of calcium because they are usually low in dairy products and other calcium-rich foods.

New Research, New Risks

Depression

New research has found that depression may cause you to lose calcium from your bones and speed up the process of osteoporosis. Scientists offer a couple of explanations. First, when you are depressed your appetite may suffer. And the less you eat, the less likely you are of not getting enough calcium. The second reason why depression may cause calcium loss is that it affects the amount of steroid cortisol, a natural substance which is believed to reduce stress. The more depressed you are, the more steroid cortisol your body produces trying to get rid of the stress you are feeling. This may literally "suck" calcium from your bones.

> **A study in the American Journal of Psychiatry
> reports that severely depressed women and men
> around the age of 60 had a 15% reduction in bone density.**

Cigarettes and Mothers

A new study from the University of California found that smoking and having a mother who broke a hip double a woman's chances of breaking a hip after the age of 65. This is true even in women who have fairly dense bones.

> **If you have 5 or more risk factors
> your chances of breaking a hip after 65 are 10%.
> If you have 2 or fewer risk factors
> your chances of breaking a hip after 65 are 1%.**

Gray Hair

What next? The Maine Center for Osteoporosis Research and Education found that men and women who begin to go gray in their 20s and who have at least half their head covered in gray hair by the time they are 40 are more than four times as likely to have thinning bones as people who go gray later in life.

The explanation may be in the fact that the genes for building bone and going grey are neighbors and affect each other.

Another study links prematurely grey hair with irregular menstrual cycles which signal a higher risk for osteoporosis.

Finally there is a link between gray hair and premature menopause and thyroid disease. Both have been associated with bone loss in other studies.

The "Biggies":
Your Highest Risk Factors

- **Asian, Caucasian, thin, small-boned frame**

- **Family history of osteoporosis**

- **Postmenopausal**

- **Early menopause (before the age of 45 years)**

- **Hysterectomy**

- **Use of medications that can cause loss of bone**

- **Lifetime of low calcium intake via diet**

- **Sedentary lifestyle–little exercise**

- **Cigarette smoking**

- **More than 2 alcoholic drinks daily**

- **Excessive amounts of caffeine (10 cups a day)**

- **More than 1 or 2 sodas daily**

****

Join The National Osteoporosis Foundation
P.O. Box 96616, Dept. M.E.
Washington, DC 20077-7456

Why Is Osteoporosis A Woman's Disease?

Good question. Why <u>is</u> osteoporosis a woman's disease? Even though men do get osteoporosis, women are eight times more likely to develop osteoporosis during their lifetime than men. Here's why:

1. Women naturally have less bone mass at adulthood, making them more vulnerable to bone loss later in life.

2. At menopause (around age 51) a woman's supply of estrogen decreases, accelerating a decrease of bone strength. Estrogen encourages the formation of new bone mass as well as the absorption of calcium from the diet. Any decrease in estrogen will affect bone density.

3. In men the male hormone testosterone offers some bone protection and since men don't experience a decrease in their hormone levels until their 60s or 70s they get extra years of bone protection.

✳✳✳✳✳✳✳✳✳

Battle of the Sexes

One out of two women suffers an osteoporosis-related fracture
One out of five men suffers an osteoporosis-related fracture

What Causes Osteoporosis?

From Bone Remodeling to Osteoporosis

Osteoporosis is the loss of bone and one of the main contributors to bone loss is the disruption of the remodeling process by which old bone is broken down and replaced by new bone. This process replaces 20% of our bone tissue every year. How does the bone remodeling work? There are five key steps:

1. Activation: a signal is sent to certain cells to get together at a meeting place along a bone site. Once there, these cells begin to remove the old bone.

2. Resorption: These cells called osteoclasts make a hole on the surface of some bones and actually drill a tunnel in other bones. Then they disappear until the next time they are needed to remove old bone.

3. Reversal: Along come different cells to get the surface of the bone ready to accept new bone.

4. Formation: New cells called osteoblasts rush to the bone holes and fill them up with calcium.

5. Quiescence: Everything is peaceful and resting until the next cycle.

If anything upsets this process, bone isn't built up as fast as it is taken apart and then the result is osteoporosis.

This entire process of remodeling takes about 4 to 8 months from start to finish and can be done as frequently as every 3 months or as rarely as every 2 years.

Types Of Osteoporosis

The National Institutes of Health proposes two major causes of osteoporosis:

#1. The lack of estrogen.

This is called <u>Type 1 Osteoporosis</u> and is caused by the lack of estrogen. Estrogen, the female hormone helps regulate the amount of calcium in our system and keeps the level of calcium in bones in balance. A lack of estrogen can lead to bone loss and a collapse of bones in the spine, producing a "dowager's hump" or what doctors call "dorsal kyphosis."

#2. The lack of calcium.

This is called <u>Type 2 Osteoporosis</u> and occurs when the body has trouble absorbing calcium. This is due to the slow reduction of bone mass. This type of osteoporosis can affect both men and women.

****

A new study in the New England Journal of Medicine says that older women can reduce their risk of hip fractures by cutting down on coffee, taking walks and getting their eyes checked.

Primary Osteoporosis

It doesn't just happen. You don't just go to bed one night without osteoporosis, and wake up with osteoporosis. It isn't like a cold, or the flu, or even a toothache. It is silent. By the time you notice something is wrong, you are in a cast, in a wheelchair, or worse.

Stage One:
Around the age of 30 is when stage one begins with gradual bone loss. This is the invisible stage. There are no warnings here. No tests can accurately tell you how much, or even if you are losing bone. How can you tell if you are in stage one osteoporosis? If you have one of the risk factors you can pretty well assume that it's happening to you as you read this. So what should you do? Eliminate as many of the lifestyle risk factors as you can. Exercise. Stop smoking. Cut back on the caffeine. Take calcium.

Stage Two:
Somewhere between the age of 35 and 50 you enter stage two. The more risk factors in your life, the greater your chances for reaching this stage. This is the stage when you might get a fracture, or you might be on thyroid medication, or you have more than two of the risk factors. If that's the case, now would be a good time to get a bone density test to see whether you have osteoporosis, and if you do, how far advanced it is.

Stage Three:
Here is where you break a bone without being in an accident or sustaining other serious injuries. Perhaps you stepped off the curb wrong. You picked up a bag of groceries or your grandchild. You reached across to scrape ice off the windshield. Something silly. And suddenly you broke a wrist, an ankle, a vertebra. You get an x-ray. And then you know. Your broken bone was the result of stage three osteoporosis. And guess what. You are only 45 years old.

Stage Four:
This is it. More fractures. Pain. Constant discomfort. You begin to walk stooped over. You may be confined to a wheelchair or a bed. Your life as you knew it is over. You develop complications. And suddenly you become another statistic... proving that osteoporosis is the fourth leading cause of death in women.

You & Your Doctor: Partners Together

You don't have to be worried about osteoporosis alone. You and your doctor can be a powerful team and between the two of you reduce the risk of osteoporosis and increase your chances of living a longer, healthier life.

<u>Here's how to be a real partner with your physician:</u>

Make sure you take time to write out a list of questions and concerns before you meet with your doctor.

Never feel rushed. If you don't understand something, keep asking until you do.

Take a pad or tape recorder with you to keep notes of what the doctor and you discuss and what decisions and actions you are going to take.

Make sure your doctor really knows about you and that includes being honest about your diet, exercise and lifestyle.

Fill out your doctor's medical history form completely and add any information you can about osteoporosis.

Make sure that your doctor discusses medication and dosage with you, especially if you are taking glucocorticoid medications for any of these diseases: rheumatoid arthritis, osteoarthritis, bursitis, asthma, liver disease, lupus, ulcerative colitis, Crohn's disease, multiple sclerosis, inflammations and severe allergies. Other medications that have been connected with bone loss include excessive doses of thyroid hormones, anticonvulsants, antacids which contain aluminum, hormones used to treat endometriosis.

Get interested. Read books, magazines, go to lectures. If you are informed and educated about osteoporosis, chances are you will be more likely to take steps to help yourself.

Bone Density Testing

Osteoporosis is a disease with few, if any, symptoms. That's scary. Early on, you may get a mild backache or spasms in your back muscles. Sometimes, because bone is lost in the jaw, your dentist may notice receding gums and ask you if your teeth seem looser. If you've fractured a bone after a seemingly minor fall, your doctor may suspect bone loss.

If you believe you are at risk for osteoporosis, see your doctor. Your family history, medical history, and lifestyle may indicate testing to measure bone mass. In addition to a complete medical workup including urine and blood tests your doctor may prescribe a bone density test.

What Can A Bone Density Test Tell You?

* If you have low bone density before you suffer a fracture

* Predict your chances for breaking a bone in the future

* Tell you whether a fracture you may have suffered was caused by osteoporosis

* Tell you pretty acurately how fast you are losing bone
    (This needs more than one time only testing.)

* Tell you if any treatments your doctor prescribed are helping
    (This needs more than one time only testing.)

****

Good News For Medicare Patients

According to the National Osteoporosis Foundation Medicare covers some tests in 41 states.
And the Medicare reimbursement for some tests has increased 91% according to the Health Care Financing Adminstration.

Is A Bone Density Test For Me?

You may decide to undergo a bone density test (they don't hurt at all) if there are things going on in your life that either you or your doctor may suspect could put you at increased risk for osteoporosis.

1. I have at least 5 major risk factors for osteoporosis.	YES	NO
2. I have to decide whether or not to start estrogen replacement therapy.	YES	NO
3. I have a thyroid condition.	YES	NO
4. I am taking steroids or medications.	YES	NO
5. I have recently fractured a bone.	YES	NO
6. I am already taking an osteoporosis treatment.	YES	NO

If you answered YES to even one question talk to your doctor about a test.

****

National Osteoporosis Prevention Week
&
Mother's Day

National Osteoporosis Prevention Week usually falls in the middle of May and often coincides with Mother's Day.

Give your mom a big bottle of calcium supplements for Mother's Day. If you are a mom, give the same gift to your daughter.

Meet The Bone Density Test Family

A diagnosis of osteoporosis can only be confirmed by a test that measures your bone-mineral density at different sites in the skeleton: the spine, hip, forearm, and wrist.

These tests use photon or x-ray energy that produce very little radiation (about one-tenth of a chest x-ray), are painless, and take from 10 to 15 minutes up to an hour. The equipment varies and depends on what type of test is done. These tests, called "bone densitometry," include the following:

DEXA (Dual-Energy X-ray Absorptiometry) uses two separate beams of x-rays to measure the hip, spine, and full body. It is the newest and fastest test doctors use and is very accurate.

DPA (Dual-Photon Absorptiometry) measures the mineral content in bone in the hip and spine. It is not as fast as DEXA.

SPA (Single-Photon Absorptiometry) measures the forearm, wrist, or heel, but doesn't measure bone density at the sites where fractures are most common: the hip and spine. The doctor might put a scanner on your arm, for example, for several minutes.

RA (Radiographic Absorptiometry) uses regular x-rays of the hand to test for bone density. These x-rays are then read by computer.

CAT Scan or QCT (Quantitative Computed Tomography) can measure the cortical bone and the trabecular bone separately. It is accurate when measuring spinal compression. The drawbacks include a higher dose of radiation and greater expense than the other tests.

Your doctor may do one test for bone density and ask you to return for a second test in six months.

****

**Call the National Osteoporosis Foundation Action Line at
1-800-464-6700
to find a testing center near you.**

Medical Therapies & Treatments

Estrogen replacement therapy/hormone replacement therapy

Women are often prescribed estrogen replacement therapy at menopause to offset symptoms, including the rapid loss of bone. In addition, estrogen may also prevent wrist, hip, and spinal fractures in older women. However, this therapy is not without some risks, including the possibility of developing cancer of the breast or uterus. In many cases doctors prescribe the hormone progesterone along with estrogen therapy to prevent the uterus from building up its lining, which may lead to cancer. This regimen is called hormone replacement therapy. If estrogen replacement therapy is used for more than 10 years, the risk of breast cancer can increase. For that reason–and because all women are individuals–only you can decide whether or not to use estrogen.

The lowest daily dose of estrogen that's shown to help prevent loss of cortical bone is 0.625 mg. Be sure to discuss all the pluses and minuses of such therapy with your doctor.

Calcitonin

If you have been diagnosed with osteoporosis, your doctor may prescribe calcitonin. Calcitonin is a hormone that occurs naturally in the body. Two types of synthetic drugs are available that act just like calcitonin does in the body. One type is based on the human calcitonin and the other is based on salmon calcitonin. Both work by slowing down bone loss and can help relieve pain caused by osteoporosis. Calcitonin is also an option for women who prefer not to or cannot take estrogen, although it is two to three times more expensive than hormone replacement therapy. Your doctor must give you calcitonin injections by using a needle and a syringe, and will start with a test dose to see if you are allergic to it.

Three products are available: Cibacalcin, Calcimar and Miacalcin.

Bisphosphonates

This is another anti-resorptive medication which slows or stops bone loss.

What You Can Do For Yourself Right Away

Calcium For All Women Through Diet And Supplements

By itself, calcium is not a prevention or "cure" for osteoporosis. It is a mineral, however, that is essential to the development of healthy bones. Many women do not get enough calcium in their diet. According to the National Institutes of Health and the National Osteoporosis Foundation, the recommended daily intake of calcium for both men and women is 1000 mg. This is the equivalent of three 8 oz. glasses of milk (preferably skim, to reduce fat intake). For postmenopausal women, 1000 mg/day is enough if you are on estrogen replacement therapy. If you are not on such therapy, this should be increased to 1500 mg/day.

Because none of us eat properly every single day we should make sure that we get at least 1200 to 1500 mg of calcium per day by adding a good supplement.

Vitamin D

Sunshine is the most obvious source of vitamin D which the body needs to absorb calcium and produce healthy bones. We need more vitamin D as we age. If you can, try to get out in direct sunlight for 15 to 30 minutes a day. Other sources include milk and cereal fortified with vitamin D, egg yolks, saltwater fish, and liver. The Recommended Daily Allowance of vitamin D is up to 200 IU (International Units) per day. Be aware that levels above 600 or 800 IU a day can be dangerous. Ask your doctor to recommend a dose if you are not sure how much to take.

Exercise

Inactivity can lead to bone loss so it's important to begin and/or continue a program of weight-bearing exercise. Ideally, try to exercise 30 to 60 minutes three to four times a week. Besides walking, weight-bearing exercises include jogging, hiking, aerobics, dancing, bicycling, rowing, jumping rope, climbing stairs, using weights or a treadmill, and any racquet sports, like tennis.

The Osteoporosis Fracture

The news is not great. One in two women and one in five men will break a bone as a direct result of osteoporosis.Women are likely to break a bone in their spinal column at some point in the twenty years between 55 and 75.

Both men and women are at risk for breaking a hip.

Spinal Fractures

Fractures in the spine, called compression fractures, often happen during routine activities such as bending, lifting or even getting up from a bed or chair. The result? Immediate and severe back pain. This pain usually fades within a few months–but some with spinal fractures are never pain-free. But, sometimes these fractures are painless and can only be found through x-rays. The tragedy is that there are women walking around right now with spinal fractures who don't know they have a broken bone. Even multiple fractures may only be perceived by a loss of body height and/or the development of a dowager's hump.

Fracture-Proof Tips

o **Use 100-watt bulbs in your lamps to provide more light.**
o **Fix sidewalk cracks around your home.**
o **Brighten up outdoor and overhead porch lighting.**
o **Replace worn out or slippery doormats.**
o **Install grab-bars in shower and toilet area.**
o **Tack down all electrical & telephone cords and tuck them behind furniture.**
o **Place nonskid underpadding under area rugs.**
o **To avoid dizziness don't get up too quickly.**
o **Make sure other drugs you are taking don't make you dizzy.**
o **Check your vision and hearing regularly to maintain good balance.**
o **Wear rubber-soled, low-heeled shoes.**

****

Falls are the leading cause of fatal injuries for people over 65.
Fifty percent of all falls happen at home,
in the bathroom or on the stairs.
Fifty percent of all older patients hospitalized because of a fall
die within the year.

Preventing & Reversing Osteoporosis: It's Never Too Late

Whether you think you are a strong candidate for osteoporosis, or whether you have already been diagnosed with osteoporosis, there are steps you can take to help yourself to live a long healthy life.

1. Take your doctor's advice and make a joint decision about hormone replacement therapy after menopause. This means you have to do your homework. Do some reading. Know your family history. Be a real partner in your own health program.

2. Get some exercise every day. Forget working out to stay in that size 10 dress, or to get into that size 10 dress. If you need motivation, just think about yourself in a wheelchair or worse. Now, go for a brisk walk.

3. Take care of your body and it will take care of you. Stop smoking. Cut back on the fatty foods. Increase the fruits and vegetables. Give your body a chance to get extra dietary calcium–which is the best kind.

4. Take calcium supplements every day. Recognize that there is probably no way you are going to get enough calcium every single day–it isn't going to happen. So make supplements as natural a part of your day as taking a shower or brushing your teeth.

5. Enjoy your life. Be happy. Reduce your stress. Stop and smell the roses.

****

There are expected to be three times the number of hip fractures by the year 2050–that is an alarming 6 million fractures a year!

A Peek Into The Future

Looking To Space

The space program may provide answers. While in space, astronauts lose bone density in much the same way women do after menopause. Scientists determined the absence of gravity leads to weightlessness and without the force of gravity on bones and muscles, calcium is drained rapidly. By giving the astronauts drugs that stop calcium loss, it is hoped that their bones remain strong and that lessons will be learned that can help the rest of us.

Osteoporosis Gene

A new study reported in Nature magazine reveals that a single gene accounts for approximately one-third of a person's risk for developing osteoporosis. Scientists are optimistic that this discovery will lead to a test to identify those of us who are at a high risk for osteoporosis and help us get on a treatment program early.

Calcium & Fluoride Combo

Several studies now show that slow-release sodium fluoride in combination with calcium can prevent vertebral fractures by as much as 50% and may increase bone density by as much as 6%.

Bone Glue

A new biomedical company in California has developed a glue that can help hold fractures together. Why is this important? Fractures, especially in older patients, take a long time to heal and sometimes heal incompletely, resulting in shortened limbs. The new glue makes fractures heal twice as fast, and it eventually dissolves leaving strong, new bone. The glue is now in clinical trials and is expected to be available soon.

New Drugs

There are over 25 new drugs lined up for approval at the FDA. These hold exciting promise for the 75 million baby boomers who are going to be at serious risk for osteoporosis.

Natural Hormones

An important new breakthrough has to do with natural estrogen and natural progersterone. These natural hormones are now available as vegetarian yam extracts. Check with your local healthfood store.

Experimental & New Drugs

- Calcitriol, a synthetic vitamin D that works by strengthening and thus preventing broken bones

- Thiazide diuretics, which are used in high blood pressure medications and help preserve bone density

- Anabolic steroids

- Progesterone

- Intermittent parathyroid hormone

- ADFR, a complex system of several drugs

- Biophosphates like etidronate

- Recombinant transforming growth factor beta

- A calcitonin nasal spray, for example

Stop The Press

The FDA has just approved two new drugs for osteoporosis. Fosamax® can increase bone density in the spine by 8% and in the hip by 7% and can reduce the number of new vertebral fractures by 48%.

Miacalcin® is the nasal spray form of calcitonin and it increases spinal bone mineral density in women who are five years past their menopause.

Check with your doctor to see if you are a candidate for either of these new treatments.

Targeting Women's Killers

The Pharmaceutical Research and Manufacturers of America report on some exciting and promising drugs under development to help fight osteoporosis and which are currently in clinical trials at the FDA.

Always ask your doctor or pharmacist about any medications

Drug	**Company**
1-alpha-hydroxyvitamin D_2	Bone Care International
Cyclophasic hormone replacement therapy	R.W. Johnson Pharmaceutical ResearchInstitute
Didronel PMO etidronate disodium	Procter & Gamble
Droloxifene	Pfizer
esterified estrogens and dydrogesterone	Solvay
estradiol/neta patch	R.W. Johnson Pharmaceutical Research Institute
estradiol patch	TeraTech
Estratab®	Solvay
Estratest®	Solvay
Estrofem®	Novo Nordisk
Evista	Eli Lilly
Fosamax (Approved)	Merck
Insulin-like growth factor (IGF-1)	Chiron
Kiliogest® Mite	Novo Nordisk
Livial™	Organon
Miacalcin Nasal Spray	Sandoz
Norethindrone acetate and ethynyl estadiol	Warner-Lambert
Premarin® MPA	Wyeth-Ayerst
Risedronate	Proctor & Gamble
Slow Fluoride	Mission Pharmacal
Systen patch	R.W.Johnson Pharmaceutical Research Institute
Tiludronate	Sterling Winthrop

Calcium & Stones

Kidney Stones

The popular wisdom was that calcium causes kidney stones. Why? Because kidney stones are 80% calcium oxalate and over 50% of the people who developed kidney stones were found to have a high level of calcium in their urine.

Well, a new study from the Harvard School of Public Health suggests that just the opposite might be true—that rather than causing kidney stones, calcium is an important factor in preventing. kidney stones from forming.

This study involved 45,619 men with no history of kidney stones. And what did researchers discover? That the men who had diets richest in calcium were the least likely to develop kidney stones.

How do scientists explain these findings? The key seems to be in oxalate. If you restrict the amount of calcium, the oxalate gets absorbed into the gastroinetinal tract and begins to form kidney stones. If you increase the amount of calcium, the oxalate is flushed out and doesn't have the chance to form kidney stones.

The Anti-Kidney Stone Diet

Increase the amount of water in your diet.
Eat potassium-rich foods.
Decrease the amount of animal protein.
Reduce alcohol consumption.

Gallstones

In a long-term study in the Netherlands it was found that the more calcium in the diet of the subjects, the less likely they were to form gallstones. Because calcium blocks the reabsorption of secondary bile acids in the colon, it offers significant protection against the formation of gallstones.

The Anti-Gallstone Diet

Reduce the sugar in your diet.
Increase the amount of vegetable protein, calcium, and fiber.

WARNING:
ALWAYS CHECK WITH YOUR DOCTOR BEFORE MAKING ANY DIETARY CHANGES, ESPECIALLY IF YOU HAVE BEEN DIAGNOSED WITH SOME MEDICAL CONDITION.

Calcium Robbers

Just getting enough calcium isn't the whole story. You may think you are taking plenty of calcium, but your body may not be absorbing the entire amount.

Research shows that we only absorb about 25% of the calcium we take in.

Why is that? Unfortunately, just as we are taking in nutrients that are good for us, we are also taking in loads of things that block the vitamins and minerals trying to get through into our cells.

This is especially true for calcium.

Because calcium is absorbed through the intestine, it runs the risk of being blocked by any number of other dietary compounds. And to make matters worse, even some of the things we take in, like medications or certain forms of antacid, can block calcium and effectively reduce the amount that gets through.

Look Out For These Calcium Blockers

* Salt
* Caffeine
* Fat
* Alcohol
* Smoking
* Protein
* Phosphoric acid
* Fiber
* Oxalic acid & phytic acid
* Medications
* Lead

Calcium Robber #1: Salt

Americans take in far too much salt every day. Salt is hidden in almost every single food we eat, and many of us are guilty of sprinkling extra amounts on all our meals from breakfast to dinner and on every between-meal snack.

Salt is a combination of two minerals—sodium and chloride. Both are the primary regulators of water in our bodies.

Calcium Going Down The Salt Drain

Research shows that 1 teaspoon of salt a day can cause a 1.5% decrease in bone mass per year because salt forces calcium out through the urine and costs you between 20 and 25 mg of calcium.

And that's not all. Researchers at Cornell University may have found another link between calcium and salt. Their findings show that calcium deficiencies trigger high blood pressure in people who are extra-sensitive to the blood-pressure-increasing effects of salt. This link is confirmed by findings at the Mayo Clinic which reports that keeping your total salt intake to 1 teaspoon per day (and that includes hidden sources of salt) may be enough to control mild or moderate high blood pressure. And Arizona State University findings show that increasing your calcium intake every day may help you lower your blood pressure, if lowering your salt intake doesn't work. And Wayne State University in Detroit, researchers showed that men on a high-sodium diet were still able to lower their blood pressure by taking additional calcium.

On the international front, a study from New Zealand found that women taking the same amount of calcium every day had very different calcium results. Those on a high salt diet lost 30% more calcium than those on a low salt diet.

Even though most calcium and high blood pressure studies have focused on calcium supplements, new research at Cornell's Hypertension Research Center shows that increasing the amount of milk you drink may work to lower your blood pressure if it is in the mild range—90 to 104. The National Heart, Lung and Blood Institute confirmed the milk & high blood pressure link in a study that showed non-milk drinking men were twice as likely to have high blood pressure as those who drank a quart of milk a day.

Lose The Salt–Gain The Calcium

It seems the more salt you take in, the less calcium you absorb. But salt is an acquired taste. If you keep eating it, you'll crave more. If you reduce your salt, your tastebuds will adjust to a lower sodium diet in about six weeks.

Health experts recommend 2400 mg of salt (1 tsp.) or less per day.

- **Get rid of that salt shaker.**
- **Look for low sodium canned foods.**
- **Taste all foods before adding salt.**
- **Experiment with various spices instead of salt.**
- **Use low-sodium salt substitutes.**
- **Take salt out of all recipes, except those using yeast.**

Become A Salt Detective

Salt by any other name is still salt.
Check for these on food labels:
Monosodium glutamate (MSG)
Sodium bicarbonate (baking soda)
Sodium aluminum sulfate (baking powder)

Get To Know Your Salt Labels

Sodium free = less than 5 mg/serving
Very low sodium = 35 mg or less
Low sodium = 140 mg/serving
Reduced sodium = 3/4 less than usual

Check Out Your Favorite Designer Water

Poland Spring	0.32 mg of sodium per glass
Evian	1.18 mg of sodium per glass
Perrier	3.04 mg of sodium per glass
Canada Dry Club Soda	44.0 mg of sodium per glass

Watch Out For These Hidden Sodium Culprits

Sauerkraut, dill pickles, chicken broth, soy sauce, ham, olives, pretzels, salami, franks, luncheon meat, American processed cheese spread, caviar–and the salt shaker. Sea salt, onion salt, garlic salt, brine, seasoned salt.

Calcium Robber #2: Caffeine

If you've been following the health news, you know that there is some confusion about caffeine and calcium. Does it or doesn't it weaken bones and contribute to osteoporosis?

Although recent studies have shown that moderate coffee drinking does not have a negative effect on calcium, drinking more than 3 cups of coffee per day can drain vital calcium stores.

Research shows that the amount of caffeine you take in may be proportional to the amount of calcium you lose. So the more caffeine you drink, the more calcium you lose. Forty mg of daily calcium loss, or the cost of drinking 6 cups of coffee, can cost you 1% bone loss if you are postmenopausal. This is a good warning for younger women, too.

Moderation seems to be a good idea here. So, you don't have to give up your first important cup of coffee of the day, or even the second one. But don't give into temptation and have a third, or fourth cup.

The famous Framingham Heart Study showed that drinking two or more cups of coffee a day increased the chances of breaking a hip by 50 percent.

And a more recent Harvard study of middle-aged women found that those who drank more than four cups of coffee a day were three times more likely to get a fractured hip than those who didn't.

Women who drink more than 6 cups of coffee per day, studies show, have 3 times the risk of developing fractures than women who drink only 1 or 2 cups a day. Researchers suspect that drinking coffee may cause an increase in the production of urine which in turn flushes out too much calcium from our systems before it can be absorbed. That results in forcing the body to get its calcium from stored sources in the bones.

Coffee may not be the only culprit. Be careful of hidden sources of caffeine, such as tea, cocoa, sodas and chocolate.

Women who had a high calcium diet throughout their lives

may be less affected by caffeine and calcium loss than

women who had a low calcium intake.

Lose The Caffeine–Gain The Calcium

- **Reduce the number of cups of coffee you drink per day.**
- **Switch to decaffeinated coffee and tea.**
- **If you must drink soda, look for sodas that don't contain caffeine.**
- **Eliminate chocolate from your diet.**
- **Drink flavored mineral waters (look for low-sodium brands).**
- **Discover the wonderful world of herbal teas.**

How Much Caffeine Are You Really Getting?

<u>Beverages</u>	<u>Caffeine in mg</u>
Coffee	
Coffee, regular drip, 1 cup	130 approx.
Coffee, instant, 1 cup	60 approx.
Coffee, decaffeinated, ground, 1 cup	5 approx.
Coffee, decaffeinated, instant, 1 cup	2 approx.
Tea	
One cup, 1 minute brewing time	20 approx.
One cup, 5 minutes brewing time	40 approx.
Instant, one cup	20 approx.
Iced, one can (12 ounces)	30 approx.
Cocoa	
Milk chocolate mix, 1 ounce	10 approx.
Soft Drinks	
Dr. Pepper (12 ounce can)	60 approx.
Mountain Dew	50 approx.
Regular cola (12 ounce can)	40 approx.
Tab	40 approx.
Diet cola (12 ounce can)	30 approx.

Watch the amount of caffeine in medications.
If you aren't sure, ask your doctor.

Calcium Robber # 3: Fat

The anti-fat lobby is alive and well and beginning to show up on our grocery shelves all over the country. All of us are now aware of the importance of keeping fat intake to no more than 30% of our total daily calories. We know that animal sources of fat are worse for us than vegetable sources of fat. We know that fat clogs up our arteries and veins, leading to heart disease, stroke and high blood pressure. We know that fat is one of the leading factors in breast cancer and cancers of the digestive system. But what we may not be aware of is that fat blocks our ability to absorb calcium, with the result that we have to go into our bone bank and deplete our reserves. Too much fat in the system combines with calcium, blocking absorption by converting the calcium to a form which can't be absorbed. The result is that vital calcium is excreted, without ever adding to our bone supply or circulating in our blood stream.

Figuring Out The Fat

1. Grams of fat per serving x 9 ÷ total calories per serving x 100 = % of calories from fat.

2. Multiply the fat grams by 30. If the number you get is smaller than the total calories listed you are getting less than 30 of your calories in that product from fat.

Check Your Cholesterol I.Q.

Total Cholesterol
Under 200	Desirable
200 to 239	Borderline-High
240 or more	High

Get The Calcium & Lose The Fat

Select nonfat or lowfat diary products.
Eat more green vegetables.
Reduce the amount of red meat in your diet.
Read food labels carefully.
Learn how to figure out the amount of fat in food.

Calcium Robber #4: Alcohol

Not all alcohol is bad. As with everything, the key is moderation. In fact, some alcohol may actually be healthful. There is evidence that moderate amounts of alcohol may have a positive effect on cardiovascular health. And there's more. A study from the University of Pittsburgh found that 3 to 6 drinks per week can actually raise estrogen levels in postmenopausal women, and help conserve calcium stores in bones.

Alcohol & Bones

However, anything more than moderate drinking has a devastatingly opposite effect. Some research shows that excessive amounts of alcohol pull calcium directly from bones. A Harvard study showed that regularly drinking a substantial number of alcoholic beverages increased the likelihood of breaking both a hip and arm. And it doesn't take much to snap those bones. Just a couple of beers a day can double your risk of breaking a hip and more than four drinks of hard liquor a day increases your odds of breaking a hip sevenfold.

Researchers believe that alcohol may affect the hormonal balance necessary to absorb and utilize calcium. Alcohol may also stimulate the increased production of urine, flushing out calcium before it can be utilized.

Alcohol & Blood Pressure

Findings from the University of California show that in light drinkers alcohol actually helped calcium to lower blood pressure, while in heavy drinkers it blocked calcium's efforts to lower blood pressure.

Lose The Alcohol, Gain The Calcium

- **Limit yourself to no more than two alcoholic drinks per day.**
- **Discover the delights of designer water.**
- **If you think you have a drinking problem, get professional help.**

Calcium Robber #5: Smoking

One of the single biggest causes of death in the United States is smoking, which kills over 300,000 people a year.

Beyond Bones

Nutritionists also point to the fact that smoking causes free radicals that can be destructive to both soft and hard tissues in the body, aging us prematurely and putting us at greater risk for a whole variety of killer diseases.

Add to this the countless studies that show smoking to be a leading cause of cancer and heart disease and there is compelling evidence to quit smoking right now.

Smoking is the leading cause of stroke. Smokers are 11 times more likely to have a stroke than nonsmokers. This is especially true for smokers under the age of 65. If you quit, your risk of stroke is cut to that of a nonsmoker after five years for men, and just two years for women. Need more reasons?

Smoking & Calcium

Smoking is especially devastating to your calcium stores.

Some studies show that smoking may damage the liver's estrogen production ability, increasing the probability of thining bones. The news just gets worse. It may be that smoking also blocks the calcium you are taking from reaching vital areas and strengthening bones. According to the Osteoporosis Center at the Hospital for Special Surgery in New York, smokers have twice as much chance of getting back fractures as nonsmokers.

New International Research

A new study from Australia found that women who smoke a pack of cigarettes a day as adults go into menopause with 5 to 10 percent less bone than their nonsmoking sisters.

****

Did You Know That

It take 39 weeks for a smoker's bone to heal after a fracture.
It takes only 21 weeks for a nonsmoker's bone to heal after a fracture.

Calcium Robber # 6: Protein

We all eat far too much protein–much more than the recommended amounts and this causes serious problems, some of which may directly affect our ability to utilize dietary calcium.

High protein intake has been found to be a significant factor in kidney damage. The kidneys act as the filter for our bloodstream. Too much protein causes kidneys to work overtime. Why? Because protein breaks down into amino acids and finally urine, causing the kidneys to excrete more water. This process also raises the fluid pressure and if this higher pressure is allowed to continue it eventually breaks down the filtering mechanism and damages the entire organ.

Too much protein consumption may also be a factor in calcium loss through the urinary tract. This research is still preliminary, and somewhat controversial. However evidence does point to the fact that the high levels of protein which Americans eat routinely may force too much calcium out of the system before it has a chance to be absorbed and utilized. This once again forces the body to take vital calcium from bones where it is stored, adding to the calcium depletion chain that eventually results in osteoporosis.

Our early ancestors ate protein only rarely, when the hunt was successful. Today, too often the major portion of each meal we eat is protein. We also eat too many large protein loads in the course of a digestive day. This makes our kidneys work harder than ever to clean up the protein by-products which are left. This is especially disasterous for people who have weakened kidney function or a family history of kidney disease. But this constant strain on even healthy kidneys can cause damage over time.

Also, most of the protein we take in is from animal sources–meat–which contains alarming amounts of fat. So our bodies are getting a double negative whammy by overloading on protein.

The Recommended Dietary Allowance for protein is 46 grams for the average woman (that's 2 cups of milk) and 56 grams for the average man. One chicken breast contains 35 grams of protein–so look out!

Get The Protein, Lose The Fat: Lessons From A Vegetarian

- Baked lentils and rice
- Macaroni & cheese
- Cereal & milk
- Cheese pizza

Calcium Robber #7: Phosphoric Acid

New studies show that while calcium can help build stronger bones and reduce the risks of fractures in later life, there are certain foods that can undo all the good that calcium is trying to do.

Chief among these are foods containing phosphorus such as sodas, packaged baked goods and processed meats. Researchers believe that these foods may increase the amount of calcium that is lost through urine and over time can result in lower bone mass.

Sodas Need Milk To Balance Calcium

The phosphorus in sodas, which all of us consume readily, is particularly dangerous for teenage girls. The more soda you drink without balancing it with milk, the greater your chances are for developing osteoporosis.

Calcium Robber # 8: Fiber

While nutritionists agree that we need to eat a higher fiber diet to keep our bowels scrubbed and clean and reduce the risk of cancer, too much fiber (and fiber cousins, oxalic acid in some vegetables and phytic acid in the outer casings of some grains) can block calcium absorption. However, scientists are still not certain about the long-term effects of too much fiber. Much more research needs to be done on the type of fiber and the level of calcium intake. These will be significant variables and still need considerable research and study.

Rule of Thumb

If there is a rule of thumb about calcium and fiber, it is this:
it is better to increase the calcium rather than decrease the fiber.
Some studies show that you may need as much as 150 more mg of
calcium for every 25 grams of fiber.

Calcium Robbers #9:
Oxalic Acid & Phytic Acid

Close cousins to fiber are two acids found in certain foods. One, oxalic acid, is found in spinach, beet and turnip greens, and green beans. This is especially important to know if you are counting on getting lots of your dietary calcium from these vegetables, which are shown to be high in calcium on food charts.

The Popeye Principle

> **Researchers at Purdue University recently discovered that only 5% of the calcium available in spinach is actually absorbed, because it is blocked by the oxalic acid.**

What can you do? Some nutritionists recommend cooking these vegetables in a little vinegar or lemon juice or serving them with a little vinegar or lemon juice. The acid in the vinegar or lemon juice helps release the calcium and make it easier to absorb–giving you more calcium value.

A similar problem exists with phytic acid which is found in the outer husks of grains. It also blocks the absorption of dietary calcium.

Foods High In Calcium & Oxalic Acid
- Greens
- Beets
- Green beans
- Rhubarb
- Spinach

Calcium Robber #10: Medications

You should be aware that there are a number of prescription and over-the-counter medications you may currently be taking that have been shown to block the absorption of calcium. You should discuss your use of medications with your physician with a view to saving as much calcium as possible.

Glucocorticoid medications
These are often prescribed for rheumatiod arthritis, osteoarthritis, bursitis, asthma, lupus, hepatitis, colitis, Crohn's disease, multiple sclerosis, glaucoma, severe inflammations.

Aluminum-containing antacids
Some antacids contain aluminum and some do not. Taking large quantities of aluminum-based antacids may, in some people, result in the extra aluminum being deposited in the bone, leaving no room for calcium. It is very important to follow your physicians' dosage instructions exactly when taking these medications.

Cholestyramine
This medication, used to control cholesterol levels, decreases the amount of vitamin D that is absorbed. This may result in less calcium being deposited and less bone mass.

Thyroid Hormones
Certain thyroid hormones need careful monitoring to make sure the dosage is exactly right in order to reduce the risk of osteoporosis.

Gonadotropin-Releasing Hormone Analogues
These are used to treat endometriosis and studies show that long-term use can result in bone loss.

Heparin
This blood-clotting medication may have a long-term adverse effect on bone mass.

Cyclosporine A
This is an immunosuppressive drug used in organ transplants and in certain immune disorders. Because it is often used in connection with glucocorticoid medications it may have an adverse effect on bone mass.

*****Alert*****
Always discuss your medications with your doctor or health professional. Do not make any changes on your own.

How To Make The Best Antacid Choice

In our fast-paced lives, when meals are snatched on the run, at our desks, or when we create strange meals based on crazy diets, the result can often be upset stomach, heartburn, acid indigestion, gas, and reflux, that uncomfortable sensation of a sourish taste in our mouths of a meal we ate hours before.

So what do you do? You pop an antacid. Terrific. You feel better. But did you know that the antacid you just took may be drawing vital calcium from your bones and that the more often you have to take antacids, the greater your risk of losing bone-calcium? Why? Because some antacids contain aluminum which binds with phosphorus and increases the amount of calcium you lose through your bowels.

Tips

1. Ask your doctor to recommend or prescribe an antacid.

2. Ask your pharmacist about over-the-counter antacids.

3. Always follow dosage instructions.

4. Read the labels and get informed.

5. Eat a lowfat, balanced diet to give your tummy a break.

Get The Lead Out

Keeping the calcium content of bones at an adequate level is also very important for another reason besides osteoporosis protection. Lead contamination.

When bones lose calcium, releasing it into the system for other uses, research shows that lead, which is also stored in bones, is released into the system at the same time. The key times that lead is released into your system are the key times that you are losing calcium–during pregnancy, lactation and menopause. This is not good because too much lead in your system is toxic and can cause serious health problems.

Check Your Lead Risk

√ You were exposed to lead as a child through lead pipes or lead-based paint.

√ There is too much lead in your drinking water.

√ Your dishes have a lead-based glaze on them.

√ Your home was built between 1978 and 1988 when plumbers used lead to solder pipes.

√ Your home was built before 1930 and has lead plumbing.

√ You drink your coffee and tea out of heavy, glazed pottery mugs.

√ You eat a lot of canned, imported products.

If you checked more than one item, you should de-lead your environment and take extra calcium to insure that calcium loss doesn't result in lead being released into your system. This is particularly important while you are pregnant.

Great Beginnings: Your Fetus & Calcium

Calcium needs begin in infancy. This is the time that determines whether we will have strong, straight, disease-free bones for life, or whether we are fated to suffer the stress, pain, and risk of death from osteoporosis and fractures. So make sure your kids get a great calcium start in life–a start that will give them protection for life.The process of building and maintaining strong bones begins before birth. The nourishment you give your unborn child will have an extraordinary and positive effect on its physical and mental development for the rest of its life. Feed your baby properly, through your own healthy and balanced diet even before your newborn sees its first sunrise. Here's why:

1. Calcium builds strong bones that give your infant a healthy foundation for life.

2. Calcium is vital for the healthy development of the nervous system. Studies have shown that calcium is a vital mineral in the transmission of nerve impulses.

3. Calcium is critical for the healthy and normal development of brain function.

4. New research shows that vision is dependent on adequate and regular amounts of calcium.

Care & Feeding Of Your Fetus: Calcium Tips

Here are some calcium-boosting tips for you and the precious life you carry inside.

- Snack on instant or cooked pudding made with skim milk.
- Sprinkle one or two teaspoons of skim milk powder into
    soups and gravies for extra calcium.
- Make all your soups with skim milk.
- Top your baked pototoes and other veggies with plain, nonfat yogurt.
- Whip up a healthy shake using frozen yogurt and skim milk instead
    of ice cream and whole milk.

Your New Baby and Calcium

Now that your baby is born, it is more important than ever to make sure the nourishment the infant gets is healthy and builds a strong foundation for life. While they are nursing or on formula, babies are getting the balance of vital nutrients they need to grow and develop both physically and mentally.

As they begin to explore new foods, and begin to wean themselves off breast milk and formula, the challenge of insuring their adequate nutrition really begins. Now is the time your baby needs all your skill and loving care. Every meal, whether breakfast, lunch or dinner, is a learning experience–not just learning how to eat, and developing likes and dislikes, but also learning how to make the right, balanced food choices for a lifetime of health. Starting the process of teaching your child to try different foods, experiment, make selections based on nutritional need, curb appetite, and develop sound, healthy eating habits, will determine to a large extent whether your child grows up healthy, fit, slim with a good mental attitude toward food and nourishment, or spends a lifetime battling food-related problems.

Nutrients and Baby's Teeth

Calcium is essential in the formation of the basic material of which teeth are made. To insure your baby's strong, firm teeth you should know that teeth are being formed in the womb from a combination of calcium and phosphorus to form calcium phosphate, the hard material of teeth. That is why it is so important that you eat only healthy foods during your pregnancy. Research shows that your baby needs the following nutrients to insure strong teeth: calcium, phosphorus, magnesium, vitamin D and vitamin C.

Your Baby's Calcium RDA

Up to six months	360 mg
Six months to 1 year	540 mg

****

8 ounces of breast milk contain 79 mg of calcium.

Calcium Plus Magnesium For Babies

Your baby needs more than calcium to build strong and healthy bones for a lifetime. If your baby is deficient in magnesium, chances are the infant will be lacking in calcium and phosphorous as well, because these three are the vital "bone" minerals.

Your Baby's Magnesium RDA

Up to 6 months	50 mg
6 months to 1 year	70 mg

Your Baby's Magnesium Diet

Getting enough magnesium is a problem, one that will probably get worse as your baby gets older. Surveys show that the majority of Americans are deficient in magnesium.

According to the U.S. Department of Agriculture, from birth to 12 months, 11% of children get less than the RDA; between 1 and 2 years of age, 26% of children get less than the RDA; and from the ages of 3 to 8, a whopping 55% of children get less than the RDA. And by the time children reach their teens, over 80% of them are getting below the minimum standard set.

Good Sources of Magnesium

1/2 cup cooked fresh spinach....................................76 mg
1/2 cup fresh cooked broccoli..................................47 mg
1/2 cup cooked okra...46 mg
1 ounce of wheat germm...91 mg
1/2 cup fresh cooked lima beans.............................63 mg

Calcium Plus Vitamin D For Babies

Vitamin D is an essential vitamin that allows calcium to do its work and build strong teeth and bones. Without vitamin D even less calcium would be absorbed, for most would be flushed out of the system.

Babies get vitamin D the way the rest of us do, through exposure to sunshine and through milk which is fortified with vitamin D. If you and your baby live in a northern climate where there are long periods without sunlight, your doctor may prescribe additional vitamin D supplements in the form of drops for your baby.

Your Baby's Vitamin D RDA

From birth to 6 months	10 mcg
From 6 months to 1 year	10 mcg
From 1 year to 3 years	10 mcg

Good Sources of Vitamin D

1 cup of fortified milk..100 IU
1 can salmon (1 1/2 ounces)....................................500 IU
1 egg...23 IU
1 cup of bran flakes...100 IU

Calcium Plus Vitamin C For Babies

Vitamin C is important in the production and maintenance of collagen, a basic protein that holds the body together. It provides a strong foundation for muscles, bones, teeth and skin and helps repair any damage to them quickly.

Your Baby's Vitamin C RDA

From birth to 6 months	35 mg
From 6 months to 1 year	35 mg
From 1 year to 3 years	45 mg

Good Sources of Vitamin C

Broccoli, 1/2 cup.............................49 mg.
Cauliflower, 1/2 cup.......................34 mg.
Vegetable juice, 1/2 cup..................33 mg.
Cantaloupe, 1/2 of whole..............113 mg.

Strong Baby Teeth

There has been a lot of controversy about the addition of fluoride to the drinking water supply. Research now shows that areas where fluoride has been added to the water supply show fewer cavities among children. Today, the addition of fluoride is recommended by the American Dental Association and the American Medical Association as well as by the United States Public Health Service.

Tooth Destroyer #1–Sugar

To some extent your baby's ability to resist tooth decay (caries) depends on heredity. Research shows that cavities and decay can also be directly attributed to lactic acid which is produced by bacteria in sugars and starches that remain on the teeth after meals and snacks. This lactic acid begins to eat away at the enamel coating of the teeth, and eventually causes cavities.

Biggest Cavity Causing Culprits
- Constant snacking between meals
- Sweet, sugary snacks
- Falling asleep with a bottle of milk or juice

Looking After Baby's & Child's Teeth

> √ Make brushing & flossing a family affair.
> √ Set a good example. Brush your own teeth after every meal.
> √ Buy a small soft brush for your baby to play with and
> get used to using.
> √Encourage the drinking of lots of water to wash away bits of food
> that remain in the mouth.

Dental Care For Your Baby

Getting your baby used to going to the dentist early can set a healthy, positive view of dentistry for life. Make sure you find a dentist who is good with children; many now have a pediatric specialty.

When you go to the dentist, take your baby along so that the child becomes used to the process, the office and the equipment.

Your child's first visit should be before the first birthday, and then every 6 months for follow-up care and careful monitoring of possible dental problems.

Kids & Calcium: Part I

Situation Desperate & Getting Worse

A shocking and desperate state of affairs exists with our kids and the critical calcium they are not getting. A major national health and nutrition survey shows clearly that between 1980 and 1991 the amount of calcium that children between the ages of 6 and 11 got dropped by 100 mg a day! This is not good news.
The less calcium our kids get now, the greater their chances for developing osteoporosis, high blood pressure and heart disease in the future. We can begin to help right now.

New Research Is Impressive: Especially for pre-teen girls

1. University of Utah School of Medicine

A new study from the University of Utah School of Medicine found that pre-teen girls who had a diet that included 1200 mg of calcium every day increased their bone density by 10 to 15 percent over girls who didn't.

Study after study showns that calcium in childhood has a significant impact on the long-term bone health of women.

2. United States Department of Agriculture Study

Increasing girls' calcium intake between the ages of 8 and 11, the age at which most bone is formed, has a maximum impact on bone density and strength. The study also found that between the ages of 10 and 14, when a girl usually begins to menstruate, there is a rapid drop in the amount of bone formation. By age 15, the study found, very little bone was added.

3. Children's Nutrition Center in Houston, TX Research

The findings of this study indicate that it is important to attain peak bone mass as early as possible. Age five is not too soon to start an anti-osteoporosis campaign using calcium. Young bones have a greater ability to use calcium to build mass. This ability greatly diminishes within the two years after the first period.

4. Penn State University's Hershey Medical Center Report

A study showed that getting girls around the age of 12 to switch back to milk from soda (like their brothers) could add 1% of bone mass a year to their frame. After five years of extra calcium girls could add 5% to their bone density and reduce their risk for osteoporosis fractures by 50%!

Kids & Calcium: Part II

> The National Institutes of Health Consensus Development Conference on Optimal Calcium Intake found that the current Recommended Dietary Allowances for calcium are too low for most age groups and that includes kids and teens.

Our Kids Are Not Getting Even The Required Amount Of Calcium

Baylor College of Medicine in Houston, Texas, studied the diets of girls between the ages of 5 and 16. These kids were just eating the way they normally would and were not given any extra calcium. The findings? All the girls were consuming much less calcium in their normal diet than the recommended amount for building strong bones. Researchers concluded that at the rate these young girls were not getting their calcium, they could enter adulthood with 10% to 15% less total body calcium and weakened bones.

Indiana University School of Medicine

This study showed that giving children slightly more calcium than the recommended dietary allowance could have a significant impact on their long-term bone health. Children in this study were given the RDA for calcium. But one group was given an extra 700 mg per day of calcium. The result? The group getting more than the RDA had significantly greater bone mass gains in the forearm and spine. This lowered their risk for later fractures, it was estimated by 30 percent. (This study was the first of its kind. The NIH meeting has since increased the amount of recommended calcium for kids. But experts feel that kids could still be taking more dietary calcium without ill effect. Always check with your doctor or pediatrician before making any changes in your child's diet.)

Bone & Mineral Metabolism Laboratory at Ohio State University

Girls between the ages of 11 and 15 have the widest window of opportunity for building bone mass. The larger and heavier bones are going into adulthood, the lower the risk for osteoporotic fractures.

****

The NIH Conference on Calcium wants you to know that the need for calcium is greatest between the ages of 9 and 18. That's when kids form a whopping 37% of the bone they will have for a lifetime.

Kids' Calcium Robbers

Smoking
More kids than ever before are smoking. The worst tragedy is that young girls are smoking even more and at an earlier age than boys.

Fat
Fast foods, hamburgers, fried snacks, cakes and cookies are all high in fat and block the absoption of calcium.

Salt
Just as guilty as their parents, kids get far too much salt in their diet.

Protein
American kids eat far too much protein, particularly in fatty red meat.

Alcohol
Here's another one of those tragedies, like smoking. Too many of our kids drink alcohol at a very early age and do serious damage to their bone strength.

Caffeine & Phosphorus
These two culprits are found in sodas, the preferred drink of girls.

Yo-Yo Dieting and Eating Disorders
Peer pressure to be slim can have disastrous nutritional effects.

Early Onset of Menstuation
The average age of the first menstruation has dropped from 16 a hundred and fifty years ago to 12 1/2 today. This gives girls less time to build bone since the greatest amount of bone growth is before the first period.

****

Calcium Counts
Scientists believe that the amount of calcium you get as a kid can make a 5% to 10% difference in how dense your bones are as an adult and can reduce your risk of hip fractures by 50%

Defending Your Kids From Calcium Robbers

Encourage them to switch from hamburgers to pizza.

Substitute air-popped popcorn for salty, fatty snacks like potato chips.

Go from sodas to juices and milk.

Buy lowfat or nonfat snacks.

Switch to frozen yogurt and frozen juice desserts.

Go from fatty cheeses to their lowfat or nonfat cousins.

Make exercise a regular part of your family routine.

Encourage kids to learn to cook and shop for healthy meals.

Look for lowfat or nonfat desserts.

Kids & Calcium Supplements

Should you run right out and buy calcium supplements for your kids? The jury is still out on that issue. However, here is what we do know. Researchers at Indiana University conducted a three-year study of identical twins. One of the twins was given a calcium supplement (1000 mg) the other twin was given a placebo. The results were sort of mixed. Some of the sets of twins had an increase in their bone density as a result of taking supplements. Others, who had gone through puberty during the course of this study, showed no change. And in addition, almost 25% of the sets of twins dropped out because they hated taking supplements.

What does this tell concerned parents?

• Calcium supplements are most effective before kids go through puberty.
• Dietary sources of calcium are still among the best for kids.
• Increasing dietary sources of calcium can help build strong bones for kids.

**The best advice on
calcium supplements for kids
is check with your doctor
before giving your kids any supplements.**

Kids & Food

Kids Are Not Little Adults

Kids have very real and very special requirements in their daily diets. Don't treat your kids like little adults, but give them the healthy, wholesome food their small bodies require for growth and health throughout the rest of their lives.

Food Groups & Your Kids

Age	Food Group	Serving Size
1 to 3 years old	Bread Group	1/2 slice
	Veggie Group	2 to 4 tablespoons
	Fruit Group	1/2 cup juice or 2 to 4 tablespoons
	Milk Group	1/2 to 3/4 cup
	Meat Group	1 to 1 1/2 ounces
4 to 6 years old	Bread Group	1 slice
	Veggie Group	1/4 to 1/2 cup
	Fruit Group	1/2 cup juice or 1/4 to 1/2 cup
	Milk Group	3/4 cup
	Meat Group	1 to 2 ounces
7 to 10 years old	Bread Group	1 to 2 slices
	Veggie Group	1/2 to 3/4 cup
	Fruit Group	1/2 cup juice or 1/2 to 3/4 cup
	Milk Group	3/4 to 1 cup
	Meat Group	2 to 3 ounces

Calories & Kids

Here are some suggested daily calorie amounts for your kids. Please use these as guidelines and always check with your doctor about your kid's diet.

Age 1 to 3 years	1300 calories per day
Age 4 to 6 years	1800 calories per day
Age 7 to 10 years	2000 calories per day

New Daily Calcium For Kids & Teens

Up to 6 months	400 mg
6 months to 1 year	600 mg
1 year to 3 years	800 mg
4 years to 6 years	800 mg
7 years to 10 years	800 to 1200 mg

Male Children

11 years to 14 years	1200 to 1500 mg
15 years to 18 years	1200 to 1500 mg
19 years to 22 years	1200 to 1500 mg

Female Children

11years to 14 years	1200 to 1500 mg
15 years to 18 years	1200 to 1500 mg
19 years to 22 years	1200 to 1500 mg

Daily Magnesium For Kids & Teens

Up to 6 months	50 mg
6 months to 1 year	70 mg
1 year to 3 years	150 mg
4 years to 6 years	200 mg
7 years to 10 years	250 mg

Male Children

11 years to 14 years	350 mg
15 years to 18 years	400 mg
19 years to 22 years	350 mg

Female Children

11 years to 14 years	300 mg
15 years to 18 years	300 mg
19 years to 22 years	300 mg

Daily Vitamin D For Kids & Teens

Up to 6 months...10 mcg
6 months to 1 year...10 mcg
1 year to 3 years..10 mcg
4 years to 6 years..10 mcg
7 years to 10 years..10 mcg

Male Children
11 years to 14 years......................................10 mcg
15 years to 18 years......................................10 mcg
19 years to 22 years..................................... 7.5 mcg

Female Children
11 years to 14 years......................................10 mcg
15 years to 18 years......................................10 mcg
19 years to 22 years..................................... 7.5 mcg

Daily Vitamin C For Kids & Teens

Up to 6 months...35 mg
6 months to 1 year...35 mg
1 year to 3 years..45 mg
4 years to 6 years..45 mg
7 years to 10 years..45 mg

Male Children
11 years to 14 years......................................50 mg
15 to 18 years...60 mg
19 to 22 years...60 mg

Female Children
11 to 14 years...50 mg
15 to 18 years...60 mg
19 to 22 years...60 mg

Let's Play Calcium Hide & Seek

There are lots of ways to sneak calcium into your kids' diet without them even suspecting. Here are some suggestions:

√ Pour them a glass of morning OJ that is calcium-reinforced.
   Try Tropicana or Minute Maid.
√ Make kids sandwiches with calcium-fortified bread.
   Try Wonder Bread or Merita.

√ If your kids hate milk try flavoring it with chocolate syrup or vanilla or
   strawberry flavoring.
√ Instead of sodas let them drink flavored water, OJ, Yoohoo, and milk.
   Try giving them Sunny Delight (300 mg calcium per 8-ounce glass) and
   Double C Hawaiian Punch (150 mg calcium per 8-ounce glass).
√ Make milk shakes and sundaes with nonfat frozen yogurt instead of ice-cream.

√ Pack individual yogurt snacks in lunchboxes. Try ones made especially for kids:
   Yoplait's "Trix" or Light n' Lively "Kid Pack" or "Sprinkl'ins" from Dannon.

√ Sprinkle extra Parmesan on pizza, popcorn and veggies.
√ Top baked potatoes with lowfat yogurt instead of sour cream.
√ Serve stuffing mix more often.

√ Let them munch on sesame seeds.
√ Encourage your kids to eat Fig Newtons.

√ Add a box of raisins to their lunch. Sprinkle raisins on their cereal and dessert.
√ Mix a couple of teaspoons of nonfat powdered milk into their pudding,
   cream soup, sauces, and hot chocolate.

Calcium Treats For Kids
&
Grown-ups Too

Super Duper Banana Split

1 ripe banana, peeled
1 small scoop lowfat frozen strawberry yogurt
1 small scoop lowfat frozen chocolate yogurt
1 small scoop lowfat frozen vanilla yogurt
3 tablespoons strawberry fruit spread
2 tablespoons whole grain cereal*
2 teaspoons raisins

Split banana in half lengthwise. Place in a longish, shallow dish, one half on each side of the dish. Arrange the frozen yogurt between the banana slices. Top with fruit spread. Sprinkle with cereal and raisins. Serve. Makes 2 servings.

Per serving:

Calories: 478   Fat: 4.3 grams   Calcium: 497 mg

* If you can, use whole grain Total® cereal. It has 250 mg of calcium per serving.
    I believe it is the only one that does.

After School Shakes

Sunshiny Day Shake

3 cups nonfat frozen vanilla yogurt
1 cup skim milk
1/2 cup orange juice*

Place all ingredients in a blender or food processor. Process until smooth. Pour into glasses. Garnish with slices of orange. Serve. Makes 8 servings.

Per serving:
Calories: 95   Fat: Trace   Calcium: 191 mg
* Use one of the calcium-reinforced juices like Minute Maid or Tropicana for maximum calcium.

Chocolate Delight

3 cups nonfat frozen chocolate yogurt
1 1/2 cups skim milk
2 tablespoons chocolate syrup

Place all ingredients in a blender or food processor. Process until smooth. Pour into glasses. Top with a Hershey's Kiss if desired. Serve. Makes 8 servings.

Per serving:
Calories: 104   Fat: Trace   Calcium: 209 mg

Strawberry Surprise

3 cups nonfat frozen strawberry yogurt
1 1/2 cups skim milk
1 sliced strawberries, fresh or frozen

Place all ingredients in a blender or food processor. Process until smooth. Pour into glasses. Top with a Hershey's Kiss if desired. Serve. Makes 8 servings.

Per serving:
Calories: 122   Fat: 2.7 grams   Calcium: 186 mg

Perfect Sweet Party Pizza

2 cups graham cracker crumbs
6 tablespoons melted margarine
6 cups nonfat frozen vanilla or strawberry yogurt, slightly
    softened
1 cup fresh sliced strawberries
1 cup fresh blueberries
1 cup pineapple packed in juice, drained
1 nectarine, peeled and sliced
chocolate syrup
coconut

Line a 12-inch pizza pan with aluminum foil. Combine crumbs and margarine in bowl. Press mixture evenly in the pizza pan. Place in freezer for 15 minutes, or until hardened. Spread yogurt on the crust. Cover with plastic wrap. Return to freezer overnight. Arrange fruits on top of the pie. Drizzle with chocolate sauce. Sprinkle with coconut. Cut into slices. Serve. Makes 16 servings.

Per serving:

Calories: 176   Fat: 5.6 grams   Calcium: 159 mg

Cheesy Zippy Popcorn

8 cups air-popped popcorn
2 tablespoon Parmesan cheese
1 teaspoon chili powder

Prepare popcorn according to package directions. Toss with Parmesan cheese and chili powder. Serve. Makes 8 servings.

Per serving:

Calories: 36   Fat: Trace   Calcium: 18 mg

Terrific Trail Mix

2 cups corn cereal squares
2 cups rice cereal squares
1 1/2 cups mini salt free pretzels
1 cup bran cereal
1/2 cup cheese nips
1/2 cup raisins
2 tablespoons margarine, melted
1 teaspoon cinnamon
1/4 cup ground nutmeg

Preheat oven to 350°F. Spray a baking pan or cookie sheet with nonstick cooking spray. Place cereals, pretzels, cheese nips in an even layer on the pan. Combine margarine, cinnamon and nutmeg in a small bowl. Mix well. Drizzle over cereal mixture and mix well. Bake for 10 to 12 minutes or until golden. Cool. Add raisins. Toss together. Serve. Makes approximately 8 servings.

Per serving:
Calories: 361   Fat: 8.3 grams   Calcium: 77 mg

Sombrero Dip

1 container (4 ounces) nonfat cream cheese
1/2 cup lowfat shredded cheddar cheese
1/4 cup medium salsa
3 teaspoons skim milk
Baked nacho chips, toasted pita bread, or fresh veggies

Combine cheeses in a small saucepan. Stir over low heat until melted. Do not boil. Stir in salsa and milk. Stirring, heat through. Use as a dip. Makes 4 servings.

Per Serving:

Calories: 75   Fat: Trace   Calcium: 128 mg

Teens & Calcium

The teenage years are particularly important as far as calcium is concerned, but, unfortunately, these are the years during which teenage girls don't take as good care of their bodies as they should. A recent Gallup Poll showed that while teens are aware of nutritional issues and what constitute good food habits, they opt for hamburgers, pizza, and luncheon meats. Teens drink too much coffee and too many caffeine-loaded sodas. They smoke. Add to that the statistics on teenage drinking–70% of teens drink and almost three quarters of those can be classified as heavy drinkers, according to the National Institute on Alcohol Abuse.

Teen Boys & Girls Are Not Calcium Equal
In a recent survey of high school students it was found that boys get an average of 1200 mg of calcium per day while girls get only 600 mg of calcium per day–half of what boys chug-a-lug down for stronger bones.

Teen Girls & Deadly Diets

A study conducted by Comprehensive Psychiatric Services in Cleveland found that 60% more females than males were dieting. Here's the shocker. Almost one-third of the teen dieters were underweight to begin with. This dieting, particularly for teenage girls can result in smaller, weaker bones and a significantly increased risk of developing osteoporosis.

Teenage Pregnancy

Today, young girls are physiologically able to get pregnant at the age of 12 1/2 or 13.
- In 1940 the birth rate for unmarried American teenagers between 15 and 19 was 7.4 per thousand.
- In 1991 the birthrate for unmarried American teenagers between 15 and 19 was 45 per thousand and there were 1.1 million teenage pregnancies, 28,000 involving girls under the age of 15.

It doesn't get better. Today it is estimated that one out of every four female teenagers will be pregnant by the age of 18.

✳✳✳✳✳✳✳✳✳

Between 1960 and 1992 consumption of diet sodas and soft drinks went up 476%. That left a lot less room for calcium-rich milk.

Teens & Calcium, Continued

Pennsylvania State University

A Penn State study reports that between the ages of 12 and 14, girls get only 70 percent of the calcium required for strong bone growth.

European Study & Teens

A study from Finland found that regular exercise and not smoking, along with a calcium-rich diet, are very important factors in the density of bone in adolescence.

How To Help Your Teenage Daughter

1. Educate her about nutrition in general & calcium in particular.
2. Set a good example. Get lots of calcium yourself. Keep calcium-rich foods in the house and get rid of the junk.
3. Communicate. Get your daughter books and literature about calcium and bone health.
4. Give your daughter a membership in the National Osteoporosis Foundation.
5. Go in for a mother-daughter exercise program with special emphasis on walking, biking, and weights.

****

The Growth Spurt
During the adolescent growth spurt your kids can add about 400 to 500 mg of calcium to their bones every single day!
Experts recommend that teens get at least 1500 mg of calcium a day in order to build bone and offset the loss of calcium from teen calcium robbers

Teen Calcium I.Q. Test

Give this test to your teenager, especially your teenage daughter. It wouldn't be a bad idea if you took it yourself.

1. Do you regularly eat breakfast away from home?	YES	NO
2. Do you regularly eat lunch away from home?	YES	NO
3. Do you regularly eat dinner away from home?	YES	NO
4. Do you eat meals at different times?	YES	NO
5. Do you prefer fast-food restaurants?	YES	NO
6. Do you drink sodas with your meals rather than milk?	YES	NO
7. Do you smoke?	YES	NO
8. Do you drink more than 2 alcoholic beverages a day?	YES	NO
9. Do have an eating disorder?	YES	NO
10. Do you think dairy products are high in fat?	YES	NO
11. Do you go on and off diets regularly?	YES	NO
12. Are you a couch potato?	YES	NO

Scoring: If you answered YES to even one of these questions chances are very good that you are not getting enough calcium and your bones are at risk.

****

**Attention Fast-food Restaurants:
Here Is An Opportunity
To Help Teens
Build Healthy Bones**

Researchers at the Unversity of Nebraska and Kansas State University determined through interviews with young women that they would be more likely to buy milk with their fast food if a picture of milk were posted and if the milk tasted fresher and was not served in cartons.

Pregnancy & Calcium

Congratulations! You are expecting. It is a wonderful, mystical time for you and a very special one as far as your health is concerned. Now is the time to focus on yourself and on the new life growing inside you and make sure both are well nourished.

During this time your baby depends on you for nutrition. Remember, you are really eating for two very special people. Your baby needs lots of vitamins and minerals to get a good start that will keep the infant healthy for the rest of its life.

You need lots of vitamins and minerals to make sure you also stay healthy and strong and don't deplete your stores of vital nutrients, leaving you at risk for vitamin deficiency.

Nutrition experts say you need at least 50 percent more calcium during this time. So take good nutritional care of yourself and start taking your calcium supplements.

Special Nutritional Requirements For Pregnant Women

Did you know that to nourish a fetus you need an extra 300 calories a day or a total of 81,000 calories during the nine months you are pregnant? That includes:

65% more protein
100% more folacin
100% more vitamin D
50% more calcium
50% more magnesium
33% more vitamin C
25% more vitamin A
25% more vitamin E
25% more zinc
100% more iron

****

Recent studies show that women between the age of 25 and 30, the age during which many women get pregnant, get less than 75% of the RDA for calcium, magnesium and iron and only 80% of the RDA for zinc.

Bone-Building Nutrients For Moms-To-Be

1. Calcium
You need at least 1200 to 1500 mg a day during your pregnancy and for breastfeeding your baby. Calcium is the main ingredient in the formation of strong bones and teeth. It is also vital in muscle contraction, nerve functioning, blood clotting, regulation of blood pressure and the development of a strong immune system. New studies show that calcium may help fight the risk of pregnancy-related high blood pressure. But one of the most important functions of calcium is the protection it provides against the fourth leading killer of women—osteoporosis.

2. Magnesium
You need at least 320 mg of magnesium a day during pregnancy and that amount increases to 355 mg during the six months you breastfeed your baby. Magnesium is a key ingredient, along with calcium, for the formation of bones and teeth. In addition, magnesium helps build vital protein links, monitors the activity of a variety of enzymes, is important in regulating muscle contraction and the transmission of nerve impulses.

3. Phosphorous
You will need 1200 mg of phosphorous a day during your pregnancy and while you are nursing your baby. Phosphorous is critical because along with calcium it makes up 75% of the total weight of minerals found in your body. This mineral, along with calcium and magnesium, is a key bone-builder. It is also important to the DNA structure of cells and helps the body produce and utilize energy.

4. Vitamin D
You will need 10 mcg (micrograms) or 400 IU (International Units) of vitamin D a day while you are pregnant and during the time you are nursing your baby.Vitamin D, the sunshine vitamin, aids in the formation of bone by controlling the amount and usage of calcium and phosphorous.

5. Zinc
While you are pregnant, the RDA for zinc is 15 mg a day. This goes up to 19 mg during the period you are nursing your baby. Zinc is important in the normal growth of bones and other tissue in the body. It helps develop your baby's sense of taste and smell. Without zinc, the immune system is at greater risk for infections and disease, and your baby risks a lower birth weight or being born prematurely.

Supplements & Pregnancy

Should you take supplements during pregnancy or not? Ask yourself:

1. I am too busy to shop and cook for myself.	Yes	No
2. I smoke (but I'm trying to quit).	Yes	No
3. I have been told I'm going to have twins.	Yes	No
4. I am under the age of 20.	Yes	No
5. I have been a yo-yo dieter all my life.	Yes	No
6. I'm allergic to milk.	Yes	No
7. I've already gained too much weight while pregnant.	Yes	No
8. I have cravings for junk food.	Yes	No
9. I feel like eating starch or clay.	Yes	No
10. I am a vegetarian.	Yes	No

Scoring: If you answered **YES** to even one of these questions you might be a strong candidate for supplements. Your physician can recommend the right nutritional supplement for you.

Self-Supplementation

Even if you don't have any apparent need for supplements and you feel your diet is adequate, you should still consider taking some additional nutrients during your preganancy and during the time you nurse your baby just to make sure that you and the baby stay healthy.

- Make sure your supplement contains no more than 100% of the RDAs.
- Don't take any individual supplements that are higher than the RDA.
- Make sure your supplement contains the RDA for iron.

When To Take Your Supplement

You should always take your calcium supplement with food. A light snack or dairy product is best. (Remember not to take your calcium at the same time you take your iron supplement.)

Menopause

Remember how confused and scared and proud you felt all at the same time when you first started to menstruate? You didn't know whether to laugh or cry, so you often did both, at the same time. Well, guess what, here it comes again. Another new frontier to cross, another set of challenges to face, and another way to relate to your own body. Just as puberty marked the age at which you began to menstruate, menopause marks the transition to your non-child-bearing years.

In the past, negative attitudes have been associated with menopause because it means a woman is aging, and aging has not always been considered something positive. However, as more "baby boomers" move into their menopausal years, the whole notion of aging is already being redefined.

Menopause Defined

Menopause is strictly defined by medical professionals as 12 months without a menstrual period, with the word menopause meaning the last such period. However, the time from when you first miss or skip a period to when you completely stop menstruating is a slow process that can take many years.

**The average age at menopause is 51.4 years.
But it most often occurs between 47 and 55.**

Remember, menopause is unique to everyone. Some women begin as early as their 30s and others not until they are in their 60s. Still others may experience menopause after their ovaries were removed by surgery.

****

In the United States today, there are 49 million women who are menopausal and 30 million who are postmenopausal. In the next decade alone, some 20 million more women will become menopausal.

The Cycle Of Change

The Beginning Of Menopause–The Menstrual Cycle

Guess what. The menopause cycle actually begins the day you have your first period. But first, let's go back all the way to the very beginning to understand what happens and why.

Get Ready, Get Set, Go!

When you are born, your body contains all the eggs that it needs for child-bearing for the rest of your life. In the first 10 to 13 years of life, however, your body is not ready to reproduce. Then, with your first period, your body enters puberty, or its reproductive phase. Some 200,000 to 400,000 eggs are present in your body when you begin to menstruate. Each month, one of your two ovaries releases an egg. This is called ovulation.

Meet The Hormones: Estrogen & Progesterone

The ovaries also release two hormones, estrogen and progesterone, to let the uterus know it's time to get ready to take care of your egg in case it is fertilized by sperm and you become pregnant. If the egg is not fertilized, it is absorbed into your uterus. Estrogen and progesterone levels then both fall, letting your body know you did not become pregnant. This is the signal for your body to let go of the lining of the uterus that it has prepared to welcome the fertilized egg. This discharged lining is your monthly period. Most women have a period anywhere from every 21 to 45 days, with 28 days, or 4 weeks, being the average. With every monthly cycle, you lose more eggs, until one day few eggs are left. The ovaries begin to produce less and less estrogen because your body no longer needs to get ready to receive the fertilized egg. This decline in estrogen marks what is called the premenopausal stage.

Enter, Calcium

Peak adult bone mass is usually achieved by age 20 with the greatest amount of bone building occuring in the pre-teen years just before puberty and your first period. But experts agree that there is an additional window of opportunity to add bone mass between the ages of 20 and 30.

Premenopause

"The Change" Is About Change

About 1 or 2 years before menopause, you may begin to notice changes in your menstrual cycle. For example, your periods may start to come closer together or farther apart. You may skip a month or two. Your menstrual flow may become lighter or heavier, and you may bleed for more or fewer days than is usual for you. All of these changes may be caused by the decline in estrogen levels, and this irregular cycle may go on for up to 4 or 5 years before you have your last period. Experts define this as perimenopause and it marks the transition into menopause. We call it premenopause.

Common Symptons of Premenopause To Watch For

- Irregular periods
- Changes in type of periods
- Mood swings
- Inability to concentrate
- Hot flashes
- Night sweats
- Temporary loss of memory

How Close Are You To Menopause?

If you have any of these symptoms of menopause, your doctor can perform a simple blood test to find out just where you are in the cycle.

This test will reveal the level of serum estradiol, or estrogen, concentration or the follicle-stimulating hormone (FSH) level in your bloodstream. The FSH hormone is manufactured by your pituitary gland and tells the ovaries to produce estrogen. Low levels of estrogen or a high level of FSH, which rises when no estrogen is present, will tell your doctor that you are probably either premenopausal or menopausal.

One Premenopause Option To Discuss With Your Doctor

Your doctor may prescribe low-dose oral contraceptives to regulate cycle and relieve mood swings and bloating. This is a fairly new use of oral contraceptives, and the FDA is considering changing its recommendations for use of such drug products. Some experts believe that use of oral contraceptives can help prevent ovarian cancer. Oral contraceptives are five times more potent than the hormones used for hormone replacement therapy.

Premenopause & Calcium

The Bone Bank

Until the time we are about 35 years old, our bodies are producing new bone faster than old bone is removed. Then, as we age, we begin to lose bone. With the decline in estrogen and the beginning of menopause, this bone loss speeds up, causing bones to become thin and brittle. Now we are seriously at risk for osteoporosis.

The good news is that osteoporosis is preventable. If you are premenopausal, now is a good time to start on a bone-saving program that will keep you feeling fit and youthful for the rest of your life.

A Premenopause Bone-Building To-Do List

√ Get a complete check-up along with a blood test to determine whether or not you have started menopause as well as a bone density test.

√ Make sure you get at least 1000 mg of calcium from foods and supplements.

√ Start an exercise program such as walking and lifting light weights.

√ If you smoke, stop.

√ Limit yourself to two cups of coffee a day, and have those with a little skim milk.

√ Switch from sodas to water or juice.

√ Start eating lowfat—no more than 30% of daily calories as fat.

√ Get at least 10 minutes of sunshine a day for vitamin D.

√ Take a multivitamin supplement daily.

****

Smoking puts you at menopause 2 to 4 years sooner than nonsmoking.

The Big M

We are now out of the closet! Menopause is no longer taboo. It has done the rounds of all the talk shows, dozens of books have been written about it, super-stars admit to having crossed into the M zone. Let's face it, it is chic!

Great. But what do we really know about menopause? And more importantly what do we know about the impact it has on calcium?

We know a lot.

1. **The first seven years after menopause bone loss speeds up alarmingly. Because as estrogen levels go down, less calcium is absorbed into our bones.**

2. **Hormone replacement therapy, exercise, and calcium can protect us from osteoporosis, the fourth leading cause of death among women today.**

****

Always discuss any treatment with your doctor.

Menopause Q & A

If you want to get a clue about what menopause might mean to you, the impact it will have on your life, and the risks it might pose to your health, ask yourself these questions:

1. How old was your mother when she experienced menopause?
2. Did your mother develop osteoporosis?
3. Did your mother appear to shrink in height and develop a "dowager's hump"?
4. Did your mother fracture a hip or wrist?
5. What is your family's history of heart disease?
6. Do you know your triglyceride levels–the "good" HDL cholesterol and the "bad" LDL cholesterol?
7. Does your family have a history of cancer? Breast cancer, colon cancer, and ovarian cancer can run in families. This may affect your decision about hormone replacement therapy, which in turn will affect your osteoporosis risk.
8. Have you ever smoked? Do you still smoke? This can increase your risk of breast cancer, cervical cancer, and cancer of the vulva (the outer lips of the vagina), put you at greater risk for heart disease and stroke and accelerate the loss of calcium, leading to osteoporosis.
9. Do you drink a lot of coffee or soda every day? Six to eight cups of coffee or an equal number of glasses of soda can make your breasts feel lumpier, leading to an increased risk of cysts and possibly an increased risk of breast cancer.
10. Are you overweight? Believe it or not, women who are slightly overweight are less at risk for developing osteoporosis. But a diet too high in fat and protein can add to the calcium loss from your bones.

Make sure you disclose to your doctor your complete medical history and lifestyle patterns including nutrition, supplements and exercise. Discussing the answers to these questions with your doctor can help you make an informed decision about your own menopause strategy.

The Estrogen Connection

Studies reveal that estrogen plays a role in nearly 300 of the body's functions. Each of these can be affected when the estrogen level declines.

Estrogen Loss or Aging?

Whether related to a loss of hormones or simply a part of aging, you may notice other changes–wrinkled skin, thinning hair (both on your head and in your pubic region), an increase in hair on your face, less full breasts, and less erect nipples. Although you may not gain weight, the fat on your body may redistribute itself. For example, your buttocks may flatten out while at the same time a "pot belly" forms and your waist seems to disappear. If you do gain weight–and it's estimated that some women will gain from 5 to 8 pounds after menopause–you should be aware that these extra pounds may put you at increased risk of heart disease.

Are You An Exception To The Rule?

Some women may experience no menopause symptoms at all because estrogen continues to be produced by glands and body fat. Therefore, a woman who is overweight may be making enough estrogen to offset the loss of what was produced by her ovaries and therefore not experience any changes.

Bone Danger

15% is lost in the first five to seven years of menopause due to the drop in estrogen.

15% is lost due to estrogen deficiency in later years.

20% is lost to other factors such as lack of understanding of nutrition.

The grand total of bone loss equals as much as 50% of total bone.

Estrogen Replacement Therapy
&
Hormone Replacement Therapy

Estrogen replacement therapy (ERT) and hormone replacement therapy (HRT) are treatments your doctor may recommend to keep you healthy through menopause.

Why ERT & HRT?

These treatments are used to eliminate hot flashes, night sweats, vaginal dryness; to prevent osteoporosis; and to protect against heart disease. Approximately 15% to 20% of women are taking estrogen at any one time.

Is Hormone Replacement Therapy For You?

Not every woman is a candidate for ERT. For example, if you have breast cancer, endometrial cancer, liver disease, a blood-clotting disorder or abnormal bleeding from the vagina you should not take estrogen.

Hormone Replacement Therapy & Calcium

Some studies indicate that if begun, this treatment should be continued for the 7 to 10 years during which bone loss occurs, while other studies suggest that it should be given for the rest of a woman's life.

You And Your Doctor: A Hormone Decision-Making Team

Your doctor may also prescribe the hormone progestin—which is similar to the progesterone produced by your body—to balance some of the risks associated with taking estrogen. While most treatment is taken in the form of tablets—there are 5 different types, including one with progestin—an estrogen patch is also available. Scientists are currently working on new and different ways to give these hormones including vaginal suppositories, injections, and implants.

What About Risks?

Most studies suggest that there is no link between HRT and breast cancer. Others note an increased risk if hormones are taken for more than 15 years.

Your Natural Alternatives To Hormone Replacement Therapy

If you and your doctor decide ERT or HRT are not for you, there are some natural ways you can help your body through menopause. For example:

Diet & Eating Habits

• Eat four to six small meals throughout the day to help prevent hot flashes and keep your sugar level on an even keel, thus preventing mood swings.

• Peas, soybeans, and other legumes have natural estrogens to help boost your body's declining levels.

• A diet low in fat can also keep your hot flashes to a minimum.

Stress Management

Alternative healers or proponents of Eastern medicine suggest herbs, acupressure and massage to help control hot flashes, and relaxation techniques such as yoga or mental imagery to help counter the stress that may be causing mood swings and depression.

Exercise

Exercise cannot be overemphasized as one of the most beneficial ways to help your body operate at its best throughout life, not only during perimenopausal, menopausal, and postmenopausal times. Even if you just walk briskly for 30 minutes a day 3 to 4 times a week, you can keep off extra fat, help prevent hot flashes, and build bone mass by improving your body's ability to absorb calcium.

Surgical Menopause

Menopause can occur at any age. For example, women who have had a hysterectomy enter menopause, as do those who have had what's called a "bilateral oophorectomy" in which their uterus and both ovaries have been removed by surgery.

There are many reasons why a woman has a hysterectomy, an operation that's performed some 590,000 times each year in the United States. These include fibroids, endometriosis, uterine prolapse, pelvic inflammatory disease, and endometrial hyperplasia. There are those who believe, however, that a hysterectomy is not an absolutely necessary operation for all women afflicted with these maladies and that it should not be performed without a second opinion. There may be ways other than a hysterectomy to treat some symptoms such as heavy bleeding.

Always get a second opinion if a surgical procedure has been recommended to you.

Postmenopause

Once 12 months go by without a period, you are considered to be postmenopausal, which means "after" menopause. Changes continue to occur in your body related to the loss of estrogen. For example, bone loss speeds up for about 7 to 10 years after menopause. Recent attention has also focused on heart disease and women. Women are at an increased risk for heart disease after menopause.

A High Quality Of Life Postmenopause Plan

1. Get regular checkups and discuss your ERT or HRT with your doctor.

2. Include a regular mammogram screening especially after age 50.

3. Don't slow down. Speed up. Get started on an exercise program.

4. Eat a lowfat, high-calcium diet.

5. Supplement your diet with extra calcium.

****

One-third of all women in the U.S. are now fifty years of age or older.

Special Menopause Dietary Needs

If you are postmenopausal you have special dietary requirements. This is true whether or not you are taking hormones. You need to be sure you are getting enough calcium and vitamin D.

Calcium

Every day you should drink enough lowfat milk and eat enough cheese, yogurt, and other dairy products or calcium-rich fish and veggies to get at least 1500 mg calcium.

Nutritionists report that without a sufficient amount of calcium, the symptoms of menopause–including depression, headaches, insomnia, and irritability–get worse.

Your bones also need a steady supply of calcium to ensure a healthy bone mass and prevent osteoporosis. If you cannot get enough calcium from what you eat and drink, you may need to take a calcium supplement.

Vitamin D

Vitamin D's most common sources are sunlight and fortified milk. However, during long winter months we may rarely see the sun. A daily supplement of 400 to 800 IU per day of vitamin D is necessary to help the body absorb calcium. Do not take a higher dose without speaking to your doctor because side effects can occur.

Lowfat

Because fat is one of most common calcium blockers, at this time of your life you need to make sure that nothing is blocking the absorption of the calcium you need to protect yourself from osteoporosis. Make lowfat choices every time.

Caffeine & Phosphates

Not only does excess caffeine pose a risk in terms of calcium loss, it doesn't do menopause symptoms any good. Try to limit your coffee drinking to those two cups in the morning, and splash a little milk in them to reduce their ill effects.

Reduce your use of sodas. All of them, including the diet one, contain phosphates that rob your body of calcium at a time when you can't afford the loss.

Protein

Try to reduce the amount of protein you are getting–especially protein from red meat, which has an added whammy of high fat, a calcium blocker.

A Menu For A Healthy Postmenopause

Breakfast

1 serving of whole grain Total® cereal or two slices calcium-enriched Wonder or
    Merita bread.
8 ounces of skim milk like Lactaid with added calcium
8 ounces of calcium-enriched orange juice like Tropicana or Minute Maid.

Snack

Nonfat fruit-flavored yogurt

Lunch

Two slices calcium-enriched bread such as Wonder or Merita topped with
canned salmon salad made with nonfat mayo, or sardines in tomato sauce, or
nonfat cheese with lettuce and tomatoes.

Snack

1/4 cup raisins
1 sliced pear

Dinner

Lowfat cheese pizza, macaroni & cheese; or
Salmon burgers; or baked perch served with
Steamed broccoli; or cooked kale; or cooked okra.

Bedtime Snack

8 ounces skim milk
1 slice toast spread with nonfat fruit yogurt

****

**Remember, calcium is not just found in dairy products. Fish and
vegetables are also good sources of this vital mineral.**

Men Are Not Exempt:
Calcium, The Great Equalizer

Osteoporosis is not exclusively a woman's disease. Men can also suffer from osteoporosis. Why, then, don't we hear more about it? One answer may be the enormous emphasis placed on the risk of osteoporosis to women. But the fact is, men are at serious risk without the advantage of menopause to trigger a warning.

Men suffer one-quarter of all the hip fractures.

On The Plus Side
Men have two things going for them in their battle against bone loss.

1. Men have more bone to begin with, so even if they lose it at the same rate as women, it takes their bones longer to weaken and thin.

2. Men retain higher levels of hormones for at least ten years longer than women. Where a woman begins to show dramatic bone eroding estrogen loss at age 50, men don't begin to show testosterone loss until their 80s. Hormones protect them and their bones for much longer.

Warning: Testosterone Level Check
Men's testosterone level stays pretty level until their 80s. But there are factors that can affect the testosterone level and put men at greater risk for osteoporosis. These factors probably warrant a testosterone level check.
√ Men who had mumps as adults.
√ Men who have undergone a course of chemotherapy.
√ Men whose testicles have shrunk.
√ Men who have lost body hair.
√ Men who take corticosteriods.

****

Men over 30 lose 1% of the bone mass in their wrists and hands per year.

Real Men Need Calcium

20% of all osteoporosis cases are men.

How Can You Tell If You Have Osteoporosis?

One of the most common complaints that could indicate osteoporosis is a chronic or persistent backache. Check any persistent problems with your doctor.

Beyond Osteoporosis

High Blood Pressure

Studies have shown that calcium seems to work better in men than in women as a factor in lowering blood pressure.

Colon Cancer

Studies show that calcium may be effective in preventing and possibly even reversing colon cancer, the second most deadly cancer after lung cancer.

Calcium Robbers For Men

Alcohol

One of the biggest calcium robbers for men is alcohol. A study at the Veterans Administration found that 47% of male alcoholics had bone loss and 31% of them were young men under the age of forty. In recent studies Cornell Medical Center and the Bone Disease Service at the Hospital for Special Surgery in New York found that male alcoholics treated with calcium supplements increased their bone mass dramatically.

Aluminum-based antacids
Smoking

Arthritis: The disease itself results in bone erosion and a medication used to treat it, corticosteroids, increases the rate at which the body excretes calcium.

Diabetes: Diabetics have abnormal vitamin D metabolism which affects routine repair of bone tissue.

Prostate cancer: This condition is often treated with a medication that blocks calcium absorption.

Heart Disease: Medications are often calcium blockers.

Calcium Plus Total Nutrition

Teamwork In The World Of Nutrients

Nutrition doesn't just happen in a vacuum. It isn't enough to eat only carrots, although carrots with their massive amounts of beta carotene and vitamin C, will protect you from certain diseases and help you live a longer, healthier life. It isn't enough to eat only sardines with bones, although research now shows that sardines are very high in calcium and can help ward off the terrors of osteoporosis, lower blood pressure and help fight off the onset of certain cancers. It isn't enough to eat only oat bran cereal, although we know that bran is a natural fiber and can help prevent the onset of colon cancer and lower cholesterol levels, protecting us against coronary artery disease. It isn't enough to eat only cabbage or only broccoli or only garlic. Why? Because nutrients work together in harmony. Like a symphony, all are needed. And nature has made the mix just right.

Scientists have identified 50 nutrients as "essential."

Calcium is critical to our health and well-being, but it is part of a total nutrient program and some nutrients play a larger role than others. Here are some of the more important nutrients that are essential with calcium.

Calcium Buddies

√ **Potassium**
√ **Phosphorous**
√ **Magnesium**
√ **Zinc**
√ **Vitamin D**
√ **Vitamin C**

Calcium Buddy Vitamins

Before we can really understand what is involved in a balanced diet with calcium as the lynchpin, it is important to get a basic understanding of the various nutrients and their roles in the total nutritional picture.

What Is A Vitamin?

Vitamins are a group of chemically unrelated organic nutrients, with a carbon base, which we need in relatively small amounts to maintain good health. Our bodies either don't produce most of the vitamins we need, or if they do, the quantities produced are insufficient for our health. That's why we have to get them from food and supplements. Our bodies then use vitamins to function from the basic cellular level on up the chain of performance and health.

Two Types of Vitamins

There are two types of vitamins. Fat-soluble vitamins and water-soluble vitamins. Not knowing the difference between them can be harmful or even potentially deadly.

Fat-soluble vitamins are vitamins that our body can store and use as it needs. These are Vitamins A, D, E, and K.

Water-soluble vitamins are not stored in our bodies, but are flushed out, so we have to keep replenishing the supply.
The water-soluble vitamins are Vitamin C and the
B vitamins: B_1 or thiamine; B_2 or riboflavin; niacin; B_6; B_{12}; folic acid; pantothenic acid; and biotin.

Calcium Buddy Minerals

What Is A Mineral?

Minerals are inorganic chemical elements, not bound to carbon, and are also essential for overall functioning of the body's sytems and total health.

Two Types Of Minerals

Just as there are two types of vitamins, there are also two types of minerals. These are grouped according to how much of each type our body needs. The basic dividing line is 100 milligrams per day. The minerals we need in a quantity higher than 100 mg of a day are simply called "minerals." The ones we need in a quantity lower than 100 mg a day are called trace elements.

The minerals we need are calcium, magnesium, phosphorous, sodium, potassium, suflur and chlorine.

The trace elements we need are iron, iodine, copper, manganese, zinc, molybdenum, selenium and chromium.

What Are The Right Amounts Of Nutrients?

Unconfusing The Confusion

There is a great deal of confusion about the right amount of various nutrients and what the recommendations mean, and where they came from and why they seem to be different. Here is a quick and easy summary.

What Are RDAs?

The National Academy of Sciences defines RDAs as "the levels of intake of essential nutrients considered, in the judgment of the Food and Nutrition Board on the basis of available scientific knowledge, to be adequate to meet the known nutritional needs of practically all healthy persons." These recommendations are re-evaluated every five years.

However, people vary in terms of their diet, their age, their lifestyle, their state of health and consequently their nutritional needs. Growing children, pregnant women, the elderly, those with a disease or chronic conditions may need more of the basic nutrients than the guidelines recommend. Therefore the RDAs try to accommodate these varying needs.

The basic standard used for women between 15 and 18 years of age is 5 feet 4 inches tall and 120 pounds. Big differences are not accounted for.

What Are USRDAs?

What's the difference between RDAs and USRDAs? USRDAs are on products as a type of shorthand because listing all the 18 RDA catagories on food labels is impractical. They usually represent the highest RDA for each nutrient, and include all individuals over the age of 4 years.

What Are RDIs?

USRDAs are being replaced by RDIs or Reference Daily Intake. These already appear on product lables and will be the new standards.

****

**The National Institutes of Health
has raised the requirements for all groups
for calcium.
Check the NIH guidelines to make sure you are getting the right amount.**

Check Your Nutritional Deficiency Risk

Those of us who need nutrients most are the ones most likely to be lacking in both vitamins and minerals. And generally if you are missing one, chances are you are missing them all.

If you fit into one of these categories you may be approaching the red zone for nutritional deficiency:

- **Pregnant women**
- **Nursing mothers**
- **Teenage girls**
- **Infants**
- **Alcoholics**
- **Seniors living alone**
- **Chronically ill**
- **Junk food junkies**
- **Smokers**
- **Drug users**
- **Couch potatoes**
- **Living below the poverty line**

Potassium

Potassium is the third most abundant mineral in the body and a kissing cousin to calcium and magnesium. The three are known as complementary minerals because they work as a team to perform critical metabolic and regulatory functions in the body.

What Does Potassium Do?

Potassium is a carrier. It is responsible for carrying electrical charges that keep muscles functioning, especially the heart. A shortage or imbalance of potassium can stop the heart instantly. Potassium transmits nerve impulses, regulates insulin, manages digestive enzymes and is a vital component of the "electrolyte soup" all our cells swim in and regulates major body functions.

The Potassium Shortage

Potassium is one of the vital nutrients shorted out of the typical diet and more so out of the typical dieter's diet. This shortage can cause serious problems. If you always feel weak and tired, it may not have anything to do with lack of sleep, but rather with a lack of potassium. One of the first signs of potassium deficiency is lack of energy, especially muscular energy.

The Potassium-Sodium Seesaw

The right balance of potassium and sodium in our bodies is more potassium and less sodium. Potassium is inside our cell walls, and sodium is outside in the liquid which surrounds our cells. The two are separated by only the thinnest of membranes. When potassium "bleeds" out of our cells, or when sodium seeps in, the electrolyte balance is thrown off and the result could be fatal. According to researchers, salt junkies run the risk of heart attack and stroke because of low levels of potassium in their bodies.

Potassium And Calcium

Potassium works with calcium as a combo, regulating key functions, including blood pressure. If you need more calcium, you probably also need more potassium to keep the balance in place.

Good Dietary Sources of Potassium

Brewer's yeast, skim milk powder, wheat germ, raisins & currants, dried apricots, almonds, peanuts, sardines, swordfish, pumpkin seeds.

Magnesium

Magnesium is one of the key "bone" minerals, along with calcium and phosphorous. Magnesium and calcium are so closely inter-connected in their functions that they are almost like Siamese twins of the mineral world. So, if you don't get enough magnesium, chances are you don't get enough calcium.

What Does Magnesium Do?

Like every nutrient, magnesium has more than one job. It works with calcium to build strong bones. It also regulates muscle contractions and nerve impulses, helps metabolize sugar, and is important in the production of proteins, the building blocks of our body. Magnesium is also a key factor in lowering blood pressure by regulating the amount of calcium that moves through the smooth muscle cells of our vascular system. Together with calcium, magnesium regulates the contractions of the blood vessels that keep blood flowing smoothly.

Magnesium Shortages

According to the U.S. Department of Agriculture, 75 percent of Americans don't get enough magnesium. In fact with our diet obsession we get about half the magnesium our ancestors did. Because magnesium deficiency is so widespread, you can probably assume that you aren't getting enough. If you fall into any one of these categories, you can be certain that you are falling very short of your magnesium requirements:

- **alcoholic**
- **teenager**
- **pregnant**
- **diabetic**
- **exercise a lot**
- **take diuretics**
- **Type A personality in terms of stress management**
- **live in an area with soft water**

Good Dietary Sources of Magnesium

Tofu
Pumpkin seeds
Nuts

Wheat germ
Whole-wheat flour
Legumes

Dried apricots
Fish

Zinc

Zinc, a trace element, is vital for proper growth, cell multiplication and tissue regeneration.

Are You Deficient In Zinc?

Real zinc deficiency is rare, but it is estimated that thousands of people have low-grade zinc deficiency that can have many destabilizing and dangerous effects on the body. One of the first symptoms of a zinc deficiency is a noticeable loss of the sense of taste and smell, a problem affecting about 4 million Americans.

Zinc deficiency has also been linked to lower immune function, birth malformation, cancer, night blindness and of course, osteoporosis.

Foods High In Zinc

Oysters
Shellfish
Wheat germ
Pumpkin seeds
Peanuts
Skim milk powder
Legumes
Whole grain cereals

Vitamin D

Of all the nutrients important for calcium absorption, vitamin D is perhaps the most important. This "sunshine" vitamin is produced in the body after exposure to the ultraviolet rays of the sun. It can also be derived from certain foods with added vitamin D.

In order to be effective, vitamin D has to be changed in the body into its hormonal form, called calcitriol. It is this calcitriol version of vitamin D that regulates the body's level of calcium.

How Much Sunshine Does It Take To Make The Sunshine Vitamin?

Studies show that as little as 10 to 15 minutes a day of sunshine on our skin can produce sufficient vitamin D to help absorb calcium. Even if you are worried about sun exposure and use heavy sunblock, try to get at least a few minutes of sun every day, especially if you don't drink vitamin D fortified milk. (Because vitamin D is so important to the utilization of calcium and is relatively scarce through food, most milk and dairy products that we purchase today are fortified with vitamin D.)

What Does Vitamin D Do?

New research shows that vitamin D may be instrumental in preventing certain forms of cancer, specifically breast and colon cancer.

Vitamin D And Calcium

Vitamin D boosts absorption of calcium in the intestines and bowel, helps kidneys reabsorb calcium from the blood, and keeps the right level of calcium in the bloodstream. It also helps the body adjust to lower levels of calcium.

Are You Deficient In Vitamin D?

While vitamin D deficiency is not widespread, several groups are at risk for not getting sufficient quantities. If you are one of these, consider taking a supplement.
- alcoholics or excessive drinkers
- seniors who take medications that may interfere with vitamin D absorption
- people who live in northern climates or who don't get out into the sunshine or who use sunscreens all the time
- anyone who dislikes milk, is allergic to it, or suffers from lactose intolerance

Good Dietary Sources of Vitamin D

Milk, canned salmon, canned sardines, shrimp, eggs, bran cereal

Vitamin C

Vitamin C has been getting a lot of press lately as an antioxidant and free radical scavenger. However, vitamin C also has another, calcium-compatible function in the body. It produces and maintains collagen, a protein-type glue that supports and repairs muscles, bones, teeth, and skin.

Are You Deficient?

Although studies show that Americans get the RDA for vitamin C, approximately 60 mg per day, nutritionists now believe this is too low to provide any real benefits. Many experts now say that at least 1,000 mg of vitamin C are needed on a daily basis.

Vitamin C is a water-soluble vitamin that is not stored in the body and therefore it has to be replenished every day. Because of our poor diets, supplements spaced throughout the day are one of the best ways to insure getting enough vitamin C.

Vitamin C And Calcium

Calcium absorption is increased with vitamin C.

Best Food Sources of Vitamin C
Red and green peppers
Broccoli
Cantaloupe
Kiwi fruit
Oranges
Strawberries
Cabbage
Brussels sprouts
Parsley
Tomatoes
Kale
Cauliflower
Papayas

Why Supplements?

Why Supplements Are Important

Even though the American Society for Bone and Mineral Research, the National Institutes of Health, and other medical and nutritional organizations recommend that nutrients be obtained from food sources, that may not always be possible. Even if you are really, really good about what you eat, and you try very hard to give yourself and your family a proper diet, getting enough calcium from food alone is difficult, if not impossible. Why?

The Calcium Gremlins

1. Fast-Food Living

There are days when we eat properly but there are also days, too often it seems, when we don't. We rush from one appointment and one crisis to the other, eating on the run or skipping meals altogether. Result? Not enough calcium.

2. Special Needs

We all have different calcium requirements at different life stages and under different conditions. If you take certain medications, have some special medical conditions, are premenopausal, pregnant, nursing or a diet junkie, your calcium requirements are going to be affected. You may need more than you are getting.

3. Calcium Blockers

Too much fat, protein, alcohol, coffee or soda can seriously block the actual amount of calcium absorbed from your diet. Add smoking, a heavy hand with the salt shaker and too few calcium-rich foods and you are a perfect candidate for being in a negative calcium position.

The Perfect Combo

A calcium-rich diet PLUS daily calcium supplements

Supplements & Bone

Let's Look At The Research

Medical experts and researchers both in the United States and in other parts of the world are undertaking major studies to determine the impact calcium supplements have on bone mass and osteoporosis. Here is a peek at some of the impressive findings that reinforce the vital role played by supplements.

Strengthening The Case For Supplements

1. In a review of some of the recent studies, the *Journal of Nutrition* reported that research involving women in their 50s who had taken calcium supplements increased their bone mass by almost 1% per year.

2. Studies of preteens and elderly women both show an increase in bone density with the addition of calcium supplements to the diet.

3. In a report from the British Medical Association it was found that adding supplements to the diets of elderly women in nursing homes substantially decreased their risk for hip fractures.

4. Further European studies point to the reduction in risk of fractures after just 18 months of supplementation.

****

Many experts agree that even a 20 percent reduction in hip fractures could spare 50,000 people from pain and possible risk of death and save the healthcare system $1.5 billion dollars a year.

Review Your Calcium Needs

New National Institutes of Health
Calcium Recommendations

I know you have seen this chart already, but believe me, you can't see it too often. Take another look to see just how important supplements may be for you.

Infants from birth to 6 months...400 mg/day
Infants from 6 months to 1 year...600 mg/day

Children from 1 to 5 years...800 mg/day
Children from 6 to 10 years...800 to 1200 mg/day

Adolescents from 11 to 24 years..1200 to 1500 mg/day
Pregnant Adolescents...2000 mg/day

Pregnant Women..1200 to 1500 mg/day
Premenopausal Women 25 to 50..1000 mg/day
Postmenopausal Women over 50 on estrogen..........................1500 mg/day
Postmenopausal Women not on estrogen.................................1000 mg/day

Men 25 to 65...1000 mg/day
Men 65 plus...1500 mg/day

****

From *The New England Journal of Medicine*

**There have been 26 studies since 1988 that have
found a link between the amount of calcium taken and bone mass.
There have been 16 studies since 1988 that found
no link between the amount of calcium and bone mass.**

Supplements Survey

If you still aren't convinced that you need calcium supplements, or if you hate to take pills, or you don't have time, or any other reasons you can think of take this little personal survey and see how you and your body stack up in the calcium department.

1. I eat out or have take-in at least three times a week.   YES   NO
2. I rarely have time for breakfast.   YES   NO
3. I am a coffee-junkie.   YES   NO
4. I am a soda-junkie.   YES   NO
5. I am almost always on a diet   YES   NO
6. I am trying to quit smoking, but still puff a few.   YES   NO
7. I can't break the salt habit.   YES   NO
8. I have more than two drinks of alcohol a week.   YES   NO
9. I am a real meat & potatoes person.   YES   NO
10. Milk? I've hated it since I was three years old.   YES   NO
11. I am allergic to dairy products. They give me pain.   YES   NO
12. I have no time to cook or shop properly.   YES   NO
13. I am so stressed that I practically live on antacids.   YES   NO
14. I get constipated, so I take laxatives frequently.   YES   NO
15. I hate veggies–especially leafy green ones.   YES   NO
16. I am not taking any hormones after menopause.   YES   NO
17. I have been on a course of chemotherapy.   YES   NO
18. Exercise? What's that? I hate it and don't have time.   YES   NO
19. I take medications for my thyroid condition.   YES   NO
21. I rarely buy calcium-enriched products at the grocery.   YES   NO
22. I am not a label-reader. I don't understand or have the time.   YES   NO
20. I take glucocorticoid for my asthma, arthritis and
     other conditions.   YES   NO

Scoring: If you answered <u>YES</u> to even one of the above questions, you need to rethink your calcium requirements. Chances are really good that you aren't getting enough from your diet and should be thinking about making up the difference through calcium supplements.

Be A Savvy Supplement Shopper

Three Quick Tips Before You Buy

There are lots of different calcium supplements on the market.
Here is how to make the best selection.

1. Read The Label

Look for a calcium supplement that contains a high percentage of elemental calcium by weight. Just because a supplement says it contains a certain amount of calcium does not always mean that is the amount your body will absorb.

2. Buy Known Brands

Look for reputable manufacturers and purchase your supplements from reliable distributors.

3. Check Out The Safety Factor

Some supplements, especially those containing bonemeal or dolomite have been known to contain lead and other impurities. Look for calcium supplements that are free from lead or other toxic elements. Alternative choices include supplements containing calcium carbonate, calcium citrate, calcium malleate or calcium lactate.

****

**The National Institutes of Health Committee
evaluating calcium needs recommended that
foods such as dairy products and leafy green
vegetables are the best sources of calcium
but
most Americans may need to supplement their diet
with calcium supplements
or
processed foods enriched with calcium.**

Know Your Supplements Part I

Unscrambling The Supplement Puzzle

There are some choices available to you in terms of the type of calcium supplements that are best suited to your needs. Check these out:

Type of Calcium	Pluses	Minuses
Calcium Carbonate	Contains the most elemental calcium (40%). Most widely used.	May cause gas. May cause constipation. Not to be taken on an empty tummy.
Calcium Citrate	Most easily absorbed. Contains the second most elemental calcium (24%). Causes fewest tummy troubles.	Need to take twice as much to get the same amount of calcium. Best taken on an empty tummy.
Calcium Lactate	Contains 13% elemental calcium. Contains lactate which helps in the absorption.	Not if you are lactose intolerant. Best taken between meals.

It's Elemental, Of Course

This chart shows how much elemental calcium you can get from each type of calcium supplement. They all have their pluses and minuses.

Type	% of calcium
Calcium carbonate	40
Calcium carbonate (from oyster shell)	28
Calcium citrate	24
Calcium lactate	13
Calcium gluconate	9

Source: National Dairy Council

Know Your Supplements Part II

To help you identify the type of calcium that is right for you, here are some of the more common brand names. Always ask your doctor to recommend the best supplement for you.

Calcium Carbonate

BioCal	Calcarb 600	Calci-Chew
Calcium 600	Caltrate 600	Chooz
Gencalc	Os-Cal 500	Oysco 500
Rolaids (calcium rich)	Super Calcium 1200	Tums & Tums E-X

Calcium Citrate
Cirtacal

Calcium Gluconate
Kalcinate

****

Quick Supplement Tip

**According to a study at the University of Miami
if you wash down your calcium supplement with a glass of OJ,
you boost the absorption of the calcium.**

****

Calcium Supplements Plus Hormone Replacement Therapy

**This combo may be the best way to prevent bone loss in women past
the age of menopause, say reports in the *Annals of Internal Medicine*.**

"Supplementals"

Dissolvability

How quickly calcium supplements dissolve is important. The faster they dissolve, the better your system absorbs them. A study at the University of Maryland found that out of 35 calcium supplements available on the market, only 14 dissolved within 10 minutes and 17 dissolved within 30 minutes.

Do The Supplement Dissolvability Test

Drop one of your supplements into a glass of vinegar. If it hasn't dissolved after 30 minutes chances are it won't be absorbed fast enough.
Also look for the letters USP on the label.

When to take your supplements

Calcium supplements should be taken between meals with a glass of milk or a little yogurt. They should be taken in even doses during the day, no more than 500 mg at any one time to help absorption and avoid constipation. Take your supplements with lots of water to help keep you regular. Save your last calcium dose for bedtime. It will be absorbed during the night, when you are at greatest risk of losing calcium from bone reserves.

Calcium Supplements and Other Nutrients

Iron: Take your calcium and iron supplements at different times of the day. Some calcium supplements may inhibit the absorption of iron.

Vitamin D: Make sure you get at least 10 minutes of sunshine, eat vitamin D fortified foods or ask your doctor about vitamin D supplements. Vitamin D is necessary for calcium absorption.

Magnesium: You also need magnesium with your calcium. The normal ratio of calcium to magnesium is 2 to 1. Some supplements combine calcium, magnesium and vitamin D.

Calcium & Calcium: Taking your calcium supplements with a food that contains calcium often helps the calcium get absorbed.

ALWAYS CHECK WITH YOUR DOCTOR OR HEALTH PROFESSIONAL TO SEE IF SUPPLEMENTS ARE RIGHT FOR YOU.

Lactose Intolerance

What Is Lactose Intolerance?

Dairy products contain a type of sugar called lactose. Each of us produced a special enzyme called lactase. This special enzyme goes to work in the small intestine breaking down the sugar or lactose in dairy products so that it can be turned into simple sugars which we can digest easily. People with lactose intolerance don't produce enough of the enzyme lactase, and so can't break down the lactose (sugars) in dairy products into a useable form.

Symptoms of Lactose Intolerance

Without this enzyme, the lactose passes directly into the colon. There it is attacked by bacteria and begins to ferment. This fermentation causes unpleasant symptoms and pain. Sometimes these symptoms start within 30 minutes of eating dairy food and sometimes they take two or more hours to develop. Products such as milk and cheese and some other forms of dairy food can cause cramps, gas, and even lead to gastrointestinal infections and inflammatory bowel disorder.

If You Are Lactose Intolerant You Have Lots Of Company

Lactose intolerance is widespread. It is also more common among certain ethnic groups. 90% of all Asian Americans and Native Americans are lactose intolerant. 75% of all African Americans and Jews; 51% of Hispanics; and 25% of Caucasians are lactose intolerant.

---
30 Million Americans Are Lactose Intolerant.

75% Of All Adults Worldwide Are Lactose Intolerant.

✳✳✳✳✳✳✳✳✳✳

New Study Says Problem May Be In The Head, Not In The Tummy

A new study found that many people who were lactose intolerant could tolerate an 8 ounce glass of 2% milk. The fat in the milk may have provided a protective effect. If in doubt try Lactaid® 100 Nonfat milk and check with your doctor.

Lactose Intolerance & The Calcium Problem

One of the biggest problems for people with lactose intolerance is getting enough calcium. Why? The best source of dietary calcium is in dairy products. Americans get 70% of their dietary calcium from dairy foods. But if you get gas, bloating, or nausea and feel wretched every time you eat dairy foods, you will naturally avoid them. The result? You will be cutting yourself off from one of the best and most popular sources of calcium.

The NIH Says Adults Need 1200 to 1500 mg Of Calcium Per Day
That Includes You
Even If You Are One Of The Lactose Intolerant.

Beyond Ice Cream Cones & Tall Glasses Of Milk

O.K. So you can't have a triple cone or a milkshake or even a slice of pizza. But that doesn't mean you can't get enough calcium. Understand that most experts use a standard glass of milk as a sort of guide to the amount of calcium we need. Skim milk has about 300 mg per glass. Most adults can get by with two glasses of skim milk and the dietary calcium they get from other sources. But your special problem is how to make up the equivalent of those two important glasses of milk. One option is to look for foods, and you will be suprised and pleased at how many there are, that will help you make up that equivalent.

About Equal To Two Glasses Of Skim Milk

6 cups of broccoli
3 waffles
2 cans sardines
1 cup tofu
6 ounces of canned salmon
2/3 cup calcium-reinforced orange juice

Lactaid® Products Are Another Good Choice

It isn't necessary to give up on dairy products as a source of calcium. Look for Lactaid® Caplets and Lactaid® 100 milk products. Both are excellent aids to help you get the dietary calcium you need from dairy products.

Selected Foods For
The Lactose Intolerant

Selected Dairy Foods	Mg Calcium
Lactaid® 100 Nonfat Calcium fortified milk	500
Yogurt, plain, nonfat, 1 cup	452
Yogurt, plain, lowfat, 1 cup	415
Yogurt, fruit-flavored, lowfat, 1 cup	314
Milk, skim, 1 cup	302
Cheese, Swiss, 1 ounce	272
Cheese, Cheddar, 1 ounce	204
Yogurt, frozen, plain, 1/2 cup	89

Protein Food Group	Mg Calcium
Tofu, 1/2 cup (with calcium sulphate)	434
Sardines, canned, with bones	324
Salmon, canned, with bones	203
Tofu, 1/2 cup (without calcium sulphate)	130
Perch, baked, 3 ounces	117
Almonds, 1/4 cup	94
Perch, cooked, 3 ounces	87
Brazil nuts, 1/4 cup	62
Beans, great northern, boiled, 1/2 cup	61
Oysters, raw, 1/2 cup	56
Filberts, 1/4 cup	54
Shrimp, cooked, 3 ounces	33
Egg, hard-cooked, one large	28
Peanuts, 1/4 cup	21
Pork chop, 3 ounces	13
Peanut Butter, 2 tablespoons	10

More Foods For The Lactose Intolerant

Fruit & Veggie Group	Mg Calcium
Spinach, fresh, cooked, 1/2 cup	122
Turnip greens, fresh, cooked, 1/2 cup	99
Kale, frozen, cooked, 1/2 cup	90
Broccoli, fresh, cooked, 1/2 cup	89
Okra, fresh, cooked, 1/2 cup	88
Beet greens, fresh, cooked, 1/2 cup	82
Bokchoy, fresh, cooked, 1/2 cup	79
Mustard greens, frozen, cooked, 1/2 cup	75
Collards, fresh, cooked, 1/2 cup	74
Dandelion greens, cooked, 1/2 cup	73
Orange, medium	52
Broccoli, frozen, cooked, 1/2 cup	47
Beans, green, frozen, cooked, 1/2 cup	31
Potatoes, mashed, 1/2 cup	28
Summer squash, fresh, cooked, 1/2 cup	24
Pear, medium, one	19
Peas, green, frozen, cooked, 1/2 cup	19
Carrots, one medium, raw	19
Raisins, seedless, 1/4 cup	18
Iceberg lettuce, 1/8 head	17

Grain Group	Mg Calcium
Waffle, 7 inches diameter	179
Pancakes, 4 inches diameter, 2	72
Hamburger roll	54
Baking powder biscuit	47
Corn tortilla	42
One slice white bread	32
Bagel	29
Hard roll	24
One slice whole wheat bread	20
Rice, 1/2 cup	11
Oatmeal, 1/2 cup	10
Egg noodles, 1/2 cup	8

Supplements & Special Foods
For The Lactose Intolerant

Supplements

If there is one group that should take a special look at supplements that's the lactose intolerant. By not being able to tolerate dairy products, those suffering from lactose intolerance are cutting themselves off from a major source of calcium and are at a potentially higher risk for developing osteoporosis and other diseases which result from a lack of calcium.

> **If You Are Lactose Intolerant**
> **AWAYS Check With Your Doctor**
> **Before Taking A Calcium Supplement.**
> **Your Doctor Can Help You Select The Best One For Your Special Needs.**

Special Foods & New Products

Good News! As more and more manufacturers start adding calcium to their products, there are more options than ever before for people who can't tolerate dairy products. Here is a partial list of products to look for:

Lactaid® 100 Nonfat Calcium Fortified
Whole Grain Total® Cereal
Tropicana Orange Juice With Calcium
Minute Maid Orange Juice With Calcium
Nature's Select Powdered Milk Substitute
Wonder Bread Enriched With Calcium
Merita Bread Enriched With Calcium

****

Lactaid® 100 Nonfat Calcium Fortified Milk Is A Calcium Bonus!

Here is an absolutely terrific idea that works for everyone, whether or not you are lactose intolerant. Look for this rich skim milk that not only tastes creamy and satisfying, but has an extra 200 mg of calcium in every glass for a total of 500 mg–that's more than regular skim milk!

Looking For Lactose?

The Higher The Number of Grams of Lactose The More Discomfort

Food	Grams of Lactose
Milk & Cream	
Dry milk, nonfat, 1/4 cup	15.6
Dry, whole milk, 1/4 cup	12.3
Skim milk, 8 ounces	11.9
2% lowfat milk, 8 ounces	11.7
Whole milk, 8 ounces	11.4
Goat milk, 8 ounces	10.9
Evaporated milk, skim, 1 ounce	3.60
Evaporated milk, whole, 1 ounce	3.20
Half & Half, one tablespoon	6.00
Heavy whipping, one tablespoon	4.00
Light whipping, one tablespoon	4.00
Cheeses (one ounce measure)	
American processed	2.50
Feta	1.16
Parmesan	0.91
Mozzarella, part-skimmed	0.78
Gouda	0.63
Swiss	0.59
Ricotta, part skim, 1/2 cup	6.37
Ricotta, whole, 1/2 cup	3.77
Cottage, lowfat, 4 ounces	3.07
Cottage, creamed, 4 ounces	3.03
Cream cheese, one ounce	0.75
Yogurt/Ice Creams	
Ice milk, vanilla, 1 cup	10.0
Ice cream, vanilla, 1 cup	9.90
Yogurt, plain, skim, 4 ounces	8.70
Yogurt, plain, lowfat, 4 ounces	8.00

Lactose Intolerance Wrap-up

There are lots of surprising places lactose can hide and catch you unawares. Here are some of the more common.

Non-Dairy Foods Containing Hidden Lactose

Hot Dogs   Pancakes
Breads   Creamy Salad Dressings
Pastries   Diet Formulas
Instant Cocoa Mix   Creamed Soups
Brownie Mixes   Powdered Eggs

Other Names For Lactose

Learn to be a savvy shopper and read and understand package labels. If you can, you will find that lactose goes by many other names and can catch the unaware with a nasty set of tummy upsets.

Milk Solids
Dry Milk
Milk Powder
Whey Powder

****

More Tips

- **Add extra servings of leafy green vegetables to your diet.**
- **A few extra slices of bread can boost your calcium intake.**
- **Avoid fat, sodium, caffeine, phosphorous and other calcium blockers.**
- **Take calcium supplements with your doctor's advice.**

Milk Allergy

Milk Allergy

Milk allergy is not the same as lactose intolerance. Milk allergy has nothing to do with the sugars in milk, but it is a sensitivity to the proteins in milk such as casein, lactalbumin and lactoglobulin.

Symptoms Of Milk Allergy

Milk allergy reactions include eczema, asthma, wheezing, mucous build-up, diarrhea, vomiting and reddish or black circles around the eyes and earlobes.

---

10 Million Americans Have A Milk Allergy.

Food Tips For Sufferers of Milk Allergy

Some of the same advice is important for those suffering from milk allergy as was offered to those suffering from lactose intolerance:

√ Try to get extra calcium from non-milk sources.

√ Become a savvy shopper and look for hidden sources of milk.

√ Talk to your doctor about the best calcium supplements for you.

****

**Always check with your doctor
if you have any upset stomach symptoms
or pain that keeps coming back.**

Do not attempt to diagnose yourself.

Vegetarians

More Than A Passing Fad

I guess it is safe to say that vegetarians are here to stay and they have some impressive health lessons to teach the rest of us. Study after study from some of the most reputable institutions in this country and worldwide indicate that a vegetarian diet can lower blood pressure, reduce cholesterol levels, offer protection against several types of cancer, diabetes and osteoporosis. It may be time for all of us to take a second look at vegetarianism and see if we can't adapt some, if not all, its ideas.

Calcium & Bone Health

A study shows that vegetarian women between the ages of 50 and 90 had only 18 percent loss of bone mass while their meat-eating sisters had a whopping 35 percent loss of bone mass!

Vegetarians, Calcium & The Protein Connection

Researchers believe that one of the major reasons that vegetarian women have a lower rate of bone loss and a lower incidence of osteoporosis, is because they have a reduced intake of protein and protein is one of the more serious calcium robbers. In addition, vegetarian women get their protein from non-animal sources and the protein in red meat is often part of a package which includes fat. Fat is also a major calcium blocker. So the animal protein/fat combo can reduce the amount of calcium that is actually absorbed in those women who get too much animal protein in their daily diet.

****

These Numbers Get Attention

More than 12.4 million Americans define themselves as full or part-time vegetarians.

60 million Americans have significantly reduced their red meat consumption.

Vegetarians Defined

Vegetarians & Vegetarians-In-Training

There are different degrees of vegetarians. And health experts are agreed that even a modified or occasional vegetarian diet or a meat-free day can have positive health benefits. Here are the different types of vegetarians. Is one of them right for you?

Total Vegetarian: The only food you consume is plant food, period. This includes vegetables, fruits, nuts, seeds, grains and legumes. Everything coming from animals or fish is excluded; that means meat of all kinds, eggs, and all dairy products.

Vegans: These folks not only eat a total vegetarian diet, but they don't use any other products that come from animals, including leather, wool and silk.

Lacto-vegetarians: This is a modified version of vegetarianism where milk and other dairy foods are allowed to supplement the entirely plant-derived diet.

Lacto-ovo-vegetarians: Here eggs are included along with the milk, dairy products and plant foods.

Pesco-vegetarians: This group includes fish in their diet along with plant food. Rice usually plays a large dietary role along with vegetables.

Pollo-vegetarians: These folks eat chicken, but omit all red meat from their diet. They also eat plant food, fish, dairy products and eggs.

****

**Guidelines From The USDA & Health & Human Services
Recommend a daily intake of 11 to 20 plant foods but
only 4 to 6 animal foods.**

Vegetarians & Good Nutrition

Pay Particular Attention To These Key Nutrients

Becoming a vegetarian doesn't just mean suddenly munching on veggies and rice. Becoming a vegetarian means getting educated to make sure that along with all the good things in your diet, you are not losing nutrients that your body needs. Here are some key nutrients you need to pay particular attention to:

Calcium

Dairy products are one of the best dietary sources of calcium. If you decide not to have any dairy products in your diet you need to make sure that you get your required amount of calcium every day. This means increasing leafy green vegetables, nuts and seeds and fruits in your diet. It also means discussing your calcium needs with your doctor or health professional to see if you need a supplement to insure healthy bones.

Vitamin D

Without sufficient Vitamin D our bodies can't use the calcium we get. If you are not going to drink fortified milk, then look for soy milk fortified with vitamin D and make sure you get at least 10 minutes of sunshine every day. You should also discuss your need for this vitamin with your doctor to see if you need to take a supplement to insure a steady supply.

Protein

While too much protein is not good for us and blocks the absorption of calcium, too little protein can also be problematic. Again, make sure your diet is reviewed by a competent health professional to make sure that you are getting the balanced nutrition you need.

****

Famous Vegetarians

There were lots of highly creative and respected people who enjoyed a vegetarian diet. Many of them lived very long, active and productive lives.

Socrates	Leonardo da Vinci	Henry Thoreau
Plato	Leo Tolstoy	Paul McCartney
Buddha	Charles Darwin	Gladys Knight
Mohammed	George Bernard Shaw	

Calcium Sources For Vegetarians

Dairy Foods	Mg Calcium
Yogurt, plain, nonfat, 1 cup	452
Yogurt, plain, lowfat, 1 cup	415
Milkshake, chocolate, 10.6 ounces	319
Yogurt, fruit-flavored, lowfat, 1 cup	314
Milk, skim, 1 cup	302
Milk, 1% lowfat, 1 cup	300
Milk, 2% lowfat, 1 cup	297
Milk, whole, 1 cup	291
Buttermilk, 1 cup	285
Milk, chocolate, 2% lowfat, 1 cup	284
Cheese, Swiss, 1 ounce	272
Cheese, cheddar, 1 ounce	204
Cheese, mozzarella, part skim, 1 ounce	183
Cheese, American, 1 ounce	174
Ice milk, softserve, 1/2 cup	137
Ice cream, softserve, 1/2 cup	118
Yogurt, frozen, plain, 1/2 cup	89
Ice cream, hardened, 10% fat, 1/2 cup	88
Cheese, cottage, 2% lowfat, 1/2 cup	7

Protein Food Group	Mg Calcium
Tofu, 1/2 cup (with calcium sulphate)	434
Sardines, canned, with bones	324
Salmon, canned, with bones	203
Tofu, 1/2 cup (without calcium sulphate)	130
Perch, baked, 3 ounces	117
Almonds, 1/4 cup	94
Perch, cooked, 3 ounces	87
Brazil nuts, 1/4 cup	62
Beans, great northern, boiled, 1/2 cup	61
Oysters, raw, 1/2 cup	56
Filberts, 1/4 cup	54
Egg, hard-cooked, one large	28
Peanuts, 1/4 cup	21
Peanut butter, 2 tablespoons	10

More Calcium Sources For Vegetarians

Fruit & Vegetable Food Group	Mg Calcium
Spinach, fresh, cooked, 1/2 cup	122
Turnip greens, fresh, cooked, 1/2 cup	99
Kale, frozen, cooked, 1/2 cup	90
Broccoli, fresh, cooked, 1/2 cup	89
Okra, fresh, cooked, 1/2 cup	88
Beet greens, fresh, cooked, 1/2 cup	82
Bokchoy, fresh, cooked, 1/2 cup	79
Mustard greens, frozen, cooked, 1/2 cup	75
Collards, fresh, cooked, 1/2 cup	74
Dandelion greens, cooked, 1/2 cup	73
Orange, medium	52
Broccoli, frozen, cooked, 1/2 cup	47
Beans, green, frozen, cooked, 1/2 cup	31
Potatoes, mashed, 1/2 cup	28
Summer squash, fresh, cooked, 1/2 cup	24
Pear, medium, one	19
Peas, green, frozen, cooked, 1/2 cup	19
Carrots, one medium, raw	19
Raisins, seedless, 1/4 cup	18
Iceberg lettuce, 1/8 head	1

Grain Food Group	Mg Calcium
Waffle, 7 inches diameter	179
Pancakes, 4 inches diameter, 2	72
Hamburger roll	54
Baking powder biscuit	47
Corn tortilla	42
One slice white bread	32
Bagel	29
Hard roll	24
One slice whole wheat bread	20
Rice, 1/2 cup	11
Oatmeal, 1/2 cup	10
Egg noodles, 1/2 cup	8
Graham crackers, 2	6
Saltine crackers, 4	3

Calcium & Exercise

Use It Or Lose It: And That Means Bone

Most of us know that exercise is important for overall good health. We also recognize that a regular exercise program can reduce stress and help keep our cardiovascular health at its peak.

But exercise is also critical in terms of saving and rebuilding bone mass and preventing the premature onset of osteoporosis. In fact, along with dietary calcium, supplements and hormone replacement therapy for women around menopause, exercise is a critical component in the fight against osteoporosis.

The Big Three

Calcium, Exercise and Hormone Replacement Therapy Fight Osteoporosis

---

Tufts University Study

According to a new study from Tufts University, pumping iron twice a week can significantly reduce the risk of osteoporosis in older women. The women in the study ranged in age from 50 to 70 and were not on hormone replacement therapy. Twenty of the women did weight training and increased their bone density by 1%.The rest did no weight training and lost 2.5% of their bone density. How hard was it to do? The women who trained with weights spent two 45-minute sessions a week working out. The added boon? The women who trained with weights came out of the 12-month program 15 to 20 years younger!

University of Heidelberg, Germany

Researchers at the University of Heidelberg found that weight lifters increased their bone density by 18 to 30 percent. When they stopped training, they immediately began to lose bone—as much as 15% after 4 weeks of inactivity.

Ohio State University

Medical experts here reported that women who rode a stationary bike regularly increased the bone mineral density in their spines by 3.5%. Women who didn't ride a stationary bike regularly reduced the bone mineral density in their spines by 2.4%. What was the winning groups' time investment in their bone health? Thirty minutes every other day.

Bones vs. Gravity

Get Out Of Bed

Seriously. The best thing you can do for your bones at any age, is get out of bed and move. Studies show that even healthy, young people can lose up to 1% of total bone for every week they are stuck in bed. What works? Gravity. Just getting up and standing or walking around for as little as three hours a day can help prevent bone loss.

Gravity Helps Build Bones

One of the big problems for astronauts is bone loss. Why? Because in space there is no gravity. And gravity, pulling on our muscles and tendons, is what helps them force calcium into bones where it can do us good. Take away the gravity and you drain away the calcium. That's why physical exercise involving gravitational stress enhances bone formation and increases bone mass.

Women & Workouts

Studies show that women between the ages of 36 and 67 who do 45 minutes of aerobic exercise three times a week can reduce their bone loss by an impressive 80%! And even if bone loss has occurred, exercise still has positive effects. A study showed that women in their 80s who did chair exercises for 30 minutes three times a week for three years regained 2% of the mineral content in their bone.

Exercise not only prevents bone loss, but has been shown to reverse and even replace lost bone mass.

Beyond Bones: Calcium & Your Workout

Being focused on bone health and the prevention of osteoporosis is terrific. But calcium plays an important role in your workout, beyond bone health.

√ Calcium controls muscle contractions, including your heart muscle.
√ Calcium activates enzymes that affect glycogen in the muscles and liver.
√ Calcium helps prevent painful muscle cramps.
√ Calcium helps stimulate fat-burning enzymes.
√ Calcium helps you get more energy to keep going.

Bone Building Workouts

Weight-bearing Exercises

The best exercises for bone-building are called weight-bearing exercises and involve forcing muscles against gravity. This allows more blood flow into muscles and bones and helps absorb calcium.

Best Weight-bearing Exercises

- brisk walking
- jogging
- hiking
- aerobics
- dancing
- biking
- rowing
- jumping rope
- stair climbing
- lifting weights
- racquet sports

****

**If you are a woman and you walked
at least one mile a day over the
course of your adulthood
you have more bone
protection.**

Create Your Own Bone-Building Exercise Program

There are three major types of exercises that should be included in your overall program.

1. Weight-bearing or Strenghthening Exercises
Strenghthening exercises build and maintain strong bones and muscles by forcing bones and muscles to move against gravity or some other resistance.

2. Flexibility Exercises
Flexibility exercises move joints through their entire range of motion and keep us limbered up and protect us from getting stiff.

3. Cardiorespiratory or Aerobic Exercises
Cardiorespiratory or aerobic exercise build overall fitness.

Getting Started

Warm-up
Spend 5 to 15 minutes stretching and doing strengthening exercises.

Aerobic
Spend 20 to 45 minutes at your target heart rate 3 times a week.

Cool-down
Spend 5 to 15 minutes slow walking and stretching.

****
Bonus Time
Research shows that women who walked five days a week for 24 weeks at an average pace of one mile every 20 minutes lost 6% body fat.
Who can resist?

Walk For Bones

Why Walking Is Terrific

Walking is one of the best all-round exercises. It requires no special or costly equipment, it can be done almost anywhere, it can be done in all kinds of weather. City people can do it and so can country folks. It can be done alone, with a friend, or with nature for company. It can be done indoors as well as outdoors. It helps our entire cardiovascular system, it burns off fat, and it builds our bones!

> ## NEVER NEVER NEVER
> ### BEGIN ANY EXERCISE PROGRAM WITHOUT YOUR DOCTOR'S APPROVAL.

Getting Started

1. Invest in a proper pair of walking shoes. Your feet & your back will thank you.
2. Pick a regular time each day to walk.
3. Start slow. Then build up speed and stamina until you can walk for 45 minutes.
4. Add a little weight to your walk buy wearing a backpack or carrying weights.
5. Vary your walk by picking different routes.
6. Enjoy it.

America's Walking

You can do yourself and others a lot of good with your walk if you participate in some of the many charity walks in cities all across the country. Watch for these in your neighborhood.

WalkAmerica	March of Dimes	800-BIG-WALK
Race for the Cure	Breast Cancer Foundation	800-653-5355
Great Strides	Cystic Fibrosis Foundation	800-FIGHT-CF
American Heart Walk	American Heart Association	800-AHA-USA-1
Memory Walk	Alzheimers Association	800-272-3900
M.S. Walk	Multiple Sclerosis Society	800-FIGHT M.S.

****

Best To Worst Bone-Building Walks On A Scale Of 1 to 10
Stairs–Uphill–Level Ground–Walking on Water–Walking on the Moon

Exercises for Osteoporosis Part I

Before You Begin

√ **Check with your doctor before beginning any exercise program.**

√ **It's a good idea to get started with a professional physical therapist to make sure you are doing the correct exercises and that you are doing them properly to avoid injury.**

√ **If you feel any pain while doing any of the exercises, stop immediately and check with your physician before continuing your program.**

Neck Exercises

Improve the flexibility of the neck. You can do these exercises sitting down or standing–whatever is more comfortable for you.

1. Bend your chin forward slowly toward your chest. Let your chin fall toward your chest. Straighten your head slowly.

2. Bend your neck toward your left shoulder. Do not force the motion. Slowly raise your head to its straight up position.

3. Bend your head back slowly and look at the ceiling. Slowly straighten your head.

4. Bend your neck toward your right shoulder. Do not force the motion. Slowly raise your head to its straight up position.

5. Turn your head slowly and look over your right shoulder. Return to your start position.

6. Turn your head slowly and look over your left shoulder. Return to your start position.

Repeat this cycle twice. Gradually work up to 10 repetitions twice a day.

Exercises For Osteoporosis Part II

Shoulder Exercises

These will increase the flexibility and strength of your shoulders and arms. You may do these exercises sitting or standing.

1. Clasp your hands behind your head. Without adding pressure to your neck, pull your elbows forward until they are as close as possible at chin level. Slowly move elbows apart as wide as you can without discomfort. Repeat. Work up to 20 repetitions twice a day.

2. Roll your shoulders in a forward-moving circle. Raise your shoulders toward your ears. Roll shoulders in a backward-moving circle. Reverse the process. Work up to 20 repetitions twice a day.

Hip Exercises

For these exercises you should lie down on a flat comfortable surface such as the floor or your bed.

1. Lie down on your back. Move your right leg away from your body as far as you can. Keep your knee pointing toward the ceiling and try not to let it turn inward. Bring your leg back. Repeat with your left leg. Work up to 20 repetitions twice a day.

2. Lie down on your back. Turn your knees in and touch your toes together. Now turn your knees and your toes out. Repeat. Work up to 20 repetitions twice a day.

3. Lie down on your back. Place both hands on your thigh behind the knee of your left leg. Now raise your knee up to your chest, using your hands to help yourself. Slowly lower your left leg. Do the same thing with your right leg. Repeat, alternating legs. Work up to 20 repetitions twice a day.

4. Lie down on your back. Pull both knees up to your chest. Hold them there for a count of 5. Rock yourself gently from side to side while your knees are against your chest. Lower your legs slowly. Repeat. Work up to 20 repetitions twice a day.

Exercises For Osteoporosis Part III
Extra Exercises

The Body Extender

Stand, spread eagle, facing a firm wall. Keep your feet and body a few inches away from the wall. Now arch your back slowly inwards toward the wall. Return to your starting position. Repeat. Work up to 20 repetitions twice a day.

The Angel

Stand comfortably. Now bend your arms and raise them up until your elbows are at shoulder height. Push your elbows back until your shoulder blades are touching. Hold for a count of 5. Lower your arms. Repeat. Work up to 20 repetitions twice a day.

Footies

1. Sit comfortably in a straightbacked chair. Place your feet flat on the floor. Now raise your toes as high as you can without lifting your heels off the floor. Repeat. Work up to 20 repetitions twice a day.

2. Sit comfortably in a straightbacked chair. Place your feet flat on the floor. Now raise your heels as high as possible, while keeping your toes on the floor. Repeat. Work up to 20 repetitions twice a day.

3. Sit comfortably in a straightbacked chair. Lift your left foot. Rotate the ankle curling your toes up and down as you complete the circle. Repeat with your right foot. Repeat, alternating feet. Work up to 20 repetitions twice a day.

Sneaking Exercise Into A Crowded Day
- Walk the dog. Walk the neighbor's dog. Walk them one at a time.
- Window shop around the mall–2 fast laps.
- Push the vacuum, even if your house doesn't need it.
- Get out the old manual lawnmower and cut the grass.
- Plant a garden.

The Nutrition Part

Why Add Calcium?

**You'll Live A Longer & Healthier Life
&
You'll Lose Weight
&
It's Easy To Add Calcium To Your Day**

If that isn't enough, here are few more good reasons to add some calcium to your life starting today.

1. Calcium has now been widely shown to have a significant impact, not just on bones, but on a wide variety of other health-related factors.

2. Calcium builds strong bones and protects us against osteoporosis, the fourth leading cause of death of women in the United States.

3. Calcium can lower blood pressure and plays an important role in reducing the risk of stroke and cardiovascular disease.

4. Calcium has been shown to provide significant protection against colon cancer, the second most deadly form of cancer.

5. Calcium may slow or even reverse the formation of cataracts.

6. Calcium can boost your brain power. And give you more energy, too!

****

**If your diet is low in calcium, chances are it is also
low in other essential nutrients.
If you increase the amount of dietary calcium you will also
increase the amount of other essential nutrients.**

Why Subtract Fat?

SAD Is Sad

Unless you spent the past twenty years in a cave without a cellular phone, cable TV or a newspaper, you know that what we are putting into our mouths is making us sick.

We know that what is called the Standard American Diet (SAD, for short) is just that, a sad excuse for nutrition. We know that potato chips, greasy fast foods, sugary snacks, cigarettes, alcohol and almost everything else that is sugar-loaded, salted, or oil and fat saturated is a food bullet heading straight for our vital organs, plugging up our arteries, chipping away at our bones and causing a lot of unnecessary pain, suffering and cost.

Make Room For The Good Stuff

The more of these fatal food bullets we swallow, the less room we have for the really good, healthy stuff that protects us from disease, premature aging and even the Grim Reaper himself. Let's face it, we've gotten to like salt, sugar, alcohol, and most of all fat. And all the foods that aren't good for us, taste great and take hardly any time at all to fix, chew and swallow. A real bonus if you're trying to get that meeting organized, that presentation written, that volunteer group started, those kids picked up, that appointment kept–and who doesn't?

Good Food Doesn't Have To Be A Lot Of Trouble

Now look at the foods that are good for us, like fruits and veggies. We would like to include them in our diet more often but they are a lot of trouble. First of all they have to be found, then washed, peeled, chopped, diced, and dipped. Anyway, we all know they take more time and trouble to fix.

But if we don't start taking the trouble to think about our food choices and make the right ones, even if they are a little more trouble, we will all be sitting in wheel chairs or lying in hospital beds years before our time, scared, hurting, and wishing we had just taken the time to peel that carrot, open that yogurt, fix that bowl of hot cereal.

✳✳✳✳✳✳✳✳✳✳

A frightening study at Brigham & Women's Hospital found that women who are 5 feet 5 inches and weigh 150 to 160 have a 30% higher risk of dying early than women who weigh 120 pounds or less.

Smart Food

There are a number of guidelines to follow in order to stay on the path that leads to smart food, lowfat and good health

USDA Dietary Guidelines

1. **Eat a variety of foods.**
2. **Maintain a desirable weight.**
3. **Avoid too much fat and cholesterol.**
4. **Eat foods that have fiber and starch.**
5. **Avoid too much sugar.**
6. **Avoid too much salt.**
7. **Drink alcohol in moderation.**

The Food Pyramid

Fats, Oils & Sweets–Use Sparingly
Milk, Yogurt, & Cheese Group–2 to 3 Servings
Meat, Poultry, Fish, Dry Beans, Eggs & Nuts Group–2 to 3 Servings
Fruit Group–2 to 4 Servings
Vegetable Group–3 to 5 Servings
Bread, Cereal, Rice & Pasta Group–6 to 11 Servings

Important: A Serving Is A Molehill, Not A Mountain

Where Does Your Calcium Come From?

Milk, Yogurt & Cheese Group supplies about 77% of your daily calcium.
Meat Group supplies about 9% of your daily calcium.
Vegetable Group supplies about 7% of your daily calcium.
Bread & Cereal Group supplies about 7% of your daily calcium.

Total
If you eat right, you should get 100% of your daily calcium every day!

How Much Calcium Is Enough? Part I

How much calcium is enough? How much is in food? How can you tell? What's the difference between RDAs and USRDAs? The National Institutes of Health Recomendations? Confused? Don't be. Here is a simple explanation and guide to follow to make sure you know how much calcium you are getting, and how much you need.

Meet The Recommended Dietary Allowances

Recommended Dietary Allowances (RDAs) are the amounts needed to prevent serious illnesses due to deficiencies.

Birth to 6 months..................360 mg
6 months to 1 year...............540 mg
1 year to 3 years....................800 mg
4 years to 6 years.................800 mg
7 years to 10 years...............800 mg
Males
11 to 14...............................1200 mg
15 to 18...............................1200 mg
19 to 22...............................800 mg
23 to 50...............................800 mg
51+..800 mg
Females
11 to 14...............................1200 mg
15 to 18...............................1200 mg
19 to 22...............................800 mg
23 to 50...............................800 mg
51+..800 mg
Pregnant...........................1200 mg
Lactating...........................1200 mg

How Much Calcium Is Enough? Part II

Meet The U.S. Recommended Daily Allowances

When you go to the store to purchase food products, you will see on the label a listing for USRDAs. The question you might ask yourself is: What's the difference between RDAs and USRDAs? Good question. Basically the USRDAs were developed as a quick reference, a convenience, because listing all the 18 RDA categories on food labels is impractical. The USRDAs are a type of shorthand. They usually represent the highest RDA for each nutrient, rather than listing all the categories. They also generally represent the RDA for individuals over 4 years.

USRDA for Calcium is 800 mg.

Meet The New National Institutes of Health
Calcium Recommendations: These Are The Ones To Follow

Infants from birth to 6 months	400 mg/day
Infants from 6 months to 1 year	600 mg/day
Children from 1 to 5 years	800 mg/day
Children from 6 to 10 years	800 to 1200 mg/day
Adolescents from 11 to 24 years	1200 to 1500 mg/day
Pregnant Adolescents	2000 mg/day
Pregnant Women	1200 to 1500 mg/day
Premenopausal Women 25 to 50	1000 mg/day
Postmenopausal Women over 50 on estrogen	1500 mg/day
Postmenopausal Women not on estrogen	1000 mg/day
Men 25 to 65	1000 mg/day
Men 65 plus	1500 mg/day

Calcium Super Foods: Dairy Group

Food	Mg Calcium
1. Yogurt, plain, nonfat, 1 cup	452
2. Yogurt, plain, lowfat, 1 cup	415
3. Milkshake, chocolate, 10.6 ounces	319
4. Yogurt, fruit-flavored, lowfat, 1 cup	314
5. Milk, skim, 1 cup	302
6. Milk, 1% lowfat, 1 cup	300
7. Milk, 2% lowfat, 1 cup	297
8. Milk, whole, 1 cup	291
9. Buttermilk, 1 cup	285
10. Milk, chocolate, 2% lowfat, 1 cup	284
11. Milk, chocolate, whole, 1 cup	280
12. Cheese, Swiss, 1 ounce	272
13. Cheese, Cheddar, 1 ounce	204
14. Cheese, mozzarella, part skim, 1 ounce	183
15. Cheese, American, 1 ounce	174
16. Ice milk, softserve, 1/2 cup	137
17. Ice cream, softserve, 1/2 cup	118
18. Yogurt, frozen, plain, 1/2 cup	89
19. Ice cream, hardened, 10% fat, 1/2 cup	88
20. Cheese, cottage, 2% lowfat, 1/2 cup	77

Don't forget Lactaid® 100 Nonfat Calcium Fortified Milk   500

Calcium Super Foods: Protein Group

Food	Mg Calcium
1. Tofu, 1/2 cup (with calcium sulphate)	434
2. Sardines, canned, with bones	324
3. Salmon, canned, with bones	203
4. Tofu, 1/2 cup (without calcium sulphate)	130
5. Perch, baked, 3 ounces	117
6. Almonds, 1/4 cup	94
7. Perch, cooked, 3 ounces	87
8. Brazil nuts, 1/4 cup	62
9. Beans, great northern, boiled, 1/2 cup	61
10. Oysters, raw, 1/2 cup	56
11. Filberts, 1/4 cup	54
12. Shrimp, cooked, 3 ounces	33
13. Egg, hard-cooked, one large	28
14. Peanuts, 1/4 cup	21
15. Pork chop, 3 ounces	13
16. Peanut Butter, 2 tablespoons	10

Calcium Super Foods: Fruit & Veggie Group

Food	Mg Calcium
1. Spinach, fresh, cooked, 1/2 cup	122
2. Turnip greens, fresh, cooked, 1/2 cup	99
3. Kale, frozen, cooked, 1/2 cup	90
4. Broccoli, fresh, cooked, 1/2 cup	89
5. Okra, fresh, cooked, 1/2 cup	88
6. Beet greens, fresh, cooked, 1/2 cup	82
7. Bokchoy, fresh, cooked, 1/2 cup	79
8. Mustard greens, frozen, cooked, 1/2 cup	75
9. Collards, fresh, cooked, 1/2 cup	74
10. Dandelion greens, cooked, 1/2 cup	73
11. Orange, medium	52
12. Broccoli, frozen, cooked, 1/2 cup	47
13. Beans, green, frozen, cooked, 1/2 cup	31
14. Potatoes, mashed, 1/2 cup	28
15. Summer squash, fresh, cooked, 1/2 cup	24
16. Pear, medium, one	19
17. Peas, green, frozen, cooked, 1/2 cup	19
18. Carrots, one medium, raw	19
19. Raisins, seedless, 1/4 cup	18
20. Iceberg lettuce, 1/8 head	17

Calcium Super Foods: Grain Group

Food	Mg Calcium
1. Waffle, 7 inches diameter	179
2. Pancakes, 4 inches diameter, 2	72
3. Hamburger roll	54
4. Baking powder biscuit	47
5. Corn tortilla	42
6. One slice white bread	32
7. Bagel	29
8. Hard roll	24
9. One slice whole wheat bread	20
10. Rice, 1/2 cup	11
11. Oatmeal, 1/2 cup	10
12. Egg noodles, 1/2 cup	8
13. Graham crackers, 2	6
14. Saltine crackers, 4	3

Other Calcium Super Foods

Food	Mg Calcium
1. Cheeze pizza, 1 slice, 1/8 of whole pie	220
2. Macaroni & cheese, 1/2 cup	181
3. Cream of mushroom soup made with milk, 1 cup	178
4. Cream of tomato soup made with milk, 1 cup	159
5. Molasses, blackstrap, 1 tablespoon	137
6. Taco	109

How Calcium-Rich Is Your Day?

Both the American Medical Association and the American Dietetic Association recommend that you get your calcium from food first. Why? Because the nutrients in food, calcium included, are balanced and in proportion to each other and in most cases, offer greater benefits combined than each nutrient can offer by itself. That being the case, how much calcium do you get from your normal daily diet and food choices? Fill in the blanks and find out. Just refer to the calcium super foods listing, or the personal calcium counter at the back of the book to get the right amount of calcium for each food and beverage.

Food or Beverage   **Amount of calcium (mg)**

<u>Breakfast</u>

_____   _____
_____   _____
_____   _____
_____   _____

<u>Lunch</u>

_____   _____
_____   _____
_____   _____
_____   _____
_____   _____

<u>Dinner</u>

_____   _____
_____   _____
_____   _____
_____   _____
_____   _____
_____   _____

<u>Snack(s)</u>

_____   _____
_____   _____

Total: _____

Try This Great Lowfat Calcium Day

Breakfast
1 serving whole grain Total or two slices calcium-enriched bread
1 glass calcium-enriched orange juice
1 cup coffee with a splash of skim milk

Lunch
Salmon salad made with nonfat plain yogurt
Two slices calcium-enriched bread
One orange

Dinner
Broiled perch (3 ounces)
One cup cooked broccoli
One baked potato with nonfat yogurt topping
One cup nonfat frozen yogurt

Snacks
One cup nonfat fruit yogurt or,
One ounce reduced fat cheddar cheese or,
1/2 cup raisins

Total Calcium: Approximately 1800 mg for one healthy day!

Dairy, Dairy, Quite Contrary

Milk

Does adding milk to coffee help bones? What's better - skim milk or 2% milk? Is dairy food the best source of dietary calcium? What about the protein in milk, doesn't it block calcium? What about vegetarians, people who are lactose intolerant, and just plain old-fashioned vanilla non-milk drinkers in bone jeopardy? Is milk just for kids, or should moms be drinking the white stuff too? And what about real men? And what about athletes? And most important of all, what about ice cream, ice milk, and those fabulous floats?

Cheese

And that's just the milk issue. What about cheese? There is soft cheese, hard cheese, French cheese, sweet cheese and goat cheese. And of course there is the familiar yellow square of American processed cheese. Finally, there is the dieters' delight, cottage cheese. How do we begin to answer these questions? Is cheese good for you? How much protein, fat, and calcium do we really get in cheese? How do we find the best cheese for our calcium and fat buck?

Yogurt

As if milk and cheese weren't enough to deal with, now we've got something relatively new–yogurt. What about yogurt? What kind is best? How often should we eat it? What does it really contribute to our bone health? Is it a fad, or is here to stay? Is it just as good frozen? Again, questions and more questions.

****

According to a study from Cornell University, dairy products take a slight edge over supplements as a source of calcium for women and children. That's because milk and cheese don't interfere with the absorption of iron. Yogurt and some calcium supplements may reduce the absorption of iron.

> **Take your iron at a different time from your calcium.**

The Fat Connection

Dairy products like cheese, milk, and yogurt have traditionally been seen as the best sources of calcium, but many of us avoided them because of the fat connection. Who could afford to gain both calcium and weight?

But there are ways to get the calcium without the fat. And the makers of milk, cheese and yogurt deserve a pat on the back for helping us do just that by taking out the fat and leaving in all the nutrients, including calcium, in the lowfat or nonfat versions of just about every single dairy product on the market.

Now, we all know that too much fat is a killer. And we also know that most of us get far more than the 30% of our total calories that is recommended by the American Heart Association and virtually every other health-promoting organization in the country. Study after study has pointed directly to fat as a major contributing factor in heart disease, stroke, high blood pressure, osteoporosis, cancer, obesity and a host of other life-shortening diseases.

So, when you go to increase your calcium intake, be smart about it and choose from the low fat or nonfat products available.

Remember, if you eat more calories than you burn off, your body will store the extra in convenient fat closets around your waist, hips, stomach, thighs and arms - and most dangerous of all, in the miles of blood vessels that bring vital nutrients to every part of your body.

Keep in mind that vitamins and minerals have no calories.

That's the good news. The bad news is that these nutrients are buried in foods that do have calories–from a high of 252 calories in one ounce of fat to 112 calories in one ounce of protein or carbohydrate. So pick the calcium-rich foods that are low in fat and get the best of all possible health worlds.

****

How Much Should You Weigh?

Women: **Count 100 pounds for the first five feet of height and 5 pounds for every inch over five feet.**

Men: **Count 106 pounds for the first five feet of height and 6 pounds for every inch over five feet.**

Fat-In-Fat Chart

Product	Grams of fat per tablespoon
Butter	12
Corn oil	14
Half-and-Half	1.7
Margarine	12
Olive oil	14
Sour cream	5.6
Whipping cream	5.6

Fat In Salad Dressings

Type	Grams of fat per tablespoon
Blue cheese	8
French	6
Mayo	11
Miracle Whip	7
Oil & Vinegar	10
Thousand Island	8

Fat In Milk

Product	Grams of fat per cup
Milk, whole	8
Milk, 2%	5
Milk, 1%	2.4
Milk, skim	0.4

Fat In Ice Cream

Product	Grams of fat per cup	
Ice milk	14	
Ice cream	24	
Sherbet	2	Source: USDA

The Milky Way

Milk & Coffee
The University of California, San Diego, found that women who drank coffee, but added at least one glass of milk to their diet every day, seemed to have sturdier bones than women who drank coffee but skipped the milk.

Dairy & Bone Density
A preliminary study shows that women who consume the most dairy products had bones that measured 20% more dense than women who consumed fewer dairy products.

The British Medical Association
The British Medical Association reports a study that found older women who had a lifetime of drinking milk had greater bone density than women who were non-milk drinkers or who didn't drink as much milk.

The Flip Side: Does Milk Contribute To Osteoporosis?
This is a controversial issue.

1. The Calcium-Drainers Count
The Physicians Committee For Responsible Medicine and some other health professionals and researchers stress factors such as smoking, lack of exercise, too much animal protein, sodium, caffeine and phosphorus contribute more to calcium loss than the fact that women don't drink enough milk.

2. The Animal Protein Factor
This group of medical experts advocates getting extra calcium from vegetable sources which are lower in animal protein than milk. Why? Because animal protein (which makes up a large part of milk) is a calcium blocker. There are some indications that countries that consume large quantities of dairy products have a higher instance of osteoporosis than countries that consume fewer dairy products.

Try To Get Your Calcium From A Wide Variety Of Foods And Ask Your Doctor Or Health Professional About Calcium Supplements For You.

Milk Is More Than Meets The Eye

Have you ever wondered what milk is made of ? Well, it's a wonderful, complex, healthy food made up of a variety of vital nutrients.

Milk Proteins

Milk proteins are composed of 20 different amino acids, 8 of which are essential because our own bodies can't manufacture them. The remaining 12 are nonessential, because we can make our own, and don't depend on a food source for them. Over 80 percent of the protein in milk is made of casein.

Minerals

Four vital minerals are found in milk: calcium, phosphorus, magnesium and zinc. These four work in marvelous harmony to insure a balance that can help prevent osteoporosis, high blood pressure, and even some forms of cancer.

Vitamins

A rich source of vitamins, milk contains the fat-soluble vitamins A and D, as well as the water-soluble, major B vitamins–thiamine, riboflavin, niacin and B_{12}. Together they change the food from fat, protein and carbohydrates into energy.

Source: National Dairy Council

New Milk With Added Calcium: Calcimilk®

Just in time. And what a great idea!
There is a wonderful new milk out there called Calcimilk.®
What makes it so special?
It has 2/3 more calcium than regular milk.
What does this mean?
Just two glasses of this terrific tasting, rich milk give you 1,000 mg of calcium.
That's the daily requirement for most of us.
Look for Calcimilk® wherever you buy milk.

Know Your Milk

Whole Milk

Whole milk must contain at least 3.25 percent milkfat and 8.25 percent milk solids. Most milk sold in the U.S. is fortified with vitamin D. The amount of vitamin D in a quart of milk is 400 International Units (IU). Vitamin D is essential because it helps calcium do its job of building strong bones.

Lowfat Milk

Lowfat milk contains anywhere from 0.5 to 2.0 percent milkfat. Lowfat milk also has 2,000 International Units (IU) vitamin A added, per quart, because the process of removing fat also removes vitamin A. Removing milkfat does not mean that there is less calcium in lowfat milk.

Skim Milk

This milk has less than 0.5 percent milkfat and is also fortified with 2,000 International Units (IU) vitamin A per quart. Removing milkfat does not mean that there is less calcium in skim milk.

Chocolate Milk

Chocolate milk is made by adding chocolate or cocoa and a sweetener to milk. Chocolate contains oxalic acid, which is a calcium blocker. There is generally not enough chocolate in chocolate milk to significantly affect calcium absorption.

Evaporated Milk

This involves evaporating enough water from milk to reduce its volume by half. The resulting milk is homogenized, fortified with 400 International Units (IU) of vitamin D per pint, canned and heat sterilized. It contains at least 7.25 percent milk solids.

Evaporated Skim Milk

This involves the same process as for evaporated milk. Vitamins A and D are added. Skim milk contains up to 0.5 percent milkfat.

Sweetened Condensed Milk

This canned concentrate of whole or skim milk is sweetened. The same vitamins and milkfat content apply as for whole or skim milk.

Cultured Buttermilk

Buttermilk is made by adding a bacterial culture to skim or lowfat milk. Salt is often added for extra flavor.   Source: National Dairy Council

Lowfat Milk vs. Skim Milk

Who Needs Whole Milk?

Please check with your own doctor, but medical experts are beginning to recommend that only infants and toddlers under the age of two really need to be drinking whole milk. That leaves the rest of us.

The Milk & Fat Wars–Be A Winner

Whole Milk	50% of its 150 calories come from fat
2% Milk	35% of its 121 calories come from fat
1% Milk	23% of its 102 calories come from fat
Skim Milk	0% to 5% of its 86 calories come from fat

Getting The Fat Out

1. Use skim milk in cooking.
2. Mix skim milk into your tea and coffee.
3. Use skim milk in your cream soups.
4. Make instant puddings with skim milk.
5. Sprinkle dry skim milk powder into your coffee as a substitute for nondairy creamers.
6. Make frosty shakes with skim milk and crushed ice.
7. Mix skim milk with assorted fruit juices in your blender.
8. Pour a little skim milk in your morning cereal.
9. Make cocoa and hot chocolate with skim milk.
10. Splash a little skim milk into your mashed potatoes.

****

Are you one of the 50% of Americans who doesn't know that skim milk has just as many nutrients as other milk, with none of the fat?

Calcium Content In Milk

Type of Milk	Calcium Content Mg
1. Sweetened condensed whole milk (4 ounces)	434
2. Evaporated skim milk (4 ounces)	369
3. Evaporated whole milk (4 ounces)	329
4. Skim milk (8 ounces)	316
5. Lowfat milk, 1% (8 ounces)	300
6. Lowfat milk, 2% (8 ounces)	296
7. Whole milk (8 ounces)	290
8. Cultured buttermilk (8 ounces)	285
9. Chocolate milk, lowfat 2% (8 ounces)	284
10. Chocolate milk, whole (8 ounces)	280
11. Eggnog (4 ounces)	165

Tips For Storing & Handling All Milk Safely

- Because fresh milk is perishable it must be refrigerated at 40°F or less.
- Pour only what you need and refrigerate the rest.
- Reseal the container to make sure other food flavors are not absorbed.
- Keep milk in the cartons in which you bought it, or in a dark container. Exposure to light can rob milk of riboflavin.
- If you open a can of evaporated milk, refrigerate it.
- If you mix up a batch of dry milk, refrigerate it the same way you would regular milk.

Not All Cheese Is Created Equal

Cheese is cheese, right? Wrong. There are dozens of different types of cheeses. Some are hard, some soft. Some are imported, some are domestic. Some go great with grapes, some go better with olives.

Just as there are differences in the cheeses themselves, there are big differences in the calcium content of those cheeses. Does a cheese sandwich made with Swiss cheese give you more or less calcium than a sandwich made with American processed cheese? And what about all of us who so virtuously nibble our cottage cheese at lunch? How are we doing in terms of calcium? Here's some shocking news. One ounce of cottage cheese has only 19 mg of calcium. American cheese has 174 and Swiss has an impressive 272.

See, you have to know your cheese if that's where you were hoping to get a lot of your daily calcium.

Cheese	Mg Calcium per ounce
Parmesan	355
Romano	301
Gruyère	287
Swiss	272
Provolone	214
Monterey	211
Mozzarella, part skim	207
Edam	207
Cheddar	204
Cottage cheese	19
Muenster	203
Tilsit	198
Gouda	198
Colby	194
Brick	191
Roquefort	188
American processed	174

Source: USDA

Fat Cheese vs. Skinny Cheese

Type	Grams fat per ounce	Calories per ounce
Cheese spread	5.9	81.2
Cheese spread (skim)	1.7	53.8
Blue cheese	8.1	98.9
Brie	7.8	93.6
Camembert	6.7	84.0
Cheddar	9.2	112.9
Processed slices	8.7	105.0
Colby	8.9	110.4
Regular cottage cheese	1.4	28.9
Cream cheese	9.8	97.8
Feta cheese	6.2	76.1
Mozzarella	7.0	89.1
Parmesan	8.4	127.7
Ricotta	3.6	48.7
Swiss	7.6	105.3

****

A recent report showed that 76 new lowfat cheese products found their way into our grocery stores between 1991 and 1992.

By the year 1997 37% of Americans are expected to buy lowfat cheese.

More Fat Cheese vs. Skinny Cheese

Type	Grams of fat per ounce	Calories per ounce
Cheese spread	5.9	81.2
Cheese spread (skim)	1.7	53.8
Processed slices	8.7	105.0
Processed slices (skim)	1.7	53.5
Cottage cheese 1%	0.3	21.0
Cottage cheese 2%	0.6	25.2
Cottage cheese 4%	1.4	28.9
Mozzarella	7.0	89.1
Mozzarella (part skim)	4.8	78.4
Ricotta	3.6	48.7
Ricotta (part skim)	2.2	38.7

Source: USDA

Cheese: A Great Dessert

The newest dessert trend in restaurants all over the country is cheese. Try some at home to give your family and guests a pleasant chance and a calcium boost besides.

Setting Up A Cheese Tray

Think of a clock when setting up a cheese tray. The mildest cheese is placed at where one o'clock would be. Then they get progressively stronger in flavor until the strongest cheese is at twelve o'clock. You follow the same pattern in tasting the cheeses. Work from the mildest to the strongest.

Cheeses To Put On Your Cheese Tray

Brie: A soft, mild cheese. It should be served at room temperature and should be slightly runny.

Gouda: Still in the fairly mild family. It can be served in a hunk.

Swiss: A family favorite. Also one of the best sources of calcium in the cheese family.

Cheddar: An aged cheddar is a terrific, full-bodied tasting cheese. Another good source of calcium. Try this with a few apple wedges.

Get To Know Goat Cheese

- **It is more easily digestible than other cheeses.**
- **It has fewer calories.**
- **Use it to replace cream cheese in most recipes.**
- **Don't store it in plastic. Wrap it in waxed paper so it can breathe.**
- **It can be frozen if tightly wrapped in foil.**
- **Try it as a flavorful alternative to regular cheese.**

The Yogurt Story

Disgusting as it sounds, yogurt is essentially sour milk. Back in the early 1900s, Dr. Metchnikoff, a Nobel prize-winning scientist and friend of Louis Pasteur, the other famous name in dairy products, conducted a series of experiments believing that sour milk contained important health elements. When his experiments showed mice fed a form of sour milk lived longest, had the healthiest babies and the cleanest insides, Dr. Metchnikoff believed he had found one of the secrets to the fountain of health and longer life. Soon, the folklore about the healing and longevity properties of this special sour milk spread, and today, contemporary scientists are rediscovering the health benefits of what we now know as yogurt.

Some Yogurt Studies

Studies show that the active cultures in yogurt act as immune system enhancers, infection fighters, possible nutritional shields against cancers, and powerful scrubbers of the digestive tract.Yogurt also offers us loads of calcium for stronger bones and teeth, and a longer life free of fractures and osteoporosis.

1. The USDA conducted a series of experiments to test yogurt's infection-fighting power by injecting rats with salmonella bacteria. The yogurt-fed rats didn't get as sick, and not as many of them died as rats that didn't get yogurt.

2. Major hospitals in Chicago and New York found that yogurt was an excellent way to stop the course of diarrhea in both adults and infants.

3. Studies at New York's Sloan Kettering Institute for Cancer Research found that yogurt had some anti-cancer properties when tested on lab animals.

4. A French study shows that women who ate yogurt had a lower risk of developing breast cancer than women who didn't.

5. Long Island Jewish Medical Center found that women who suffered from recurring yeast infections found major relief by eating just one cup of yogurt with active yeast cultures a day.

Check Out Yogurt Cheese

Don't knock it until you've tried it. Remember the goal is to get as much calcium as possible without the fat. Yogurt cheese (the recipe is in the cookbook part of this book) is fun to make, tastes great, and is loaded with calcium. Make it out of nonfat yogurt and you lose the fat, too.

	Fat	**Calcium**
Yogurt cheese made from nonfat yogurt	0 gm	10 gm
Cream cheese	50 gm	5 gm
Sour cream	26 gm	2.5 gm

Source: National Dairy Council

****

Remember, yogurt must contain live cultures to give you real health benefits. Look for L. acidophilus, L. bulgaricus or S. thermophilus on the container.

Add A Little Yogurt To Your Life

- Bored with breakfast? Skip the jam, jelly or peanut butter, and spread a little fruit-flavored yogurt on your toast, muffin, or bagel.

- For a fast breakfast or snack, toss a handful of your favorite cereal into a container of nonfat or lowfat fruit-flavored yogurt.

- Yogurt makes a great marinade. Mix up a little nonfat yogurt with garlic, lemon juice, or any of your favorite marinades. Brush on your meat before grilling.

- Looking for a way to zip up tired, old vegetables? Mix a spoon of Dijon-style mustard with some nonfat yogurt. Heat slowly. Spoon over vegetables.

- Try a couple of frozen yogurt sandwiches for a special frozen treat. Just put some lowfat frozen yogurt between two graham crackers or vanilla wafers. Freeze. Serve anytime.

- Got a yen for a shake? Substitute frozen yogurt, or regular fruit-flavored yogurt and ice for the ice cream you might normally use.

- Dessert was never this good, and this good for you. Cover an angel-food cake with fruit-flavored yogurt. Put on your best serving platter. Garnish with fresh fruit and sprigs of mint. And guess what? You are a lowfat cooking sensation!

✳✳✳✳✳✳✳✳✳

The University of California reports that yogurt eaters have 25% fewer colds.

The *International Journal of Immunotherapy* reports that studies show that yogurt may boost the immune system by aiding in the production of gamma interferon.

Calcium From The East: Soy & Tofu

Before you skip this section, stop. There are some very compelling reasons to introduce yourself and your family to the soy family, especially when it comes to your bone health and calcium nutrition. And the soy and tofu lessons aren't as complicated as you think. In fact, if you think these products are only for vegetarians or nutrition freaks, just check out the produce and other sections of your local supermarket. You'll find them well stocked with dozens of soy products.

A Basic Primer

Soy:
This is a bean that is made into a variety of different soyfoods. It is high in calcium, non-animal protein and generally low in fat. It is the staple in most Eastern and Oriental diets.

Tofu:
Also known as beancurd this is a soy product that looks like white cheese. It is found in the produce section of most supermarkets and is stored chilled in water. It has many uses and comes in a variety of different textures and consistencies.

Soy sauce:
There's more to soy sauce than you would think just from opening those little packets that come with Chinese food. That's right. Soy sauce is also made from soybeans. It is made by fermenting soybeans.

Soy milk:
This is what you get when you process soybeans with water. When it curdles, it becomes tofu.

There are other soy products, but these are the most familiar to us here in America and these are the ones that lend themselves to many American recipes.

****

The soybean was first used as a food source in China over 4000 years ago.

Soybeans & Your Health

Soybeans are a wonderful source of protein and make a good alternative from animal sources of protein. Besides protein they contain fiber, many B vitamins, and calcium. These soybean products are rich in iron, potassium and vitamin E. They are nutrient dense and have little fat.

1. Some studies show that soybeans are a very good source of protease inhibitors, which have been shown to "quiet" pre-cancerous cells or normalize them.

2. Soybeans and the products derived from them such as tofu have been shown to help those who suffer from lactose intolerance and allergies. Tofu and soy milk can be used to replace the dairy products normally found in some of our favorite foods.

3. Tofu is a good choice for those on a low sodium diet. It contains just 2 to 15 mg of sodium per 100 grams.

4. A study at the University of Texas showed that 50% less calcium is lost through urine when eating soy-based protein products than when eating animal-based proteins. This may be one explanation for the fact that Asian women retain more calcium and suffer less from osteoporosis.

5. Researchers at the University of North Carolina found that soy products contain a natural estrogen which acts to prevent bone loss and may protect women from osteoporosis.

****

Looking for a healthy alternative to ice cream?
Try Tofutti, a frozen dessert made from tofu.

In The Kitchen With Tofu

What Kind To Buy?

O.K. You decided to buy one container of tofu. But you are puzzled. There seem to be different kinds. Here's how to decide which type is just right. It depends on what you want to use it for.

Firm and Extra Firm: This is best for stir-fry, stews and hearty dishes like casseroles where it is important the tofu hold its shape. For the more adventurous, tofu can be slit and the pocket formed can be stuffed. This is best accomplished with firm or extra firm tofu.

Soft and Silken: This is best for desserts, sauces, dips and dressings or a good substitute for cottage or ricotta cheese. If you only have the soft type and need the hard simply squeeze out the extra water through a cloth.

How To Shop For And Store Tofu

√ Always check the date and don't buy any tofu that is past its freshness stamp.

√ Make sure it is cool to the touch when you buy it.

√ Store unopened in your fridge, but don't use it past the freshness date.

√ After opening, store leftover tofu in a clean bowl covered with fresh water.

√ Change the tofu water every day to insure freshness.

√ You can freeze tofu by rinsing it first and wrapping in foil. Lasts 4 to 5 months.

****

1/2 cup of tofu without calcium sulphate has 130 mg of calcium.
1/2 cup of tofu with calcium sulphate has 434 mg of calcium.
Check the label.

Cooking With Tofu 101

If you've never cooked with tofu and don't know how to start, these few recipes should get you started, give you confidence and introduce you to a whole new calcium source.

**Tofu has little flavor of its own.
It "borrows" flavors from other ingredients.**

Dilly Tofu Dip

1/2 pound soft tofu
3 medium dill pickles, chopped
1 tablespoon fresh dill
1 tablespoon pickle juice

Toss all the ingredients into a food processor or blender. Blend until smooth. Serve chilled with fresh veggies, crackers or lowfat chips.

Tofu Spaghetti Sauce

3 large tomatoes, diced
1/2 pound fresh, thinly sliced mushrooms
1 red pepper, diced
1 green pepper, diced
1 cup water
2 onions, diced
2 cloves garlic, minced
1 pound extra firm tofu
1 tablespoon vegetable oil
1 tablespoon soy sauce
pepper to taste

Sauté onions and garlic in oil until soft. Add tomatoes, peppers, and mushrooms. Sauté for 3 to 5 minutes. Add the tofu, water, salt, soy sauce and pepper. Cover and bring to a boil. Reduce heat and simmer for 1 hour stirring occasionally. Serve. Makes 4 servings.

Tofu Ideas For A Calcium Change

Chop firm tofu into chunks and toss it into your salad.

Try soy cheese for a snack or sandwiches.

Mix a little tofu with eggs and scramble as usual.

Substitute firm tofu for chicken or beef in your stirfry recipes.

Switch from ground beef to tofu in chili.

Make a shake by replacing milk with soft tofu and blend.

Slice firm tofu and fry. Top with tomato sauce and pretend it's veal.

Make a tofu meatloaf or hamburgers.

Toss a few chunks of firm tofu into your favorite soups.

✳✳✳✳✳✳✳✳✳✳

**Don't forget to look for and try the dozens of
other soy and tofu products in
your grocery store**

Calcium & Veggies

Although dairy products are among the richest sources of calcium, vegetables are another calcium source. But before you say "great" you should know that some of the highest sources of vegetable calcium also contain oxalic acid. Oxalic acid blocks the absorption of calcium.

Spinach and greens like beet greens, turnip greens, mustard greens, and green beans provide a healthy amount of calcium, but because of the oxalic acid the calcium doesn't get into our system where it can do us the good it should. Some studies have shown that only as little as 5% of the calcium in spinach gets absorbed.

That doesn't mean you should give up on vegetables as a source of dietary calcium. Some experts recommend adding a teaspoon of vinegar or lemon juice to the cooking water of the oxalic-heavy vegetables as a way of releasing the calcium and making it easier to absorb.

But even so, there are many vegetables like broccoli, okra, bokchoy (Chinese cabbage), and carrots that will give you calcium, plus loads of other vitamins and nutrients for good health.

Best Veggie Bets For Calcium

Broccoli 1 cup	178 mg of calcium
Okra 1 cup	176 mg of calcium
Bokchoy 1 cup	158 mg of calcium
Green beans 1 cup	62 mg of calcium
Potatoes 1 cup	56 mg of calcium
Carrots 1 medium	19 mg of calcium

****

**Watch for water soluble nutrients.
Steam vegetables whenever you can.
Steaming can save vitamin C, calcium,
magnesium and phosphorous.**

Beans	**10 to 15 minutes**
Broccoli	**10 to 15 minutes**
Carrots	**10 to 15 minutes**

Let's Go Calcium Shopping

"Be prepared" is a great motto, not just for the cosmic things in life, but also for the everyday things, like grocery shopping. For many of us, grocery shopping has become a rushed, hectic process squeezed in between dozens of other daily committments. We often run into the store, reach for the items that will give us the fastest meals possible, and rush out again.

But when it comes to shopping not just for food, but for health and a longer life, it's not a bad idea to take a little time to make the best choices.

√ Always make a list. Keep it on the fridge or tacked up on a kitchen cupboard and add items to it as you run out.

√ Make a little note beside each item on your shopping list to indicate its key nutritional elements. For example, items like milk, cheese, yogurt, etc. could have a small letter c beside them, to remind you they are calcium-rich.

√ In order to insure freshness, shop for vegetables more than once a week.

√ Always check the expiration date on dairy products to make sure you are buying them at the peak of their nutritional life.

√ Always pick milk and yogurt containers that are closest to the bottom of the refrigeration unit. Dairy products need consistent lower temperatures to retain their freshness.

√ Be creative. Add your own fresh or frozen fruit to plain, nonfat yogurt.

√ Try not to shop for groceries when you are overtired, hungry or upset. You need to be as relaxed as possible to make wise selections.

√ Think about the items you are buying. Make sure they are low in fat, salt, and sugar. Try to purchase foods in as close to their natural state as possible. Do most of your shopping from the aisles around the outside edges of the supermarket. Many stores keep the highly processed foods in the inside lanes.

Calcium-Rich Shopping List

Plain, nonfat yogurt
Fruity lowfat yogurt
Lowfat frozen yogurt desserts
Skim milk
Skim milk powder
Evaporated skim milk
Buttermilk
Grated Parmesan cheese
Lowfat mozzarella cheese
Lowfat cottage cheese
Lowfat cream cheese
Lowfat Cheddar cheese
Lowfat Swiss cheese
Lowfat sour cream
Lowfat mayonnaise
Canned sardines packed in tomato sauce
Canned salmon
Canned mackeral
Smelts, fresh or frozen
Bokchoy cabbage
Turnip greens, fresh
Collard greens, fresh or frozen
Kale, fresh or frozen
Spinach, fresh or frozen
Broccoli, fresh or frozen
Tofu
Instant oats
Almonds
Filberts

****

Look for and buy calcium-enriched products such as Total, Tropicana Orange Juice, Sunny Delight, Wonder Bread, Merita Bread, Hawaiian Punch, Minute Maid Orange Juice, and others that help you get your daily calcium.

Eating Out

It's almost a conspiracy. Eating out is often a minefield of fat, sugar, salt, so that even the most careful of us can get caught with a lunch or dinner that causes us to break many of our good eating intentions.

Here are some suggestions that will help you make calcium-rich choices on your evening out.

Ordering Tips For Calcium Rich Eating Out . . . Go For–

Italian

Pizza with cheese topping
Pasta primavera
Pasta with clam sauce
Pasta marinara
Parmesan cheese

French

Oysters on the half shell
Salad Nicoise
Bouillabaisse
Chicken in wine
Broiled fish
Fresh salads, no dressing
Fresh fruit

Chinese

Stir fried veggies
Stir fried chicken or fish
Vegetarian dishes
Plain rice

Mexican

Chicken taco
Corn tortillas
Chicken or bean burrito
Chicken fajitas
Shredded lettuce and tomato
Rice
Salsa

Indian

Chicken marinated in yogurt
Chicken, vegetable or fish curry
Salad with yogurt dressing
Lentils, chickpeas, cucumbers

Japanese

Sushi
Chicken teriyaki
Tofu
Rice and noodles
Miso soup
Japanese vegetables

Sneaking In The Calcium Part 1

√ Add lowfat dry milk to hot, cooked cereals.

√ Add a slice of cheese to a sandwich.

√ Try using tofu instead of meat in stirfry recipes.

√ Use lowfat cream cheese or cottage cheese instead of butter on sandwiches.

√ Put a jar of Parmesan cheese on the table. Better than salt.

√ Toss a couple of cubes of cheese into your favorite soup just before serving.

√ Start buying the dark green varieties of lettuce like romaine. The darker the green, the bigger the calcium punch.

√ All you picklers, make your pickle brine with calcium chloride instead of sodium chloride (table salt).

√ Throw 1/4 cup of powdered nonfat dry milk into all your baking recipes. It won't damage the recipe, and it will build your bones.

√ Use your leftover vegetable cooking water in soups and stews.

√ If you can't give up mayo completely, mix it half and half with lowfat yogurt.

√ Have a cup of skim milk cocoa before bedtime or anytime.

√ Look for low-sodium products in the supermarket.

Sneaking In The Calcium Part II

√ Mix up some salsa with nonfat yogurt and use on baked potatoes and vegetables.

√ Add evaporated skim milk to sauces and puddings right out of the can for a creamier taste.

√ Add yogurt to your mashed potatoes.

√ Add lowfat powdered milk to your dry pancake mix.

√ Add lowfat powdered milk to your mashed potatoes.

√ Mix up a batch of nonfat yogurt, your favorite cereal, nuts, raisins and fresh fruit. Add sweetener. Put the mixture into a plastic wrap-lined loaf pan. Freeze. Slice and serve.

√ If you hate the skin on hot milk, beat the milk with a whisk while it cooks.

√ Throw some fresh or frozen fruit into a blender. Add nonfat yogurt. What do you have? A great sauce for fresh fruit, puddings, cakes or desserts.

√ Keep some buttermilk on hand to substitute for milk in any recipe. Just add 1/2 teaspoon baking powder for each cup you substitute.

√ Even if your milk has gone sour it can still be used in recipes.

√ Get a can of nonfat evaporated milk. Pour it into a shallow dish. Put it into the freezer, just until ice crystals form around the edges. Transfer it to a chilled bowl. Beat with chilled beaters until fluffy. Add a couple of teaspoons of confectioner's sugar. Beat again. Serve as a topping.

15 Ways To Keep The Calcium & Lose The Fat

1. Use cottage cheese and lowfat mozzarella cheese instead of ricotta and regular mozzarella in your favorite lasagne recipe.

2. Use nonfat yogurt in your tuna, chicken, potato and macaroni salads. Great for coleslaw, too.

3. Go for lowfat frozen yogurt or sherbert instead of ice cream.

4. Sprinkle Parmesan cheese instead of butter on your popcorn.

5. Make puddings with skim milk.

6. Use powdered skim milk in your coffee or tea.

7. Buy sardines packed in water or tomato sauce, not oil.

8. Make all your cream soups with skim milk.

9. Add nonfat powdered milk to gravy stock, stews, and soups to thicken them.

10. Always use nonfat cream cheese.

11. Substitute Neufchâtel for cream cheese.

12. Make dips with lowfat or nonfat yogurt instead of sour cream.

13. Top your veggies and baked potatoes with yogurt.

14. Take your own yogurt-based dressing to restaurants. If they care about you as a customer, they won't mind.

15. Top cakes and desserts with lowfat or nonfat fruit-flavored yogurt.

The Cookbook Part

Yogurt Bran Muffins

1 1/2 cups wheat bran
1/2 cup boiling water
1 1/3 cups whole wheat flour
1 1/4 teaspoons baking soda
1/2 teaspoon ground cinnamon
1/4 teaspoon ground cloves
1/4 teaspoon ground nutmeg
1 egg
1/3 cup honey
1/2 cup DANNON® Plain Nonfat Yogurt
3 tablespoons vegetable oil
3/4 cup fresh or frozen and drained blueberries

Preheat oven to 350° F. Line muffin cups with paper baking cups. In a medium bowl combine the wheat bran and boiling water. Let stand 10 minutes to soften. In a large bowl combine flour, baking soda, cinnamon, cloves and nutmeg. In a small bowl combine egg, honey, yogurt and oil. Stir well. Add to bran mixture. Add egg mixture all at once to flour mixture. Stir just until dry ingredients are moistened. Batter will be stiff. Fold in blueberries.

Fill prepared muffin cups 2/3 full. Bake 20 to 25 minutes or until toothpick inserted into center comes clean. Serve warm.

Makes: 12 muffins   Serving size: 1 muffin

Per serving: Calories: 138   Fat: 4.6 grams   Calcium: 32 mg

****
**The University of California reports that
yogurt lovers have 25% fewer colds and
suffer less from hay fever symptoms.**

Pineapple Carrot Raisin Muffins

1 cup whole wheat flour
3/4 cup all-purpose flour
1 tablespoon baking powder
1/4 cup firmly packed brown sugar
1 1/2 cups KELLOGG'S® ALL-BRAN® cereal
1 can (8 ounces) crushed, unsweetened pineapple,
1/2 cup unsweetened orange juice
2 egg whites
1/4 cup vegetable oil
3/4 cup shredded carrots
1/3 cup seedless raisins

Line 12 muffin cups with paper liners. Stir together flours, baking powder, and sugar. Set aside. In a large mixing bowl combine cereal, pineapple (including juice) and orange juice. Let stand five minutes or until cereal is softened. Add egg whites and oil. Beat well. Stir in carrots and raisins. Add flour mixture. Stir until just combined.

Fill prepared muffin cups 2/3 full. Bake at 400°F for 25 minutes or until lightly browned on top. Serve warm.

Makes: 12 muffins   Serving size: 1 muffin

Per serving: Calories: 175   Fat: 5.1 grams   Calcium: 108 mg

****
Studies show that calcium is an antioxidant.
Add the 20,000 IU of betacatotene from the carrots in this
recipe and you have a good source of major protection
from premature aging and disease.

Classic Bran Muffins

1 1/4 cups all-purpose flour
1/2 cup sugar
1 tablespoon baking powder
2 cups KELLOGG'S ® ALL-BRAN® cereal
1 1/4 cups milk
1 egg
1/4 cup vegetable oil

Line muffin cups with paper baking cups. In a large bowl stir together flour, sugar and baking powder. Set aside. In a separate bowl, combine bran cereal and milk. Let stand about five minutes or until cereal is softened. Add egg and oil. Beat well. Add flour mixture. Stir until just combined.

Fill prepared muffin cups 2/3 full. Bake 20 minutes at 400°F or until lightly browned. Serve warm.

Makes: 12 muffins

Serving size: 1 muffin

Per serving: Calories: 178   Fat: 6.2 grams   Calcium: 131 mg

****

**The State University of New York reports that milk contains vital
E2 prostaglandins that coat the stomach lining with a
vaseline-type substance to protect it from damage from
ulcer-causing foods and cigarette smoke pollution.
How much milk do you need to produce a batch of E2 prostaglandins?
Two cups a day of whole milk, whole milk yogurt or low fat milk.
Careful. Skim milk has no E2's . . . Seems the little
darlin's love to live in the fatty part of milk.**

Classic Lowfat Bran Muffins

1 1/4 cups all-purpose flour
2 tablespoons sugar
1 tablespoon baking powder
2 cups KELLOGG'S ® ALL-BRAN® cereal
1 1/4 cups skim milk
2 egg whites
2 tablespoons liquid Butter Buds®

Preheat oven to 400°F. Line muffin cups with paper baking cups. In a large bowl stir together flour, sugar and baking powder. Set aside. In a separate bowl, combine bran cereal and milk. Let stand about five minutes or until cereal is softened. Add egg whites and Butter Buds®. Beat well. Add flour mixture. Stir until just combined.

Fill prepared muffin cups 2/3 full. Bake 20 minutes at 400°F or until lightly browned. Serve warm.

Makes: 12 muffins   Serving size: 1 muffin

Per serving: Calories: 106   Fat: 0.5 grams   Calcium: 130 mg

****

**The American Heart Association
recommends that no more than
30% of your daily calories
be from fat.**

Cheddar Cheese Omelet

3 eggs
3 tablespoons water
1/2 cup shredded cheddar cheese
1 tablespoon margarine
pepper to taste

With a fork, mix eggs, water, 1/4 cup of cheese and pepper in a mixing bowl. Heat margarine in an 8-inch omelet pan until hot enough to sizzle a drop of water. Pour in the egg mixture. Draw the edges of the mixture away from the sides of the pan toward the center letting the uncooked portion flow underneath. Shake skillet to keep mixture from sticking. When mixture is no longer runny, sprinkle the rest of the cheese on top. Fold in half. Serve hot.

Makes: 2 servings

Per serving: Calories: 277   Fat: 22.6 grams   Calcium: 244 mg

Courtesy: United Dairy Industry Association™

****
Researchers at the University of Toronto
found that cheddar cheese can
cut cavities by 56%.
How?
Cheddar cheese stimulates the production
of saliva and increases plaque pH levels.

Cheese & Vegetable Frittata

1 tablespoon margarine
2/3 cup sliced zucchini
1/2 cup chopped fresh tomato, seeded and peeled
1/3 cup green pepper, cut into strips
1/3 cup onion, cut into rings
1/2 teaspoon basil
1/2 teaspoon oregano
8 eggs
1/2 cup skim milk
pepper to taste
1 tablespoon margarine
1 cup (4 ounces) shredded part skim mozzarella cheese

Preheat oven to 350°F. Melt 1 tablespoon margarine in 10-inch omelet pan or heavy skillet. Sauté zucchini, tomato, green pepper, onion, basil, and oregano until tender, about 5 minutes. Remove from heat. Transfer vegetables to bowl.

Combine eggs, milk, and pepper. Wrap handle of skillet with aluminum foil. Melt 1 tablespoon margarine in omelet pan until hot enough to sizzle a drop of water. Pour in egg mixture. Carefully draw cooked portion in at edges toward the center using a spatula so uncooked portion flows to the bottom. Tilt skillet to speed up the flow of uncooked eggs. Shake pan to keep mixture from sticking. While top is still moist, sprinkle with the reserved vegetable mixture and the cheese. Transfer to oven. Bake at 350°F for 3 to 5 minutes or until cheese is melted. Slide onto a heated serving plate. Cut into wedges. Serve at once.

Makes: 4 servings

Per serving: Calories: 303   Fat: 20.8 grams   Calcium: 314 mg

Courtesy: United Dairy Industry Association™

Zesty Cheese Muffins

1 3/4 cups flour
3 teaspoons baking powder
1 tablespoon sugar
1/2 cup lowfat grated cheddar cheese
1 egg
1 cup skim milk
2 tablespoons margarine, melted

Preheat oven to 400°F

Prepare muffin tins and line with paper muffin cups or spray with vegetable spray.

Combine the flour, baking powder, sugar and cheese in a bowl. Mix well. In a small bowl mix together the egg, milk and margarine. Add the egg mixture to the flour mixture. Mix until all ingredients are combined.

Pour into prepared muffin tins filling each 2/3 full. Bake at 400°F for 20 minutes. Serve warm.

Makes: 32 2-inch muffins   Serving Size: 1 muffin

Per serving: Calories: 43   Fat: 1.1 grams   Calcium: 56 mg

****

Tired?
Snack on some high-calcium foods.
Research shows that calcium can give you an energy boost
and make you feel less tired.

Orange Fig Muffins

1 1/2 cups all-purpose flour
1/4 cup sugar
1 tablespoon baking powder
2 cups KELLOGG'S® COMPLETE® Bran Flakes cereal
1 1/4 cups orange juice
1 egg
1/4 cup vegetable oil
2/3 cup chopped dried figs
1 teaspoon grated orange peel

Line muffin cups with paper baking cups. Stir together flour, sugar, and baking powder. Set aside. Measure cereal, orange juice, egg, oil, figs, and orange peel into a large mixing bowl. Beat well. Add dry ingredients to cereal mixture. Stir until just combined.

Fill prepared muffin cups 2/3 full. Bake at 400°F about 25 minutes or until golden brown. Serve warm.

Makes: 12 muffins   Serving size: 1 muffin

Per serving: Calories: 197   Fat: 5.6 grams   Calcium: 118 mg

****

Calcium Boosts Brain Power.

Recent studies show that not getting enough calcium and magnesium can cause mental confusion.

Lowfat Orange Fig Muffins

1 1/2 cups all-purpose flour
2 tablespoons sugar
1 tablespoon baking powder
2 cups KELLOGG'S® COMPLETE® Bran Flakes cereal
1 1/4 cups orange juice
2 egg whites
2 tablespoons vegetable oil
2/3 cups chopped dried figs
1 teaspoon grated orange peel

Line muffin cups with paper baking cups. Stir together flour, sugar, and baking powder. Set aside. Measure cereal, orange juice, egg, oil, figs, and orange peel into a large mixing bowl. Beat well. Add dry ingredients to cereal mixture. Stir until just combined.

Fill prepared muffin cups 2/3 full. Bake at 400°F about 25 minutes or until golden brown. Serve warm.

Makes: 12 muffins

Serving size: 1 muffin

Per serving: Calories: 164   Fat: 2.9 grams   Calcium: 116 mg

****

Don't kid yourself.
If you don't get enough calcium from your diet or supplements
your body "steals" what it needs from your bones.

Shrimp Creole Eggs

1 cup chopped cooked shrimp
1/4 cup green pepper, chopped
1/4 cup onion, chopped
1 tablespoon margarine
8 eggs, slightly beaten
1/2 teaspoon Worcestershire sauce
1 cup (4 ounces) cheddar cheese, shredded
1 tomato, cut into wedges

Sauté shrimp, green pepper and onion in margarine in large skillet about 3 minutes or until tender, stirring frequently. In a bowl, combine eggs and Worcestershire sauce. Pour over shrimp mixture. Cook to desired doneness stirring occasionally. Top with cheese. Let stand until cheese begins to melt. Slide onto heated plate. Garnish with tomato wedges. Serve hot.

Makes: 6 servings

Per serving: Calories: 238   Fat: 15.4 grams   Calcium: 190 mg

Courtesy: United Dairy Industry Association™

****

**What two minerals are the most deficient in the
American woman's diet?
Give up?
<u>Calcium</u> and <u>Iron</u>.**

Leftover Chinese Rice Muffins

1 egg substitute
1 cup cooked white rice
1 1/4 cups skim milk
1 tablespoon liquid Butter Buds®
1 1/2 cups flour
1 tablespoon sugar
2 teaspoons baking powder
2 egg whites

Preheat oven to 400°F.

Line muffin tins with paper muffin liners or spray with nonstick vegetable spray.

In a medium bowl combine all the ingredients except the egg whites. Beat until well mixed. In a small bowl beat the egg whites until stiff. Fold the egg whites into the mixture. Pour into prepared muffin tins until 2/3 full. Bake at 400°F for 20 minutes. Serve warm.

Makes: 30 muffins   Serving Size: 1 muffin

Per serving: Calories: 59   Fat: 0.4 grams   Calcium: 42 mg

****

Can't quite quit the egg habit cold turkey?
Even though eggs are loaded with cholesterol
they are also filled with vital nutrients.
Try mixing egg substitutes half-and-half
with the real thing.
You'll be getting your vitamins and giving your heart a break.

Homestyle Instant Breakfast I

1 banana
1/2 cup skim milk or nonfat yogurt
1 teaspoon honey
1 tablespoon natural bran

In blender or food processor, combine banana, milk or yogurt, honey and bran. Process until smooth. Pour into tall glass.

Makes: 1 serving

Per serving: Calories: 177   Fat: 0.9 grams   Calcium: 161 mg

****

Milk Tips

√ **Make milk the last thing you pick up before heading for the check-out counter to keep it cold and fresh for as long as possible.**

√ **Always keep your milk in the dark. Daylight can change the delicate, distinctive taste of milk.**

√ **Milk gone sour? It may taste terrible to drink, but it's still good for cooking. So don't toss it out too fast.**

√ **Hate the skin on hot milk? Put a lid on the pot while it cooks or give it a few quick stirs with a whisk.**

Homestyle Instant Breakfast II

1 cup DANNON® plain nonfat yogurt
1/2 cup orange juice
1/2 cup fresh or frozen unsweetened strawberries
1 ripe banana
2 tablespoons honey
1 tablespoon wheat germ

In a blender or food processor combine all ingredients. Process until smooth. Serve immediately.

Makes: 2 servings

Per serving: Calories: 230   Fat: 1 gram   Calcium: 244 mg

****

**The U.S. Department of Agriculture conducted a major ten-year study
of over 50,000 Americans and their eating habits. And the
results are not so good. The results show that 68% of
the U.S. population doesn't meet the RDA for calcium.
It gets worse.
The people who need calcium the most
are the ones who get the least.**

**87% of girls between 15 and 18 are deficient in calcium.
84% of women 35 to 50 are deficient in calcium.**

Mixed Fruit Muesli

1 cup rolled oats
1/2 cup raisins
2 cups nonfat yogurt
2 tablespoons honey
1 cup fresh apples, sliced

In a large bowl combine rolled oats, raisins, honey, and yogurt. Stir until mixed. Cover and refrigerate overnight. Top with fresh fruit before serving.

Makes: 4 servings

Per serving: Calories: 216   Fat: 1.7 grams   Calcium: 247 mg

****

**The *New England Journal of Medicine*
reports that just one single extra serving
of fresh fruit or vegetables every day
can reduce your risk of stroke by
an impressive 40%.**

A Taste of the Tropics

1 cup DANNON® nonfat yogurt
1 cup crushed pineapple in juice, undrained
1/2 cup orange juice
1 ripe kiwi fruit, peeled & sliced
2 tablespoons wheat germ

In blender or food processor combine yogurt, pineapple, orange juice, kiwi fruit and wheat germ. Cover and process on high speed until smooth. Serve immediately.

Makes: 2 servings

Per serving: Calories: 89   Fat: 0.7 gram   Calcium: 126 mg

****

The *New England Journal of Medicine* reports that women with osteoporosis can reduce the amount of bone loss with estrogen-replacement therapy. But, estrogen can't bring back bone that's already gone. So researchers recommend taking estrogen as soon as possible after the beginning of menopause.

Blueberry Lemon Muffins

1 3/4 cups all-purpose flour
1/3 cup sugar
1 1/2 teaspoons baking powder
1 egg, beaten
1 cup DANNON® plain nonfat yogurt
1/3 cup vegetable oil
2 tablespoons milk
1 teaspoon grated lemon peel
3/4 cup fresh or frozen blueberries

Preheat oven to 400°F. Line muffin cups with paper baking cups. In a large bowl combine flour, sugar and baking powder. In a medium bowl combine egg, yogurt, oil, milk and lemon peel. Stir mixture well. Add egg mixture all at once to flour mixture. Stir until dry ingredients are moistened. Batter should be lumpy. Gently fold blueberries into batter.

Fill prepared muffin cups 2/3 full. Bake 20 to 25 minutes or until golden and a toothpick inserted into center comes out clean. Serve warm.

Makes: 12 muffins   Serving size: 1 muffin

Per serving: Calories: 165   Fat: 6.8 grams   Calcium: 89 mg

****

Scientists believe that most of us reach our peak bone mass between the ages of 15 and 30.

Lowfat Blueberry Lemon Muffins

1 3/4 cups all-purpose flour
2 tablespoons sugar
1 1/2 teaspoons baking powder
2 egg whites, lightly beaten
1 cup DANNON® plain nonfat yogurt
2 tablespoons vegetable oil
2 tablespoons skim milk
1 teaspoon grated lemon peel
3/4 cup fresh or frozen blueberries

Preheat oven to 400°F. Line muffin cups with paper baking cups. In a large bowl combine flour, sugar and baking powder. In a medium bowl combine egg, yogurt, oil, milk and lemon peel. Stir mixture well. Add egg mixture all at once to flour mixture. Stir until dry ingredients are moistened. Batter should be lumpy. Gently fold blueberries into batter.

Fill prepared muffin cups 2/3 full. Bake 20 to 25 minutes or until golden and a toothpick inserted into center comes out clean. Serve warm.

Makes: 12 muffins

Serving size: 1 muffin

Per serving: Calories: 96   Fat: 0.3 grams   Calcium: 51 mg

****
Do you know how many calories there are in one ounce of . . .
Carbohydrate–112
Protein–112
Fat–252
Alcohol–196

Creamy Cheese Breakfast Sandwich

1/3 cup lowfat cottage cheese
2 slices whole wheat bread (plain or toasted)
1/4 cup sliced strawberries, blueberries or peaches
low calorie sweetener to taste

Spread equal amounts of cottage cheese on whole wheat bread. Top with fruit. Sprinkle with sweetener if desired.

Makes: 1 serving

Per serving: Calories: 272   Fat: 4.4 grams   Calcium: 112 mg

****

The Sunshine Vitamin D

√ **Boosts the absorption of calcium making sure we get as much as we can.**

√ **Helps our kidneys re-absorb calcium from the bloodstream and put it to use.**

√ **Keeps the right level of calcium in our bloodstream.**

Oatmeal Plus

1 cup water
1/2 cup quick cooking oatmeal
1/4 cup lowfat cottage cheese

Cook oatmeal according to package directions. After 3 minutes of cooking time stir in cottage cheese and bring to a boil. Serve with brown sugar or artificial sweetener. Serve warm.

Makes: 1 serving

Per serving: Calories: 190   Fat: 3.0 grams   Calcium: 272 mg

****
Beat the morning blahs with this terrific topping.
Throw fresh fruit into the blender
or food processor. Process until smooth.
Mix it up with a little nonfat yogurt.
Spoon it on
oatmeal,
or
cold cereal.

Simply Surprising Yogurt Omelet

6 egg substitutes
1/2 cup plain, nonfat yogurt
Salt, pepper to taste

Beat ingredients together in a bowl. Spray a nonstick skillet with vegetable cooking spray. Cook egg mixture gently over low heat, lifting the edges and letting the liquid portion flow underneath until cooking is complete.

For a different taste add a pinch of fresh, finely chopped dill or parsley.

Makes: 4 servings

Per serving: Calories: 332   Fat: Trace   Calcium: 256 mg

****
Can you use egg substitutes in most recipes
that call for whole eggs?
Yes!

Ever wonder what egg substitutes are made of?
Mostly egg whites.

Elegant Eggs

4 eggs
4 thin slices Canadian bacon
1 cup DANNON® plain nonfat yogurt
1/2 teaspoon dry mustard
dash of ground red pepper
2 English muffins, split & toasted

Spray a large skillet with vegetable cooking spray. Fill half full with water. Bring to a boil. Reduce heat until water simmers. Break eggs, one at a time, into a small dish and slide into the water. Simmer 3 to 5 minutes or until yolks are firm.

In a large skillet over medium-high heat cook bacon 3 to 4 minutes until heated through, turning once. Set aside. In a small saucepan whisk together yogurt, mustard and red pepper. Cook and stir over low heat until just warm. Do not boil. Top each English muffin half with bacon slice, egg and 1/4 cup sauce. Serve immediately.

Makes: 4 servings

Per serving: Calories: 194   Fat: 6.6 grams   Calcium: 189 mg

✳✳✳✳✳✳✳✳✳

**Studies show that you should limit your caffeine
to 300 mg a day or less.
That's about 3 cups of coffee.**

Cheesy Cinnamon Toast

2 cups nonfat cottage cheese
2 tablespoons lemon juice
1/4 cup skim milk
2 tablespoons sugar
1 teaspoon cinnamon
4 slices whole wheat toast

In blender or food processor mix together cottage cheese, lemon juice, milk, sugar and cinnamon until smooth. Spread over toast. Serve at room temperature.

Makes: 2 servings

Per serving: Calories: 384   Fat: 3.6 grams   Calcium: 389 mg

****

The *New England Journal of Medicine* says
that women who get 1,000 mg of calcium a day
before menopause and 1,500 mg of calcium a day
after menopause, exercise regularly,
and are on hormone replacement therapy
might never get osteoporosis at all.

Buttermilk Pancakes

1 cup flour
1 teaspoon sugar
3/4 teaspoon baking powder
1/2 teaspoon baking soda
1 egg substitute
1 cup buttermilk
1 tablespoon liquid Butter Buds®
vegetable cooking spray

Sift together the flour, sugar, baking powder and baking soda. Beat egg lightly. Add the buttermilk and Butter Buds® to the egg. Add the egg mixture to the dry ingredients. Spray a nonstick pan with vegetable spray. Using a ladle, pour batter into hot pan making pancakes of approximately 4 inches. Fry on both sides until golden. Serve hot.

Makes: 10-4 inch round pancakes   Serving size: 2 pancakes

Per serving: Calories: 160   Fat: 2.4 grams   Calcium: 138 mg

****

How can you tell if you aren't getting enough calcium?
Minor irritability and occasional muscle spasms might
be your only clues. Get some insurance.
Take calcium.

Country Breakfast For A Crowd

1 tablespoon vegetable oil
1 large onion, chopped
8 cups cooked, diced potatoes
1 1/2 cups egg substitutes
1 cup skim milk
2 tablespoons flour
4 ounces lowfat shredded cheddar cheese
pepper to taste
nonstick cooking spray

Preheat oven to 350°F.

In a medium skillet heat oil. Sauté onion until soft. Add potatoes and fry until golden on all sides. In a large bowl mix the remaining ingredients together. Fold in the potato and onion mixture. Pour into an 8 x 12 baking dish treated with nonstick cooking spray. Bake at 350°F for 45 minutes. Serve hot.

Makes: 8 servings

Per serving: Calories: 173   Fat: 4.4 grams   Calcium: 176 mg

****

Skim Milk Savvy

2 cups of skim milk per day could protect you against colon cancer.

2 cups of skim milk a day could stop potential ulcers from forming.

2 cups of skim milk a day can give you a mental energy boost.

Chinese Breakfast In A Hurry

2/3 cup leftover white rice
1/3 cup skim milk
1/4 cup raisins
2 tablespoons maple syrup
dash of ground cinnamon

Combine all ingredients in a microwave-safe bowl. Cook on high for 2 1/2 minutes. Serve hot.

Makes: 1 serving

Per serving: Calories: 389   Fat: 1.2 grams   Calcium: 179 mg

****

Attention Smokers
New research from Johns Hopkins University shows that smokers
who smoke one or more packs a day and who don't drink
milk have a 60% greater chance of developing bronchitis
than heavy smokers who drink their milk every day.

"Nuked" Eggs

1/2 red pepper cut into strips
1/4 cup scallion, chopped
1/4 cup broccoli
egg substitute for 4 eggs
2 tablespoons skim milk
2 tablespoons shredded, lowfat cheddar cheese
pepper to taste

Place red pepper, scallion and broccoli in microwave-safe bowl. Cook until soft. Stir. Cook another 60 seconds. Add remaining ingredients except cheese. Cook, uncovered 2 minutes. Stir. Add cheese. Cook for another 2 minutes. Serve hot.

Makes: 1 serving

Per serving: Calories: 230   Fat: 8.6 grams   Calcium: 176 mg

****
Meet that great calcium trio . . .
Broccoli
Collards
&
Kale

Skinny, Spicy Muffins

2 cups all-purpose flour
3 tablespoons sugar
1 1/2 tablespoons baking powder
1/2 teaspoon cinnamon
1/4 cup Butter Buds®
1 cup skim milk
1 egg white

Preheat oven to 425°F. Line 12 muffin tins with paper liners or spray with nonstick vegetable spray.

In a large bowl, combine all the dry ingredients. In a smaller bowl, combine the milk and liquid Butter Buds®. Add the milk and Butter Buds® to the dry mixture. Stir gently until just combined. Beat the egg white until stiff peaks form. Fold the beaten egg white into the mixture. Fill prepared muffin cups, 2/3 full. Bake at 425°F for 20 minutes. Serve warm.

Makes: 12 muffins   Serving size: 1 muffin

Per serving: Calories: 103   Fat: 0.3 grams   Calcium: 32 mg

****

Myth: Too much calcium causes kidney stones.

**Fact: Studies show that just the opposite may be true . . .
too little calcium may cause kidney stones.**

Apple Cinnamon Oatmeal

1 apple, unpeeled, chopped
2/3 cup rolled oats
1 cup skim milk
cinnamon to taste

Put the milk, apple and rolled oats into a medium saucepan and bring to a boil stirring often. Reduce heat and simmer until oatmeal thickens. Stir in cinnamon before serving. Serve hot.

Makes: 2 servings

Per serving: Calories: 187   Fat: 2.2 grams   Calcium: 170 mg

****
Need another reason to drink your skim milk? Here's a great one.
New research from Vanderbilt University uncovered a
"skim milk factor" that can reduce the amount of
cholesterol in the bloodstream.
How does it work?
In addition to getting cholesterol from what we eat,
our bodies produce cholesterol.
The "skim milk factor" tells our liver, which
makes cholesterol, to cut back on production.

Slim Crêpes

1/2 cup skim milk
2 tablespoons skim powdered milk
4 egg whites

In a medium bowl or blender combine ingredients and mix until smooth. Coat a nonstick crepe pan with vegetable spray. Using a ladle pour enough batter to coat the bottom of the pan. Cook on one side, about 1 minute. Turn. Cook on other side. Serve hot.

Makes: 8 crêpes

Serving size: 1 crêpe

Per serving: Calories: 2.0   Fat: Trace   Calcium: 43 mg

****
Did you know that . . .
The average adult absorbs only about 20 to 30 percent of the calcium
in food. Why? Because the older we get, the less able we
are to absorb calcium. The irony is, the older we
get the more we need calcium.

Basic Omelet

egg substitute for 3 eggs
1/4 cup lowfat cottage cheese
1/4 cup powdered skim milk
pepper to taste

In a blender or food processor combine egg and cottage cheese until smooth. Spray a nonstick skillet with vegetable spray and heat. Pour in the egg mixture. Stir until set. Turn over onto serving platter. Serve hot.

Makes: 2 servings

Per serving: Calories: 391   Fat: 12.9 grams   Calcium: 405 mg

****

How safe are egg substitutes from the salmonella
that plagues real eggs?
Very safe, say the folks at the
U.S. Department of Agriculture,
because the manufacturers of egg substitutes
are required to pasturize their product and
the pasturization process kills any
salmonella bacteria.

Yogurt Cheese

2 containers (16 ounces) plain, nonfat yogurt

Line a colander or strainer with a single coffee filter or double thickness of cheesecloth. Place over a large bowl, but not touching bottom. Pour yogurt into the coffee filter or cheesecloth. Cover and refrigerate overnight. Liquid can be saved and used for soups.

Makes: 1 cup   Serving size: 1 tablespoon

Per serving: Calories: 16   Fat: 0 grams   Calcium: 56 mg

****

**The *International Journal of Immunotherapy*
says that yogurt boosts our
body's production of
gamma interferon, a
major immune system
powerhouse of protection.**

Party Canapé Spread

1 cup plain nonfat yogurt
1 cup grated Parmesan cheese
1 cup lowfat shredded Swiss cheese
1 large onion, chopped
1 tablespoon skim milk
10 slices whole wheat bread cut in quarters

Combine yogurt, cheeses, onion and milk. Mix well. Refrigerate until well chilled, about 2 hours.

Spread toasted quarters of bread with cheese mixture. Broil 4 inches from heat for 2 to 3 minutes until golden and bubbly. Serve hot.

Makes: 20 servings   Serving size: 2 pieces

Per serving: Calories: 88   Fat: 2.4 grams   Calcium: 152 mg

****
It's never too soon to charge your calcium batteries.

It's never too late to charge your calcium batteries.

Start today.

Cheese Squares

1/2 cup margarine
4 ounces lowfat, shredded cheddar cheese
1 egg white, beaten
1 1/2 teaspoons milk
dash of paprika
1/2 pound white bread, unsliced, crust removed, cut into
1-inch cubes

Preheat oven to 350°F.

Combine margarine and cheese. Beat until creamy. Add egg white, milk and paprika. Mix well. Dip bread cubes into cheese mixture, coating all sides except bottom. Place on ungreased cookie sheet. Bake at 350°F for 10 minutes or until toasted.

Makes: 24 servings   Serving size: 1 cube

Per serving: Calories: 45   Fat: 0.7 grams   Calcium: 44 mg

****

Myth: Chocolate milk is bad for you because
it has less calcium than plain milk.

Fact: Milk is milk. While it is true that the chocolate in
chocolate milk contains oxalic acid
which blocks calcium absorption,
there isn't enough oxalic acid in
chocolate milk to really cause any
harm. So, if chocolate milk is the
only kind you or your kids like . . .
go ahead, drink up.

Splendid Spinach Dip

2 cups DANNON® plain nonfat yogurt
1 package (10 ounces) frozen chopped spinach, thawed and
   squeezed
1/3 cup finely chopped fresh onion
2 tablespoons lowfat mayonnaise
1 package instant vegetable soup mix

In a medium bowl combine yogurt, spinach, onion, mayonnaise and vegetable soup mix. Mix well. Serve immediately or cover and chill up to 3 hours. Serve with assorted fresh vegetables for dipping.

Makes: 24 servings (3 cups)   Serving size: approx. 2 tablespoons

Per serving: Calories: 21   Fat: 0.6 grams   Calcium: 53 mg

****

A study from the University of California shows
that women who breast-feed their babies for
over a year and have babies very close together . . .
every couple of years . . . are at risk for
developing osteoporosis.
Protect yourself.
Take calcium.

Chunky Chili Dip

2/3 cup DANNON® plain nonfat yogurt
1/3 cup lowfat mayonnaise
1/4 cup finely chopped green bell pepper
1/4 cup chili sauce
2 tablespoons finely chopped green onion
1 tablespoon prepared horseradish

In a medium bowl combine yogurt, mayonnaise, bell pepper, chili sauce, green onion and horseradish. Mix well. Cover. Chill before serving. Serve with assorted vegetables for dipping.

Makes: 12 servings (about 1 1/2 cups)   Serving size: approx. 2 tablespoons

Per serving: Calories: 32   Fat: 2.4 grams   Calcium: 25 mg

****
Did you know that . . .

Every year 200,000 folks over 35 break a hip because of osteoporosis.
Every year 100,000 folks over 35 break a wrist because of osteoporosis.

Cheese Lovers' Curry Dip

2/3 cup lowfat cottage cheese
1 tablespoon skim milk
1 tablespoon lemon juice
1/2 teaspoon curry powder

Blend all ingredients in blender or food processor until smooth. Serve with fresh vegetables.

Makes: 16 servings   Serving size: approx. 1 tablespoon

Per serving: Calories: 8   Fat: Trace   Calcium: 7 mg

****
People who don't drink milk are twice as likely to
have high blood pressure as people who
drink a quart of milk a day.
Who says?
Cornell University's Hypertension Research Center
&
The National Heart, Lung and Blood Institute.

Yogurt Lovers' Curry Dip

**1 cup plain nonfat yogurt
3 tablespoons mayonnaise
2-3 teaspoons curry powder**

Drain yogurt in coffee filter or cheesecloth. In a bowl mix all ingredients together. Serve with fresh vegetables.

Makes: 2 servings

Per serving: Calories: 16   Fat: 1 gram   Calcium: 20 mg

****
Avoid excessive amounts of these calcium robbers:

- **caffeine**
- **fiber**
- **smoking**
- **salt**
- **stress**

Cucumber Yogurt Dip

1 cucumber
1 cup plain, nonfat yogurt
dash of Worcestershire sauce

Peel and grate cucumber. Drain very well. Drain yogurt. Combine cucumber, yogurt and Worcestershire sauce. Serve with fresh vegetables.

Makes: 16 servings   Serving size: 1 tablespoon

Per serving: Calories: 1.0   Fat: 0 grams   Calcium: 31 mg

****

Did you know that the bone mass in the racquet arm
of a tennis player is higher than the bone mass
in the other arm?
A great reason for getting some
bone-building exercise.

Artichoke Dip

1 16-ounce can artichoke hearts
1/2 cup low fat mayonnaise
1/2 cup plain, nonfat yogurt, drained
1 cup grated Parmesan cheese

Drain artichoke hearts and mash with fork. Add mayonnaise, yogurt and Parmesan cheese. Combine well. Serve with fresh vegetables.

Makes: 2 cups (32 tablespoons)   Serving size: 1 tablespoon

Per serving: Calories: 33   Fat: 2.0 grams   Calcium: 48 mg

****

Most of us only get 500 mg of calcium a day from our diet.
That's only half of what we need for strong bones and
good health.

South-of-the-Border Bean Dip

1 cup canned, drained, rinsed kidney beans
2 tablespoons minced onions
1 garlic clove, minced
1 tablespoon plain nonfat yogurt
1 teaspoon lowfat mayonnaise
1/8 teaspoon dry mustard powder
1 teaspoon sugar
2 teaspoons tomato paste

Place all ingredients into blender or food processor. Process until smooth. Pour into bowl. Cover. Refrigerate. Serve with fresh vegetables, crackers or as a sandwich spread.

Makes: 8 servings

Per serving: Calories: 84   Fat: 0.4 grams   Calcium: 39 mg

****
According to
some studies there is a link between nearsightedness
and the levels of calcium and chromium in
our systems.
Calcium could be as good for your
eyes as carrots.

Antipasto

2 red peppers, roasted, skinned & halved
1/2 pound part skim mozzarella, cut into four 1/2 inch slices
8 sardines in tomato sauce
2 tablespoons extra virgin olive oil
2 tablespoons fresh parsley, chopped
1 lemon cut into 4 wedges
freshly ground black pepper

Arrange the red peppers on 4 plates. Place a slice of mozzarella on each red pepper. Arrange two sardines on the cheese. Drizzle with olive oil. Sprinkle with fresh ground pepper and parsley. Garnish with lemon wedges.
Serve at room temperature.

Makes: 4 servings

Per serving: Calories: 374   Fat: 25.8 grams   Calcium: 645 mg

****

How important is it to get enough calcium early in life?
Very important.
Research shows that the more bone mass
you have created in early adulthood,
the more is available later on
when your body starts to
use up its bone reserves.

Zippy Cheese

1 cup lowfat cottage cheese
3 tablespoons plain, nonfat yogurt
1 tablespoon chopped scallions
1 tablespoon chopped parsley
1/4 teaspoon Italian spices
black pepper to taste

Place all ingredients in a blender or food processor. Process until smooth. Serve with fresh vegetables or crackers.

Makes: 1 1/2 cups   Serving size: 1 tablespoon

Per serving: Calories: 8   Fat: 0.1 grams   Calcium: 12 mg

****

The signs of calcium deficiency are no picnic:
- **Frequent fractures**
- **Hump in your spine**
- **Seizures**
- **Muscle cramps**
- **Low backache**

Veggie Bites

1/3 cup biscuit mix
1/4 cup grated Parmesan cheese
1 egg substitute, beaten
1 egg white, beaten lightly
2 cups zucchini, unpared & shredded
1 medium onion, chopped
1 tablespoon margarine
dash of pepper to taste

In a large bowl, combine the biscuit mix, Parmesan cheese and pepper. Stir in egg substitute and egg white. Add zucchini and onion.

In a medium skillet melt the margarine. Spoon 2 tablespoons of the mixture into the hot margarine. Cook until brown. Turn. Cook on the other side. Serve warm.

Makes: 4 servings

Per serving: Calories: 164   Fat: 8.1 grams   Calcium: 148 mg

****

From the international research community . . .

**Japanese studies have linked the drinking of milk
to a lower risk of stomach cancer.**

**European studies have linked the drinking of milk
to a lower risk of lung cancer.**

Sliced Tomato & Mozzarella Italian

3 large tomatoes, sliced thick
3 ounces lowfat mozzarella cheese part skim, sliced thin

Arrange alternative slices of tomato and mozzarella cheese on a salad plate. Garnish with fresh basil leaves or parsley.

Makes: 6 servings

Per serving: Calories: 53   Fat: 2.6 grams   Calcium: 107 mg

****
Super Foods That Contain Less Than 20% Fat

- **Skim milk**
- **Nonfat yogurt**
- **Lowfat yogurt**
- **Lowfat milk**
- **Lowfat cottage cheese**
- **Lowfat cream cheese**

Savory Marinated Veggies

1 lb. cauliflower, cut in florets
1 lb. broccoli, cut in florets
12 cherry tomatoes
1 cucumber, pared and sliced
3 zucchini, sliced
1 can (10 ounces) black olives, drained
1 can (10 ounce size) artichoke hearts, drained
1 cup low calorie Italian salad dressing

Combine all ingredients in a large mixing bowl. Refrigerate, covered overnight. Stir thoroughly before serving.

Makes: 6 servings

Serving size: 1 cup

Per serving: Calories: 181   Fat: 5.8 grams   Calcium: 95 mg

****

The National Research Council says that the amount of calcium you build while you are young can protect you from bone loss when you get older.

Mushroom Blues

**12 large fresh mushrooms
1 bunch scallions, chopped
2 tablespoons margarine
1/4 cup blue cheese, crumbled
1 teaspoon Worcestershire sauce
1/3 cup seasoned breadcrumbs**

Clean mushrooms. Remove and chop stems. Set them aside. In a medium skillet over medium heat, sauté scallions and chopped mushroom stems in margarine until tender. Add blue cheese, Worcestershire sauce and one-half breadcrumbs to the mixture. Stir until all ingredients are well combined. Spoon the mixture into the prepared mushroom caps. Sprinkle with remaining breadcrumbs. Arrange on a nonstick cookie sheet. Bake at 350°F for 10 to 12 minutes.

Makes: 12 servings

Serving size: 1 mushroom

Per serving: Calories: 43   Fat: 2.9 grams   Calcium: 18 mg

****

**Got the "blues?"
The U.S. Department of Agriculture
reports that extra calcium may reduce
menstrual cramps, bloating,
water retention and those
period "blues."**

Tomato Soup

1 can condensed tomato soup
1 can skim milk (measured in soup can)
1 can (14 ounces) low-sodium, seasoned tomatoes, chopped
pepper to taste

Combine all ingredients in a saucepan over medium heat. Cook until hot, do not boil. Serve hot.

Makes: 4 servings   Serving size: 1/2 cup

Per serving: Calories: 55   Fat: 0.7 grams   Calcium: 94 gm

****
How can we be dying of obesity and starving to death at the same time?
Give up?
Because we are filling our bodies with too much fat, salt, sugar,
cholesterol, alcohol and empty calories.
And that doesn't leave any room for the good things like vitamins,
minerals and other nutrients.

Cheese Soup

1 can condensed cream of potato soup
1 can condensed chicken broth
1 1/2 cups skim milk
1/2 cup shredded lowfat cheddar cheese
pepper to taste

Combine all ingredients in saucepan. Cook over medium heat until cheese melts, stirring often. Serve hot.

Makes: 6 servings   Serving size: 1/2 cup

Per serving: Calories: 75   Fat: 1.7 grams   Calcium: 148 mg

****
Think you might not be getting enough calcium?
Here are some symptoms of serious calcium deficiency to watch for:
• Irregular heartbeat
• Muscle spasms
• Rickets

Creamy Potato Soup

1 tablespoon unsalted margarine
1/2 cup finely chopped onion
1/4 cup chopped celery
1 large potato, peeled and diced
1 cup low-sodium chicken broth
1/4 cup chopped fresh parsley
1/4 teaspoon dried thyme
ground black pepper to taste
1 1/2 cups skim milk

Melt margarine in saucepan over medium-high heat. Add onion and celery and cook, stirring often, until soft. Add potatoes, chicken broth, parsley and spices. Bring to a boil. Reduce heat. Cover and simmer until potatoes are tender. Add milk. Simmer uncovered for 5 minutes. Pour the mixture into a blender or food processor and process until smooth. Return to saucepan and heat.

Makes: 4 servings

Per serving: Calories: 100   Fat: 3.2 grams   Calcium: 189 mg

****
Meet the Calcium Team

Did you know that calcium is a team player?
It needs the help of phosphorous, potassium, magnesium,
vitamin A, vitamin C and vitamin D
in order to score bone-building points.

Satin Salmon Chowder

1 tablespoon margarine
1/2 cup chopped onion
1 clove garlic, minced
2 cups water
1 large potato, peeled & diced (1 cup)
1 envelope low-sodium instant chicken bouillon
1 can (8 ounces) corn kernels, drained
1 can (7 1/2 ounces) salmon, drained and flaked
1/4 cup diced green pepper
1/4 cup diced red pepper
fresh ground black pepper to taste
2 cups DANNON® plain nonfat yogurt
1/4 cup all-purpose flour

In a large saucepan melt margarine over medium heat. Add onion and garlic. Cook and stir until just tender, about 2 minutes. Stir in water, potatoes, and chicken bouillon. Bring to a boil and simmer, stirring occasionally, 4 to 5 minutes or until potatoes are tender. Reduce heat to low. Add corn, salmon, bell peppers and ground pepper. Do not allow to come to a boil. In a medium bowl, combine yogurt and flour. Blend well. Gradually add to soup, stirring constantly until smooth and slightly thickened. Serve hot.

Makes: 4 servings

Per serving: Calories: 269   Fat: 6.8 grams   Calcium: 363 mg

****
Fish without bones
has little or no
calcium.
So go for sardines and salmon.

Corny Chowder

2 tablespoons liquid Butter Buds®
1/4 cup chopped onion
1/4 cup mixed chopped red and green bell pepper
1 tablespoon all-purpose flour
2 cups skim milk
1 can (8 ounces) corn kernels, drained
1/4 cup dried thyme
ground black pepper to taste
vegetable cooking spray

Spray saucepan with vegetable cooking spray. Place over medium heat. Add onion and peppers and cook, stirring often until soft, about 4 minutes. Add flour, stirring constantly, about 1 minute. Gradually add milk, corn, Butter Buds®, thyme and pepper. Reduce heat to low. Cook 5 minutes more or until slightly thickened. Serve hot.

Makes: 4 servings

Per serving: Calories: 114   Fat: 0.8 grams   Calcium: 161 mg

****

Hold the salt
and
Save your bones.

Cream of Asparagus Soup

1 can condensed cream of asparagus soup
1 can low sodium condensed chicken broth
1 1/2 cups skim milk

In a medium saucepan combine all ingredients. Heat, stirring, until smooth and hot. Serve hot.

Makes: 5 cups   Serving size: 1 cup

Per serving: Calories: 41   Fat: 0.5 grams   Calcium: 99 mg

****
Number of Americans deficient in calcium: 68%
Number of teenage girls deficient in calcium: 87%
Number of American women deficient in calcium: 84%
Get your calcium every day.

Tomato Corn Chowder

1 can condensed tomato soup
1 can skim milk
1/2 cup cream-style corn
pepper to taste

In a medium saucepan, combine all ingredients and heat, stirring constantly. Do not allow to boil. Serve hot.

Makes: 3 cups   Serving size: 1 cup

Per serving: Calories: 88   Fat: 1 gram   Calcium: 106 mg

****

**A study from Harvard University reports that
college students who drank milk regularly while
in school were less likely to
get ulcers after graduation
and were less likely to suffer
from adult stress.**

Cream of Broccoli Soup

1 large onion, chopped
1 medium carrot, sliced
1 stalk celery, chopped
1 clove garlic, chopped
3 cups low-sodium chicken broth
1/4 cup uncooked rice
3 cups broccoli, chopped
2 cups skim milk
black pepper to taste

Combine onion, carrot, celery, garlic and chicken broth in a large saucepan and bring to a boil. Add rice. Cover and simmer for 20 minutes or until rice is tender. Add broccoli. Cover and simmer until broccoli is tender, about 5 minutes. Transfer the soup to a blender or food processor. Process until smooth. Return to saucepan. Add milk. Season with pepper. May be served hot or cold.

Makes: 8 servings

Per serving: Calories: 68   Fat: Trace   Calcium: 112 mg

****

**The national average for calcium intake by women
is below 500 mg per day.
That's half of what's needed.**

Russian Summer Beet Soup

1/2 cup nonfat yogurt
1/2 cup lowfat cottage cheese
4 cups buttermilk
4 beets, cooked, peeled and cubed
1/2 cucumber, peeled, seeded and diced
2 hard-boiled eggs
1/2 cup chopped fresh parsley
1/3 cup radishes, sliced thin
3 tablespoons chopped chives
black pepper to taste

In blender or food processor combine yogurt, cottage cheese and buttermilk. Blend until smooth. Chill. Add remaining ingredients. Reserve a tablespoon of chopped egg and chives to sprinkle on top as garnish. Serve.

Makes: 8 servings

Per serving: Calories: 118   Fat: 2.8 grams   Calcium: 252 mg

****
**New studies show that high blood pressure may be
linked to calcium deficiency.**

No-Dairy Clam Chowder

3 medium potatoes, peeled & diced
2 cups low-sodium chicken bouillon
1 cup clam juice
1 can (6.5 ounces) clams, drained and rinsed
white pepper to taste

In a medium saucepan combine potatoes and chicken bouillon and bring to boil. Cover and simmer for 20 minutes or until potatoes are tender. Transfer to blender or food processor and process until liquid. Return to saucepan. Add clam juice, clams and pepper. Heat. Serve hot.

Makes: 2 servings

Per serving: Calories: 310   Fat: 2 grams   Calcium: 112 mg

****

Lactose Intolerance Facts

5 to 20 percent of whites are lactose intolerant.
80 to 100 percent of nonwhites are lactose intolerant.
Why?
Because in nonwhites the enzyme that breaks down lactose
is not present.
The result?
Pain and possible gastrointestinal infections.

Mock Cream-of-Chicken Soup

2 cups chicken bouillon
2 potatoes, peeled and diced
1 large carrot, peeled and diced
1 stalk celery with leaves, chopped
pepper to taste

In a medium saucepan bring bouillon to a boil. Add potatoes, carrot, and celery. Return to boil. Reduce heat. Cover and simmer for 20 minutes. Pour into blender or food processor. Process until smooth. Serve hot.

Makes: 8 servings

Per serving: Calories: 30   Fat: Trace   Calcium: 10 mg

****

30 million Americans are lactose intolerant.
10 million Americans have a milk allergy.

Dilly Vichissoise

6 white potatoes, pared and diced
5 leeks, rinsed and chopped
1 1/2 cups skim milk
2 tablespoons dill
pepper to taste
3 tablespoons nonfat yogurt
2 tablespoons liquid Butter Buds®

In a medium saucepan cover potatoes and leeks with water until just covered. Cook potatoes and leeks until tender. Add a touch of salt to the cooking water. Add milk, dill and pepper. Simmer for 15 to 20 minutes or until soup thickens and potatoes begin to fall apart. Stir in yogurt and liquid Butter Buds®. Heat thoroughly. Serve hot.

Serves: 8   Serving size: 1 cup

Per serving: Calories: 139   Fat: 0.5 grams   Calcium: 133

****

**If you lowered your salt intake in order to
get your blood pressure down and
that strategy isn't working, there's good news
from researchers at Arizona State University
who say that increasing calcium may
help to lower the blood pressure
of people whose blood
pressure doesn't respond
to reducing salt alone.**

Chilled Casbah Soup

1 ripe cantaloupe
1 cup nonfat yogurt
3 tablespoons lemon juice
1/4 teaspoon dried ginger
fresh mint leaves for garnish

Peel and seed cantaloupe and cut into chunks. Put cantaloupe, yogurt, lemon juice and ginger into blender or food processor. Process until smooth. Serve chilled. Garnish with fresh mint leaves.

Makes: 4 servings

Per serving: Calories: 82   Fat: 0.5 grams   Calcium: 129 mg

✳✳✳✳✳✳✳✳✳

What Should You Weigh?

Women: 100 pounds for the first five feet of height, and then 5 pounds for each inch over five feet.

Men: 106 pounds for the first five feet of height, and then 6 pounds for each inch over five feet.

Chilly Cucumber "Soop"

4 cups cucumbers, peeled, seeded, chopped
2 cups nonfat yogurt
1 cup water
1 tablespoon honey
dash of white pepper to taste
1/4 teaspoon dried mint
1 garlic clove, pared

Put all ingredients into a blender or food processor. Process until smooth. Refrigerate at least 4 hours before serving. Serve chilled.

Makes: 6 servings   Serving size: 1/2 cup

Per serving: Calories: 58   Fat: Trace   Calcium: 158 mg

****

Good news from the Mayo Clinic!
New research shows that restricting your
salt intake to 1 teaspoon a day may be
enough to control mild or moderate
high blood pressure.
So put that salt shaker away, and
watch out for hidden sources of salt.

Turkey Vegetable Soup

1 pound ground turkey
3 medium onions, peeled & chopped
8 cups water
1 can (8-oz.) low-sodium tomatoes
1/3 cup barley
3 carrots, peeled and sliced
3 potatoes, peeled, and diced
3 celery ribs, chopped
1/2 cup fresh parsley, chopped
pepper to taste

In a large saucepan, cook turkey, onions and water until done. Add tomatoes, barley, carrots, potatoes, celery, parsley and pepper. Simmer covered for one hour. Serve hot.

Makes: 8 servings   Serving size: 1 cup

Per serving: Calories: 187   Fat: 5.3 grams   Calcium: 119 mg

****

Here's some news from the
Calcium Information Center at New York Hospital-
Cornell Medical Center.
Researchers report that 25% of American women
over the age of 20 are calcium deficient.

Hearty Minestrone

1/2 cup dry navy beans
1 cup low-sodium chicken stock
8 cups water
2 carrots, pared, cut in strips
1 potato, pared, diced
1/2 head of cabbage, shredded
1 8-oz can tomatoes, low-sodium
1 onion, peeled, sliced
1 celery rib, sliced
1 tablespoon olive oil
1 pound zucchini, sliced
2 garlic cloves mashed
pepper to taste
1/2 teaspoon basil
1/4 teaspoon marjoram
1 bay leaf
2 tablespoons parsley, chopped
1/2 cup tomato sauce, low-sodium
1/2 cup spaghetti, broken

In a large saucepan, combine beans, chicken stock and water. Cook for 1 hour. Add carrots, potato, cabbage and canned tomatoes. Cook for 30 minutes. Reserve. In a skillet, sauté the onion in the olive oil, until tender. Add celery, zucchini, garlic, and spices. Sauté until tender. Stir into the bean mixture. Add parsley and tomato sauce. Add spaghetti. Cook for 10 minutes more until spaghetti is tender. Serve hot.

Makes: 8 servings   Serving size: 1 1/2 cups

Per serving: Calories: 114   Fat: 2.2 grams   Calcium: 95 mg

Bouillabaisse

4 ounces raw clams, shucked
1 celery rib, chopped
1 onion, peeled & chopped
16 cups water
1 garlic clove, peeled & mashed
1 leek rinsed, sliced thin
1/2 teaspoon fennel
1/2 cup dry white wine
1 large tomato, peeled, seeded, diced
1 lobster tail, quartered
1/4 pound red snapper, quartered
1/4 pound frozen shrimp, shelled, deveined
1/4 pound scallops
pepper to taste

In a large kettle, simmer clams, celery, onion in water for 10 minutes. Strain. Reserve liquid and clams. In a large saucepan heat the garlic for a minute and discard. Add the leek, fennel seed and wine. Sauté for 3 minutes. Add the tomato. Sauté for 3 minutes more. Add the mixture to the reserved liquid. Bring to boiling. Add the lobster, shrimp, scallops, snapper, and pepper to taste. Simmer for 10 minutes. Add the clams. Serve hot.

Makes: 4 servings   Serving size: 2 cups

Per serving: Calories: 223   Fat: 2.3 grams   Calcium: 141 mg

Stuffed Tomatoes

6 large tomatoes
1 package frozen spinach, thawed, squeezed out, chopped
8 ounces Ricotta cheese, part skim
2 1/2 cups grated fontina cheese
3/4 cup grated Parmesan cheese
fresh black pepper to taste
1/2 cup chopped parsley
1/2 teaspoon anchovy paste
2 garlic cloves, peeled & pressed

Preheat oven to 400°F.

Peel tomatoes by dipping into boiling water for a minute, letting cool and pulling skin off. Cut top off each tomato and scoop out seeds and pulp. Mix spinach and cheese together. Add pepper, parsley, anchovy and garlic. Stuff each tomato with the mixture. Bake in oven for 5 minutes until heated through. Serve warm.

Makes: 6 servings

Per serving: Calories: 335   Fat: 21.5 grams   Calcium: 635 mg

****

**Cornell University reports that if your blood pressure
goes up with salt, you might be able to
bring it down with milk.**

Broccoli-Lovers' Salad

1 pound broccoli cut into bites
1/2 cup fresh mushrooms, chopped
1/2 cup grated Parmesan cheese
1/2 cup pickle relish
1/2 cup plain, nonfat yogurt
1 onion, peeled, sliced into rings
2 hard-cooked eggs, chopped
pepper to taste

In a large bowl, toss all the ingredients. Refrigerate until chilled.

Makes: 8 servings   Serving size: 1 cup

Per serving: Calories: 90   Fat: 3.1 grams   Calcium: 139 mg

✳✳✳✳✳✳✳✳✳

The University of Washington reports that women who are
post menopausal can reduce their risk of stroke
by going on estrogen replacement therapy.
This is especially true for former smokers.

Traditional Greek Salad

3 large tomatoes cut into chunks
2 cucumbers, peeled and cut into chunks
1 red onion, peeled and cut into chunks
6 leaves of romaine lettuce torn into bite-size pieces
1/4 cup olive oil
4 teaspoons lemon juice
1 1/2 teaspoons dried oregano
fresh pepper to taste
1 cup crumbled feta cheese
6 black olives, whole
6 large whole leaves of romaine lettuce

In a mixing bowl combine all ingredients except the romaine lettuce. Toss gently until well mixed and evenly coated. Place one large leaf of romaine lettuce on each of 6 individual salad plates. Divide the salad evenly and place on the romaine leaf. Serve at room temperature.

Makes: 6 servings

Per serving: Calories: 235   Fat: 15.9 grams   Calcium: 441 mg

****

Got hard water? Great!
Hard water contains as much as 375 mg of calcium per liter.

Love the calcium but hate the washing problems of hard water?
Connect your water softener only to your hot water supply for
the best of both worlds.

Tasty Tofu Salad

1/4 cup vegetable oil
2 tablespoons red wine vinegar
1 garlic clove, peeled & minced
1/2 teaspoon dried oregano
black pepper to taste
8 ounces tofu, drained and cubed
2 large tomatoes, chopped
2 cups mushrooms, sliced
1 large stalk celery, sliced
1/4 cup green bell pepper, chopped
1/4 cup red bell pepper, chopped
1/2 cup fresh parsley, chopped
1 small onion, chopped

In a large salad bowl combine oil, vinegar, garlic, oregano, and black pepper. Combine. Add tofu. Toss to coat evenly. Cover and refrigerate until chilled, about 2 hours, stirring occasionally. Before serving, remove from fridge, add all vegetables. Toss.

Makes: 6 servings

Per serving: Calories: 147   Fat: 11.4 grams   Calcium: 134 mg

****
Did you know that . . .

One million pounds of tofu is consumed in the U.S. every year.
Tofu by any other name is bean curd.
Tofu is a great fat cutter.
Four ounces of tofu add 82 calories but deliver 145 mg of calcium.

Waldorf Plus Salad

2 small apples, cored and chopped
2 small pears, cored and chopped
1 small banana, sliced
1 small avocado, peeled and sliced
2 stalks celery, chopped
1/4 cup raisins
1/4 cup chopped walnuts
1/4 cup Grape-Nuts® cereal
1/2 cup plain, nonfat yogurt
1 teaspoon lemon juice

In a large bowl combine all ingredients. Toss until well coated. Cover and refrigerate until chilled, about 2 hours. Serve with graham crackers.

Makes: 6 servings

Per serving: Calories: 211   Fat: 8.7 grams   Calcium: 64 mg

****

Calcium supplements can relieve leg cramps.
Especially good news if you are pregnant.

Yogurty Slaw

2 cups shredded cabbage
1/2 cup shredded carrots
1 minced onion
2 tablespoons plain nonfat yogurt
2 tablespoons lowfat mayonnaise
1 1/2 teaspoons skim milk
1 1/2 teaspoons lemon juice
1/4 teaspoon sugar
black pepper to taste

In a large bowl combine all ingredients. Toss to coat well. Cover and chill for about 2 hours.

Makes: 4 servings

Per serving: Calories: 59   Fat: 2.7 grams   Calcium: 56 mg

****

There is almost no way to get all the calcium you need
every single day from your diet alone.
Some days you may get more, some days less.
So take a calcium supplement.

Pasta Salad Supreme

4 ounces cooked bowtie pasta
1 hard boiled egg
1 tablespoon lowfat mayonnaise
2 tablespoons skim milk
1 tablespoon grated lowfat cheddar cheese

Cook bowtie pasta according to package directions. Drain. Set aside. Chop egg. Combine chopped egg with mayonnaise, milk and cheddar cheese. Add the pasta. Toss well to coat. Serve chilled or at room temperature.

Makes: 1 serving

Per serving: Calories: 575   Fat: 12.4 grams   Calcium: 132 mg

****

Economists estimate the cost of 225,000 new fractures a year
at a whopping $5 billion!

Hearty Chicken Salad

2 cups cooked chicken, chopped
1 cup spinach leaves, torn into bits
1/4 cup carrots, chopped
1/4 red bell pepper, chopped
1/4 cup Grape-Nuts® cereal
1/4 cup plain, nonfat yogurt
2 tablespoons lowfat mayonnaise
1 clove garlic, minced
1/4 teaspoon rosemary
whole spinach leaves or romaine lettuce leaves

In large bowl combine all ingredients except whole greens. Toss well to coat. Cover and chill for about 2 hours. Divide equally among four small salad plates which have been covered with a large leaf of fresh spinach or romaine lettuce.

Makes: 4 servings

Per serving: Calories: 172   Fat: 5.8 grams   Calcium: 59 mg

****

The University of Minnesota reports
that people who ate loads of
fruits and vegetables had the
lowest stroke rates.
That means eat
more
veggies.

Super Duper Spinach Salad

4 cups spinach leaves, cleaned, torn into bits
1/2 head romaine lettuce, cleaned, torn into bits
1/4 pound mushrooms, sliced
1 large tomato, cut into wedges
1 large onion, sliced
1/2 cup feta cheese, crumbled
1 cup buttermilk
2/3 cup nonfat yogurt
1/4 cup lowfat Italian salad dressing
1 tablespoon white vinegar
1 teaspoon dried dill
1 clove garlic, minced
1 teaspoon Dijon-style mustard
pepper to taste

In a large bowl, combine all ingredients. Toss well to coat. Chill for about 2 hours. Serve cold.

Makes: 2 servings

Per serving: Calories: 291   Fat: 11.5 grams   Calcium: 646 mg

****

Hint

Spinach is high in calcium. But it is also high in oxalates
which block the absorption of calcium.
To get the calcium benefit from your
spinach, add a little vinegar or lemon juice.
Experts say this releases the calcium and lets it
go to work to build strong bones.

Quicky Potato Salad

6 large potatoes, cooked, peeled and cubed
1 cup plain, nonfat yogurt
1/4 cup scallions, chopped
salt & pepper to taste

Combine all ingredients in a large bowl. Toss to coat. Refrigerate. Serve chilled.

Makes: 5 servings

Per serving: Calories: 133   Fat: Trace   Calcium: 103 mg

****

Can Milk Put You To Sleep?

According to researchers at MIT, milk, especially skim milk,
triggers your body to produce more dopamine which is
a mind stimulant.
So drink your milk for a brain boost
but
try a little herbal tea at bedtime.

Russian Potato Salad

2 pounds potatoes
4 tablespoons liquid Butter Buds®
1 large onion, sliced
4 ounces of mushrooms, sliced
1 container (8 ounces) plain, nonfat yogurt
3 tablespoons chopped chives
salt & pepper to taste
vegetable cooking spray

Scrub potatoes and boil until just tender. Drain. Cool. Peel. Slice.

Spray a skillet with vegetable cooking spray. Add onion. Cook over medium heat until onion is soft. Do not brown. Add the mushrooms. Cook until juices run. Add the potatoes and brown. Season with a little salt and pepper. Turn over and brown potatoes on the other side. Add the yogurt, chives, and Butter Buds®. Mix gently until coated. Heat yogurt and potato mixture. Serve warm.

Makes: 4 servings

Per serving: Calories: 244   Fat: 0.6 grams   Calcium: 149 mg

****

Another Good Reason To Take Calcium
From The Land Down Under.

A study from Australia showed that people who drank
less than 2 1/2 cups of milk a week
were more likely to develop
colorectal cancer.

Thousand Island Dressing

1 cup plain nonfat yogurt
3 tablespoons lowfat mayonnaise
2 tablespoons pickle relish
1 tablespoon skim milk
1 tablespoon onion, finely chopped
1 tablespoon green bell pepper, finely chopped
1 tablespoon red bell pepper, finely chopped
garlic powder and black pepper to taste

Combine all ingredients in a small bowl. Cover. Refrigerate for at least 2 hours. Toss with favorite salad, or serve on the side.

Makes: 12 servings

Serving size: approx. 2 tablespoons

Per serving: Calories: 27   Fat: 1.3 grams   Calcium: 40 mg

****
Did you know?
There are 200 bones in the human skeleton and they
make up about 14% of the total body weight.

Tofu Dressing

2/3 cup tofu, drained
3 tablespoons lemon juice
3 tablespoons olive oil
pepper to taste
2 teaspoons low-sodium soy sauce

Put all ingredients into a blender or food processor. Process until blended.

Makes: 1 cup   Serving size: 1/4 cup

Per serving: Calories: 114   Fat: 11.7 grams   Calcium: 36 mg

****

Guess which bone loses calcium first?
The jawbone.
That means that the foundation in which
teeth are set begins to erode and
tooth loss may be a signal of
advanced osteoporosis.

Basic Buttermilk Dressing

1 cup buttermilk
1 tablespoon Dijon-style mustard
1 small minced onion
2 teaspoons chopped parsley
1/4 teaspoon dried dill
black pepper to taste

Combine all ingredients in a jar. Shake to mix. Store in fridge tightly covered. Use within a week of making.

Makes: 1 cup   Serving size: 1 tablespoon

Per serving: Calories: 9   Fat: Trace   Calcium: 25 mg

****
Become a mini-vegetarian.
Go meatless a couple of days a week.

Basic Yogurt Dressing

1/2 cup plain, nonfat yogurt
2 tablespoons lemon juice
dash of tabasco

In a covered jar, mix all ingredients together. Store in fridge.

Makes: 2/3 cup   Serving size: approx. 1 1/4 teaspoons

Per serving: Calories: 71   Fat: 0.2 grams   Calcium: 228 mg

****

Become a calcium nut.
• Almonds
• Brazil Nuts
• Filberts
are all good sources of calcium.

Blue Cheese Dressing

1/2 cup crumbled blue cheese
1 cup plain, nonfat yogurt
1 clove garlic, mashed
dry mustard and pepper to taste

In a jar combine all ingredients. Shake to combine. Cover and store in fridge.

Makes: 1 1/2 cups   Serving size: approx. 1 1/2 teaspoons

Per serving: Calories: 14   Fat: 0.7 grams   Calcium: 32 mg

****

**Did you know that new studies show that
heavy alcohol intake contributes to
the development of osteoporosis
as early as 30 or 40?**

Parsley Herb Dressing

1/2 cup chopped fresh parsley
1 cup lowfat cottage cheese
1 teaspoon Dijon-style mustard
1 teaspoon lemon juice
pepper to taste

Place all ingredients in blender or food processor. Process until combined. Cover and store in fridge.

Makes: 1 cup   Serving size: approx. 1 tablespoon

Per serving: Calories: 16   Fat: Trace   Calcium: 36 mg

****

Go Japanese.
Sea vegetables, sesame seeds and tahini
are all good sources of calcium.

Five Fabulous Fakes

The "Other" Hollandaise

1 cup plain, nonfat yogurt
2 teaspoons lemon juice
3 egg yolks
1/2 teaspoon Dijon-style mustard
pinch of salt and pepper to taste

Beat together yogurt, lemon juice and egg yolks in top of double-boiler. Heat, stirring often until the sauce begins to thicken. Remove from heat and stir in remaining ingredients. Serve warm.

Makes: 1 cup   Serving size: approx. 1 tablespoon

Per serving: Calories: 19   Fat: 1 gram   Calcium: 33 mg

****

Watch your labels.
Lite, slender, lowfat, part-skimmed
may not be as low in fat as you think.

Sinless Sour Cream

2 tablespoons skim milk
1 tablespoon lemon juice
1 cup lowfat cottage cheese

Put milk, lemon juice and cottage cheese into blender or food processor. Process until smooth. Store in covered container in fridge.

Makes: 1 cup   Serving size: approx. 1 tablespoon

Per serving: Calories: 11   Fat: Trace   Calcium: 11 mg

****
Are You In The "Disability Zone"?

The U.S. Department of Agriculture
Human Nutrition Research Center
at Tufts University
says you need to exercise when you hit middle age
to avoid falling into the "disability zone"
of premature aging.

Tartar Sauce

1 teaspoon hotdog relish
2 teaspoons lemon juice
1 cup lowfat cottage cheese

Put lemon juice and cottage cheese into blender or food processor. Process until smooth. Add relish. Stir until mixed. Store in covered container in fridge.

Makes: 1 cup   Serving size: approx. 1 tablespoon

Per serving: Calories: 11   Fat: Trace   Calcium: 9 mg

****
Only one in 7 girls gets 100% of the RDA for calcium.
Is your daughter one of the calcium
winners–or losers?

Mock Mayo

1 teaspoon Dijon-style mustard
2 teaspoons lemon juice
1 cup nonfat cottage cheese

Put all ingredients into a blender or food processor. Process until smooth. Store in covered container in fridge.

Makes: 1 cup   Serving size: approx. 1 tablespoon

Per serving: Calories: 13   Fat: Trace   Calcium: 10 mg

****
Cigarette smoking lowers estrogen levels
and increases your risk of
developing osteoporosis.

Fake Cream Cheese

1 cup lowfat cottage cheese
1/2 cup margarine, softened

Put ingredients into blender or food processor. Process until smooth.

Makes: 1 cup   Serving size: 1 tablespoon

Per serving: Calories: 61   Fat: 5.8 grams   Calcium: 11 mg

****
Both animal fat and vegetable fat contain
9 calories per gram
or
260 calories per ounce.
Cut the fat.

Creamy Cauliflower

2 cups fresh or frozen cauliflower
1 tablespoon unsalted margarine
1 tablespoon chopped onion
1 garlic clove, chopped
1 tablespoon all-purpose flour
1/2 cup skim milk
pepper to taste
1 tablespoon grated Parmesan cheese

Steam fresh cauliflower until tender but crisp. If using frozen broccoli, prepare according to package directions.

Melt margarine in small saucepan over low heat. Add onion and garlic. Stir often. Cook until tender. Add flour. Cook, stirring often, about 1 minute. Gradually add milk and pepper. Cook until thick and smooth. Remove from heat. Stir in grated cheese. Pour over cauliflower just before serving.

This sauce works well with broccoli, brussels sprouts, carrots and boiled potatoes.

Makes: 4 servings

Per serving: Calories: 63   Fat: 3.4 grams   Calcium: 70 mg

****

Here's A Bone Formula

Estrogen supplementation + exercise = calcium absorption + stronger bones

Creamed Peas

1 cup DANNON® plain nonfat yogurt
2 tablespoons all-purpose flour
2 tablespoons finely chopped fresh or 1 teaspoon dry dill
1 jar (2 ounces) pimientos, drained
pepper to taste
1 1/2 cups fresh or frozen peas
3 tablespoons chicken broth

In a small bowl combine yogurt, flour, dill, pimiento and pepper. Stir until smooth. Set aside. In a small saucepan combine peas and broth. Cover and bring to a boil. Reduce heat and simmer 5 minutes until peas are tender. Stir in yogurt mixture. Cook over low heat until thick, stirring constantly.

Makes: 4 servings

Per serving: Calories: 98   Fat: 0.6 grams   Calcium: 156 mg

✱✱✱✱✱✱✱✱✱✱

A study conducted at the University of Pittsburgh
found that 3 to 6 glasses of wine per week
boosted the amount of estrogen
in postmenopausal women
and reduced the risk of
osteoporosis
and
heart disease.

Texas Potato Topper

1 cup DANNON® plain, nonfat yogurt
1/3 cup mild or medium chunky salsa
1/3 cup chopped stuffed green olives (optional)

In a small bowl combine yogurt, salsa and olives. Cover. Chill until ready to serve. Top baked potatoes with the mixture.

Makes: 10 servings   Serving size: approx. 3 tablespoons

Per serving: Calories: 22   Fat: 0.9 grams   Calcium: 50 mg

****
Take a walk.
Women who walk one hour per day,
five days a week at a pace of 3 miles per hour
can raise their HDL (good cholesterol) levels.

Two-Cheese Spaghetti Squash

4 cups cooked spaghetti squash
4 tablespoons grated Romano cheese
4 tablespoons grated Parmesan cheese
4 teaspoons chopped parsley
pepper to taste

In a large bowl combine all ingredients. Toss. Serve warm.

Makes: 4 servings

Per serving: Calories: 87   Fat: 4 grams   Calcium: 185 mg

****

Studies show that 44% of those taking
1,000 mg of calcium supplements per day
may lower their blood pressure.

Lean Creamed Spinach

2 packages (10 ounces each) frozen spinach
vegetable cooking spray
1 teaspoon finely chopped onion
2 cloves garlic, minced
1 tablespoon all-purpose flour
3/4 cup skim milk
1 tablespoon grated Parmesan cheese
black pepper to taste
nutmeg to taste (optional)

Prepare spinach according to package directions. Drain well. Chop fine. Set aside. Spray a saucepan with vegetable cooking spray. Place over medium heat. Add onion and garlic. Cook until tender. Stir in flour. Stir constantly. Cook for 1 minute. Gradually add milk, stirring constantly until thick. Add pepper and Parmesan cheese. Continue cooking until cheese is melted. Pour over hot spinach. Mix well. Serve warm.

Makes: 6 servings

Per serving: Calories: 44   Fat: Trace   Calcium: 156 mg

****

Milk Tip

Drink your milk before your meal.
This gives the milk time to get through the blood-brain barrier
before other nutrients compete for space.
The result?
A brain boost.

Baked Leeks With Cheese

4 leeks
2 tablespoons liquid Butter Buds®
2 tablespoons dry white wine
3/4 cup grated Muenster cheese
black pepper to taste

Preheat oven to 350°F. Wash leeks, trim away the green part. Cut the white part into 1/4 inch rounds. In a small uncovered casserole combine leeks, Butter Buds®, wine and pepper. Bake for 30 minutes. Remove from oven. Sprinkle with cheese. Place under broiler until cheese is bubbly. Serve hot.

Serves: 4

Per serving: Calories: 168   Fat: 6.8 grams   Calcium: 226 mg

****
Women who have osteoporosis are twice as likely
to develop high blood pressure
as women of the same age
who don't have osteoporosis.
Take your calcium.
Take a walk.

Summery Vegetable Casserole

4 large garlic cloves, minced
2 tablespoons extra virgin olive oil
2 large tomatoes, peeled and chopped
1/2 pound green beans cut into small chunks
1/2 pound fresh peas
3/4 cup feta cheese, crumbled
pepper to taste
1 tablespoon oregano

In a large skillet sauté garlic in the oil until softened, about 2 minutes. Add tomatoes, beans, peas and black pepper. Cover and simmer until beans and peas are tender, about 10 minutes. Add the cheese and oregano. Heat until cheese is melted. Serve warm.

Makes: 4 servings

Per serving: Calories: 200   Fat: 11.9 grams   Calcium: 166 mg

****

Who has the most protection against osteoporosis? Answer:
1. Black men
2. Caucasian men
3. Black women
4. Caucasian women

Savory Mashed Potatoes

1 tablespoon olive oil
1 tablespoon minced garlic
4 cups water
4 medium potatoes, peeled and cut into quarters
1 cup DANNON® plain, nonfat yogurt
1/4 cup skim milk
1/4 cup chopped scallions
fresh pepper to taste

In a large, heavy saucepan heat oil over medium heat. Add garlic. Cook and stir 1 minute, stirring constantly, until fragrant, but not browned. Add water and potatoes. Cover and bring to a boil over high heat. Reduce heat to medium-low and simmer 15 to 20 minutes until potatoes are tender. Drain. Return potatoes to saucepan and mash. Add yogurt and milk. Stir until creamy. Stir in scallions and pepper. Serve hot.

Makes: 6 servings

Per serving: Calories: 107   Fat: 2.4 grams   Calcium: 102 mg

****

Couch Potatoes Beware

**You need to exercise against gravity to prevent bone loss and
increase the bone mass you already have.
So get moving.**

Tomato-Zucchini Yogurt Surprise

3 small zucchini, washed and sliced
1 large tomato, peeled and seeded
1 small onion, sliced into rings
2 teaspoons liquid Butter Buds®
1/2 cup plain, nonfat yogurt
4 teaspoons fresh, chopped parsley
fresh pepper to taste
1/4 teaspoon oregano
1/4 teaspoon basil
vegetable cooking spray

Spray a heavy saucepan with vegetable cooking spray. Place over medium heat. Add onion and cook until tender. Add zucchini and tomato, stirring often. Cook until tender, about 5 minutes. Remove from heat. Stir in yogurt, parsley, Butter Buds®, and spices. Mix well to coat. Serve warm.

Makes: 6 servings

Per serving: Calories: 34   Fat: Trace   Calcium: 74 mg

****

Bone is living tissue.
It keeps growing and repairing itself
all the time.

Cheese-Filled Potato Shells

4 medium potatoes, baked
1 cup lowfat cottage cheese
1/2 cup skim milk
1 onion, minced
1 tablespoon chopped parley
pepper to taste

Cut potatoes in half, lengthwise. Scoop out inside. Transfer to blender or food processor. Add cottage cheese, milk and onion and 1/2 parsley. Process until mixed. Spoon mixture back into the shells. Bake until golden. Garnish tops with remaining parsley. Serve hot.

Makes: 8 servings

Per serving: Calories: 75   Fat: Trace   Calcium: 55 mg

✳✳✳✳✳✳✳✳✳

How Should You Take Your Calcium?

Calcium is best absorbed if you take it in
divided doses throughout the day.
Try taking your calcium supplements between meals with a glass of
skim milk or a few spoons of yogurt.
Remember to take the last of your calcium
just before bedtime.
While you are sleeping, that's when calcium is being lost.

Eggplant Parmesan

**1 medium-sized eggplant, peeled and sliced into 1/4 inch
    rounds
1/2 pound part skim mozzarella cheese
2 tomatoes, sliced
1/4 cup vegetable oil
1/2 cup bread crumbs
1 egg, beaten slightly
1 cup low-sodium tomato sauce**

Preheat oven to 450°F. Heat skillet over medium heat. Add oil. Dip eggplant slices
into egg and then breadcrumbs. Sauté eggplant turning once, until golden.
Remove from oil. Drain well on paper towels. Layer casserole with eggplant
slices. Top with a layer of tomato slices, then tomato sauce and finally a layer of
mozzarella cheese. Bake in preheated oven for 15 to 20 minutes until cheese is
brown and bubbly. Serve hot.

Makes: 6 servings

Per serving: Calories: 271   Fat: 17.3 grams   Calcium: 299 mg

****

**Did you know that studies show that people with
high blood pressure
eat fewer calcium-rich foods
than people with normal blood pressure?**

Spinach Cheese Casserole

1 package frozen spinach, chopped, drained
1 medium onion chopped
2 medium tomatoes sliced
1 large container (16 ounces) lowfat cottage cheese
1/3 cup grated Parmesan cheese
1/2 teaspoon basil
1/2 teaspoon oregano
pepper to taste

Preheat oven to 350°F. Place cottage cheese, onion, oregano and basil into blender or food processor. Process until smooth. Place alternative layers of spinach, cottage cheese mixture, and tomatoes into a casserole. Top with Parmesan cheese. Bake at 350°F, uncovered for 25 to 30 minutes. Serve warm.

Makes: 6 servings

Per serving: Calories: 95   Fat: 2.4 grams   Calcium: 154 mg

****

Add A Little Calcium To Your Life

Have a glass of milk instead of coffee for breakfast.
Have yogurt and fruit for your lunch.
Snack on a piece of lowfat cheese and whole wheat crackers.
Pick pizza over burgers when eating on the run.

Carrots and Raisins Revisited

2 cups DANNON® plain, nonfat yogurt
1 tablespoon packed brown sugar
1/4 teaspoon grated orange peel
2 tablespoons orange juice
1/4 teaspoon ground nutmeg
6 medium carrots, peeled and shredded (3 cups)
1/4 cup raisins
3 tablespoons chopped cashews, almonds or pecans

Spoon yogurt into large strainer lined with double thickness of cheesecloth or a coffee filter. Place bowl beneath, but not touching strainer to catch liquid. Chill 1 1/2 hours. Scrape yogurt into a medium bowl. Discard liquid. Add brown sugar, orange peel, juice and nutmeg. Stir until smooth. Add carrots and raisins. Toss to coat. Cover. Chill 20 to 30 minutes. Sprinkle with nuts just before serving. Serve cold.

Makes: 6 servings

Per serving: Calories: 129   Fat: 2.7 grams   Calcium: 189 mg

****

More from the folks at the
U.S. Department of Agriculture
Human Nutrition Research Center on Aging
at Tufts University,
who say that postmenopausal women who don't get enough
calcium from their diet can reduce their bone loss by bringing
their calcium intake up to the recommended level.

Cheese & Tomato Rice

1 cup rice
1/2 cup lowfat shredded cheddar cheese
1 cup condensed tomato soup

In a medium saucepan cook rice according to package directions. When the rice is almost done add the cheese and tomato soup. Stir until combined and cheese is melted. Serve hot.

Makes: 6 servings

Per serving: Calories: 152   Fat: 1.2 grams   Calcium: 77 mg

****
Did you know that studies show that
1,000 mg of calcium per day
can reverse periodontal bone loss
after just 18 months?
This was the case in 40% of the people studied.

Baked Macaroni & Cheese

1 cup cooked macaroni
1 cup lowfat shredded cheddar cheese
1 egg substitute
2/3 cup skim milk
1 tablespoon grated onion
pepper to taste

Preheat oven to 350°F.

In a nonstick baking dish arrange the cooked macaroni in a layer. Sprinkle the macaroni with the cheddar cheese. In a medium bowl combine the remaining ingredients. Using a whisk or fork, beat until combined. Pour over the macaroni and cheese layers. Bake at 350°F for 30 to 40 minutes or until bubbly. Serve hot.

Makes: 4 servings

Per serving: Calories: 241   Fat: 4 grams   Calcium: 288 mg

****

The U.S. Department of Agriculture
reports that magnesium, a mineral
important to calcium absorption,
may reduce the risk of heart disease
and lower blood pressure in males.

Scalloped Potatoes In A Hurry

3 cups potatoes, pared, sliced thin
1 can cream of celery soup
1 can skim milk
1/4 cup lowfat, shredded cheddar cheese

Preheat oven to 350°F.

Prepare soup according to directions on can, using the skim milk instead of water. Add the cheese and heat until melted. Stir often. Place potatoes in the bottom of a nonstick baking pan. Pour the hot soup mixture over the potatoes. Bake at 350°F for 1 hour. Serve hot.

Makes: 4 servings

Per serving: Calories: 107   Fat: 2.1 grams   Calcium: 139 mg

****
Why do women need extra calcium after menopause?
Because women lose a lot of calcium
from their bones
during menopause.

Veggie Pizza

1 1/2 cups whole-wheat flour, divided
1 teaspoon active dry yeast
1 teaspoon sugar
1/2 cup warm water
1 tablespoon olive oil, divided
2 1/2 cups sliced mushrooms
1 small onion, chopped
1 can (8 ounces) low-sodium tomato sauce
1 small green pepper cut into rings
1 small red pepper cut into rings
1 cup cooked broccoli
1 cup cooked spinach, drained, chopped
4 ounces shredded part skim mozzarella cheese
1 tablespoon grated Parmesan cheese
vegetable cooking spray

In a bowl combine 3/4 cup flour, yeast and sugar. Add water and 2 teaspoons oil. Mix until flour is moistened. Gradually stir in rest of flour to make a soft dough. On a lightly floured surface, knead dough until smooth and elastic, about 5 minutes. Spray a bowl with vegetable spray. Place dough into sprayed bowl and turn, coating dough with spray. Cover with a towel. Set aside in a warm place to rise until double in volume, about 45 minutes.

In a large nonstick skillet heat remaining oil over medium heat. Add mushrooms and onion. Cook until tender, about 5 minutes.

Punch down dough. Spray a 12-inch round pizza pan with vegetable cooking spray. Spread dough to reach edges of pan. Spread tomato sauce over dough. Spread with mushroom and onion mixture, and remaining vegetables. Sprinkle with mozzarella and Parmesan cheese. Bake 15 to 20 minutes until crust looks golden. Makes: 8 servings

Per serving: Calories: 364   Fat: 6.1 grams   Calcium: 167 mg

Meatless Lasagne

1 medium eggplant, cut into 1/4 inch rounds
1 tablespoon extra virgin olive oil
1 medium onion, chopped fine
1 pound sliced mushrooms
1 package lasagne noodles
1 jar low-sodium, meatless spaghetti or marinara sauce
1 cup lowfat ricotta cheese, part skim
1 cup shredded mozzarella cheese, part skim
2 tablespoons grated Parmesan cheese
vegetable cooking spray
pepper to taste

Preheat oven to 350°F. Cook lasagne noodles according to package directions.

Brown eggplant in a nonstick skillet coated with vegetable cooking spray. Blot with paper towels. Set aside. Add olive oil to skillet. Add onion and cook, stirring often until tender, about 3 minutes. Add mushrooms. Cook, stirring often until tender, about 5 minutes.

Spoon 1/4 cup sauce into lasagne pan. Arrange layers alternating noodles, ricotta, mushroom mixture, mozzarella cheese, eggplant slices, sauce and Parmesan cheese. Top with remaining sauce and sprinkle with Parmesan. Cover and bake 30 to 40 minutes.

Makes: 8 servings

Per serving: Calories: 209   Fat: 8.9 grams   Calcium: 230 mg

****

Mineral balance is just as important as taking a single nutrient.

Spinach Pierogi Pizza

1 can (10 oz.) Pillsbury® Refrigerated All Ready Pizza Crust
1 can (9 oz,) pkg. Green Giant®Harvest Fresh®Frozen
     Spinach thawed, squeezed to drain
1/2 cup chopped onion
2 tablespoons margarine
1 1/2 cups mashed potatoes
2 tablespoons vegetable oil
1/2 teaspoon garlic salt
4 ounces (1 cup) shredded mozzarella cheese, part skim
2 ounces (1/2 cup) shredded cheddar cheese, lowfat
1 small onion, sliced, separated into rings

Heat oven to 425°F. Grease a 13 x 9-inch pan. Unroll dough and place in greased pan. Starting at center, press out with hands. Bake at 425°F for 7 to 9 minutes or until golden brown.

Meanwhile in a large skillet cook spinach and chopped onion in margarine until onion is crisp tender. Stir in mashed potatoes. Mix well. In a small bowl combine oil and garlic salt. Mix well. Brush over partially baked crust. Top with spinach mixture. Sprinkle with mozzarella cheese and then cheddar cheese. Top with onion rings.

Bake at 425°F for 15 to 20 minutes or until cheese is melted and edges of crust are golden brown.

Makes: 8 servings

Per serving: Calories: 195   Fat: 9.9 grams   Calcium: 204 mg

Courtesy of the Pillsbury Bake-Off® Contest

Beef & Bean Chili

1 pound dry lentils, soaked overnight, drained
1 cup chopped celery
1 medium onion, chopped
1 pound lean ground beef
1 can (28 ounces) tomato paste
1 large red pepper, chopped
1 teaspoon chili powder
1 teaspoon cayenne pepper
1 can (16 1/2 ounces) kidney beans

Place lentils, celery and half the onion in saucepan. Add enough water to cover. Cook over medium heat until water is absorbed and lentils are tender, about 1 to 1 1/2 hours. In a skillet, brown the beef with the remaining onion. Add tomato paste, pepper, chili powder and cayenne pepper to the beef. Cook uncovered over low heat for 30 minutes. Add kidney beans to the lentil mixture and add the entire bean mixture to the beef. Stir to combine. Cook uncovered for 30 minutes or until thick.

Makes: 8 servings

Serving size: 1 cup

Per serving: Calories: 358   Fat: 13.2 grams   Calcium: 83 mg

****

Peak bone mass is reached by the age of 30.

Broccoli Cauliflower Tetrazzini

8 ounces spaghetti, broken into thirds
1 (16 ounce) package Green Giant® American Mixtures ®
Heartland Style Frozen Broccoli, Cauliflower and
Carrots
2 tablespoons margarine
3 tablespoons flour
2 cups lowfat milk
1/2 cup grated Parmesan cheese
dash pepper
1 (4.5 ounce) jar Green Giant® Sliced Mushrooms, drained
2 tablespoons grated Parmesan cheese

Cook spaghetti to desired doneness as directed on package. Drain. Rinse with hot water. Keep warm. Set aside. Cook vegetables until tender crisp as directed on package. Drain. Set aside.

Preheat oven to 400°F. Grease 13 x 9-inch pan. Melt margarine in medium saucepan. Stir in flour. Mix until smooth. Gradually add milk. Blend well. Cook over medium heat for 6 to 10 minutes until mixture thickens and boils, stirring constantly. Stir in 1/2 cup Parmesan cheese and pepper. Spoon cooked spaghetti into greased pan. Top with cooked vegetables and sliced mushrooms. Pour milk mixture over mushrooms. Sprinkle with 2 tablespoons Parmesan cheese.

Bake at 400°F for 15 to 20 minutes or until mixture bubbles at edges and is thoroughly heated.

Makes: 6 servings

Per serving: Calories: 314   Fat: 8.3 grams   Calcium: 243 mg

Courtesy of the Green Giant® Company.

Light Chicken Cordon Bleu

1/2 cup seasoned dry bread crumbs
1 tablespoon grated Parmesan cheese
1 teaspoon chopped fresh parsley
1/2 teaspoon paprika
1 egg white
1 package (1 1/4 pounds) Perdue Fit 'n Easy® fresh skinless &
boneless Oven Stuffer Roaster thin-sliced breast
1 package (6 ounces) lowfat Swiss cheese slices
1 package (6 ounces) turkey ham slices

In a shallow bowl, combine bread crumbs, Parmesan cheese, parsley and paprika. In another shallow bowl, beat egg white lightly. Set aside. On each chicken breast slice, place 1 slice of cheese and 2 overlapping slices of ham. Roll up jelly-roll style. Secure with toothpick. Dip each roll in egg white and then bread crumbs, coating all sides.

In a microwave-safe utensil, arrange chicken rolls, seam side down, in circular pattern. Cover with wax paper. Microwave at medium-high (70% power) for 5 minutes. Rearrange chicken rolls. Cover with double thickness of paper towels. Microwave at medium-high for 8 minutes. Let stand, uncovered, 5 to 10 minutes before serving.

Makes 6 servings.

Per serving: Calories: 235   Fat: 4.9 grams   Calcium: 308 mg

****

Some experts feel that you need to burn 285 calories per day
via aerobic exercise to reduce your risk of heart disease.

Curried Chicken

1 3-pound frying chicken, cut-up
2 containers (8 ounces each) plain, nonfat yogurt
2 teaspoons curry powder
1/4 teaspoon cayenne pepper
2 cups hot cooked rice

Place chicken in heat-proofed shallow glass casserole. Combine yogurt, curry powder and cayenne pepper. Coat chicken evenly with the mixture. Refrigerate overnight.

Preheat oven to 375°F. Bake uncovered for 50 to 60 minutes, or until chicken is tender. Baste chicken several times. Serve over hot cooked rice.

Makes: 4 servings

Per serving: Calories: 945   Fat: 31.7 grams   Calcium: 300 mg

****
Calcitriol, one of the most potent forms of vitamin D,
has been shown in some studies to be an effective
treatment for osteoporosis, because it has
the ability to increase the amount
of calcium that is absorbed
through the intestine.

Baked Chicken With Yogurt

4 chicken breasts, skinless
2 tablespoons Butter Buds®
1/4 cup plus one tablespoon flour
1/2 cup chicken stock
1/2 cup mushrooms, sliced
1 cup plain, nonfat yogurt
1/2 cup dry white wine
pepper to taste
vegetable cooking spray

Place chicken pieces in baking dish. Bake at 350°F for 30 minutes. Drain. Combine flour and Butter Buds® in a saucepan. Add chicken stock, stirring until thick and smooth. In a small skillet, sprayed with vegetable cooking spray, sauté mushrooms. Add them to the chicken stock mixture. Add the yogurt, wine and pepper to the stock mixture. Mix. Pour over the drained chicken. Bake at 350°F for 35 or 40 minutes or until tender.

Makes: 4 servings   Serving size: 1/4 chicken

Per serving: Calories: 411   Fat: 4 grams   Calcium: 150 mg

****

It is never to late to start building better bones.
Take calcium.
Work out.

One-Step Oven Fish

4 pounds of whitefish fillets
2 cups plain, nonfat yogurt
1/4 cup chopped parsley
pepper to taste

Preheat oven to 350°F.

Place fish in single layer in nonstick baking pan. Top with yogurt. Cover with lid or foil. Bake at 350°F for 45 minutes. Remove to serving platter. Garnish with chopped parsley. Serve warm.

Makes: 8 servings

Per serving: Calories: 223   Fat: 1.7 grams   Calcium: 177 mg

****
The benefits of canned fish:

√ Heart disease fighting omega-3 fatty acids.
√ Calcium for strong bones and colon cancer protection.

Lite Macaroni & Cheese

1 package (8 ounces) elbow macaroni
2 cups (8 ounces) shredded lowfat cheddar cheese
1 can evaporated skim milk
pepper to taste

Cook macaroni according to package directions. Drain. Add cheese, milk and pepper. Mix well. Put into casserole. Bake, uncovered at 350°F for 30 minutes or until heated through, stirring occasionally. Serve warm.

Makes: 6 servings

Per serving: Calories: 260   Fat: 3.3 grams   Calcium: 341 mg

****

Real men drink milk

In a twenty-year study at the University of California researchers found that men who drank 2 1/2 glasses of milk a day had one-third the rate of colon cancer of non-milk-drinkers.

Lite Tuna Casserole

2 cups cooked peas
1 can condensed cream of chicken soup
1 cup plain, nonfat yogurt
2 cans (7 ounces each) water-packed tuna, drained
1 tablespoon Butter Buds®

Combine all ingredients. Toss to coat well. Put into casserole. Bake, uncovered at 350°F for 30 minutes or until heated through. Serve warm.

Makes: 6 servings

Per serving: Calories: 157   Fat: 2 grams   Calcium: 99 mg

****

There's more to good bones than just calcium.
A mineral balance is important
so that we can absorb
the calcium
we do
get.

Italian Tuna Casserole

1 medium onion, chopped
1 garlic clove, minced
1 can (8 ounces) tomato sauce
1/2 teaspoon oregano
2 cups spaghetti, cooked
1 can (7 ounces) water-packed tuna, drained
1/2 cup cooked peas
1 cup lowfat cottage cheese
1 egg, slightly beaten
pepper to taste
vegetable cooking spray

Spray a saucepan with vegetable cooking spray. Place over medium heat. Add onion and garlic. Cook, stirring occasionally about 3 minutes. Add tomato sauce and oregano. Bring to a boil. Reduce heat. Cover and simmer, stirring occasionally, about 15 minutes.

Cook spaghetti according to package directions. Drain. Place in bowl. Add tuna and peas. Toss together.

Preheat oven to 375°F. Spray 1 1/2 quart casserole with cooking spray. In a small bowl, combine cottage cheese, egg and pepper. Pour over spaghetti. Mix. Place mixture in baking dish. Pour sauce over mixture. Bake 30 minutes or until hot and bubbly.

Makes: 4 servings

Per serving: Calories: 349   Fat: 4 grams   Calcium: 114 mg

****

**You will probably reach menopause
the same time your mother did.**

Sole Florentine

1 package (10 ounces) frozen spinach, cooked, chopped,
    drained
1 medium onion, chopped
4 sole fillets (1 pound)
2 tablespoons all-purpose flour
1 cup skim milk
1 teaspoon grated Parmesan cheese
black pepper to taste
dash of ground nutmeg
vegetable cooking spray

Preheat oven to 350°F. Spray baking dish with cooking spray. Arrange spinach in baking dish. Arrange fish in single layer over spinach.

Place a small saucepan sprayed with vegetable cooking spray over low heat. Add onion and cook, stirring often 3 minutes, or until onion is soft. Add flour and cook, stirring often, about 1 minute. Gradually add milk, pepper and nutmeg and cook, stirring constantly until thick. Pour over fish. Sprinkle with cheese. Bake 15 minutes or until fish is flaky.

Makes: 4 servings

Per serving: Calories: 135   Fat: 1.3 grams   Calcium: 241 mg

✳✳✳✳✳✳✳✳✳

**A study at UCLA found that milk may aggravate your existing ulcer.
It seems that milk stimulates the production of stomach acid
and can irritate the ulcer you already have.**

Baked Salmon Loaf

1 can (15 1/2 ounces) water-packed salmon
2 slices whole wheat bread, crumbled into crumbs
1 cup cooked rice
2 egg whites, slightly beaten
1/4 cup skim milk
1 small onion, minced
1 tablespoon lemon juice
1/2 teaspoon dill
pepper to taste
vegetable cooking spray

Preheat oven to 375°F.

In a large bowl, combine all ingredients. Mix well. Spray a 9 x 5 loaf pan with cooking spray. Spoon mixture into pan. Bake for 45 minutes or until a knife inserted into the center comes out clean. Invert onto a serving platter. Serve warm.

Makes: 8 servings

Per serving: Calories: 146   Fat: 3.9 grams   Calcium: 147 mg

****

The Osteoporosis Center at the Hospital for Special Surgery in New York says that smokers have twice as much chance of getting a spinal fracture as nonsmokers.

Salmon Burgers To Go

1 can (16 ounces) salmon
1 medium onion, chopped fine
vegetable cooking spray
1/3 cup crushed Total® cereal
2 egg substitutes, beaten
1 teaspoon dry mustard
1/2 cup dry bread crumbs

Spray a medium skillet with vegetable cooking spray. On high heat, sauté onion in the coated skillet until soft, about 2 minutes. In a large bowl combine salmon, cereal, eggs, and mustard and onion. Mix well. Shape into patties. Roll each patty in the bread crumbs. Place patties in the microwave and cook 5 to 6 minutes, rotating microwave dish one-quarter turn halfway through cooking cycle. Set aside for 5 minutes before serving. Serve warm.

Makes: 4 servings

Per serving: Calories: 345   Fat: 12.2 grams   Calcium: 341 mg

****
Acidophilus milk, a form of liquid yogurt, has been shown
to actually block cancer-causing
impurities in the colon.

Curried Shrimp

1 large green pepper, chopped
1 large onion, chopped
1 can (10 3/4 ounces) condensed tomato soup
1 cup evaporated skim milk
1 tablespoon curry powder
pepper to taste
1 1/2 pounds (about 30-35) shelled, deveined, cooked shrimp
vegetable cooking spray

Coat a large skillet with vegetable cooking spray. Add the chopped pepper and onion. Cook slowly over medium heat until tender. Add soup, milk, curry powder and pepper. Simmer, stirring occasionally for 20 minutes. Add shrimp. Cook over low heat for 10 minutes. Serve hot.

Makes: 4 servings   Serving size: 1 cup

Per serving: Calories: 256   Fat: 2.8 grams   Calcium: 278 mg

****

Sloan Kettering Memorial Cancer Center says
that calcium detoxifies bile acids and
appears to calm down the
growth of cancer
cells in
high-risk people.

Mini Salmon Pot Pie

6 prepared individual pie shells
1 cup canned salmon, drained
1 can cream of celery soup
1/2 cup skim milk
2 tablespoons fresh, chopped parsley
dash of Worcestershire sauce
pepper to taste

Preheat oven to 350°F.

Place individual pie shells in preheated oven for 10 minutes until hot. Remove.

In a medium saucepan combine the salmon, celery soup, skim milk, parsley and spices. Heat, stirring constantly. Pour the mixture into the heated pie shells. Serve hot.

Makes: 6 servings   Serving size: 1 individual pie

Per serving: Calories: 214   Fat: 11.5 grams   Calcium: 150 mg

****

The University of California says that if you are looking for a major calcium boost, pick skim milk or nonfat yogurt over cottage cheese.

Italian Manicotti With Spinach

5 manicotti shells
1 package (10 ounces) frozen spinach, thawed, chopped,
  drained
1 cup lowfat cottage cheese, drained
1 egg substitute plus 1 egg white, beaten
1 small onion, chopped
1/2 teaspoon garlic powder
1 teaspoon oregano
1/8 teaspoon thyme
1 cup tomato sauce
4 ounces lowfat mozzarella cheese part skim, shredded
vegetable cooking spray

Cook manicotti according to package directions. Drain.

Combine spinach, cottage cheese, eggs, onion, garlic and spices in a large bowl.
Mix well. Stuff the shells with the mixture. Arrange in nonstick baking pan coated
with vegetable spray. Pour tomato sauce over shells. Top with mozzarella cheese.
Cover. Bake at 350°F for 25 minutes or until done.

Makes: 5 servings   Serving size: 1 shell

Per serving: Calories: 250   Fat: 6.6 grams   Calcium: 300 mg

****
A calcium cooking tip: Add a teaspoon of vinegar
to homemade stock made with soup bones.
During cooking the vinegar draws out the calcium
locked in the bones.
If you open the lid of the pot, the
vinegar smell and taste will
fade away.

Quick Broccoli Quiche

1 (16 ounce) container lowfat cottage cheese
1/2 cup skim milk
equivalent of 4 eggs, egg substitute
1 medium onion, chopped
1 package (10 ounces) frozen broccoli, thawed
1 9-inch prepared pie crust shell
1/4 teaspoon paprika
pepper to taste

Preheat oven to 400°F. In blender or food processor mix cheese, milk and egg substitute. Process until smooth. Add onion and pepper, and broccoli. Pour mixture into prepared pie crust shell. Sprinkle with paprika. Bake at 400°F for 50 minutes. Serve warm.

Makes: 6 servings

Per serving: Calories: 353   Fat: 14.6 grams   Calcium: 214 mg

****

**Did you know that one-quarter of the weight of our bones
is water? Another quarter is collagen, a special
connective tissue.
Half the weight of
our bones is calcium phosphate.
See how important calcium is?**

Pasta With White Clam Sauce

4 ounces spaghetti
vegetable cooking spray
1 small onion, chopped
2 garlic cloves, chopped
1/2 cup parsley, chopped
pepper to taste
1 can (6 1/2 ounces) minced clams with liquid reserved
2 tablespoons grated Parmesan cheese

Cook spaghetti according to package instructions. Drain. Set aside. Keep warm. In a small saucepan cook onion and garlic in vegetable spray until soft, about 2 minutes, stirring often. Add parsley, pepper, and reserved liquid from the minced clams. Simmer about 5 minutes. Add clams. Heat about 1 minute. Pour sauce over cooked spaghetti. Toss well to mix. Divide onto two dinner plates. Sprinkle each serving with 1 tablespoon grated Parmesan cheese. Serve warm.

Makes: 2 servings

Per serving: Calories: 427   Fat: 4.9 grams   Calcium: 420 mg

****
Osteoporosis is more common than arthritis and diabetes.

Chicken Divine

4 whole chicken breasts, split, boned & skinned
1 package (10 ounces) frozen broccoli, cooked & drained
1 medium onion, chopped
1/4 cup all-purpose flour
1 1/2 cups skim milk
1 teaspoon margarine
2 tablespoons grated Parmesan cheese
dash nutmeg (optional)
black pepper to taste
vegetable cooking spray

Preheat oven to 400°F. Spray nonstick skillet with vegetable cooking spray. Brown chicken breasts over medium heat. Pat with paper towels to remove excess fat. Arrange broccoli in baking pan. Place chicken in single layer over broccoli.

In medium saucepan melt margarine over low heat. Add onion and cook until tender, stirring often, about 3 minutes. Stir in flour. Cook, stirring often, about 1 minute. Gradually add milk, nutmeg and pepper. Cook, stirring constantly until thick. Pour over chicken and broccoli. Sprinkle with cheese. Bake at 400°F for 20 minutes, or until bubbly. Serve hot.

Makes: 4 servings

Per serving: Calories: 405   Fat: 4.7 grams   Calcium: 236 mg

****
Kids who drink sodas instead of milk aren't getting enough calcium.

Chicken Mushroom Casserole

4 chicken breasts, without skins
1 tablespoon margarine
1 medium onion, chopped
1/2 pound fresh sliced mushrooms
1 tablespoon flour
2/3 cup low-sodium chicken stock
pepper to taste
1/2 cup plain, lowfat yogurt

Preheat oven to 300°F.

In a skillet, brown the chicken in the margarine. Remove chicken and place in nonstick baking dish. Add the onion and mushrooms to the skillet. Cook until onion is transluscent. Remove from heat. Slowly add the flour, stock and pepper, stirring constantly to avoid lumps. Pour the mixture over the chicken. Cover and bake at 300°F for 45 minutes. Warm the yogurt slightly, over low heat. Add to the chicken. Heat again. Serve hot.

Makes: 4 servings

Per serving: Calories: 357   Fat: 4.2 grams   Calcium: 105 mg

****
Smoking may double your risk of developing osteoporosis.

Turkey Meat Loaf

1 1/2 pounds ground turkey
1 cup fresh whole wheat bread crumbs (2 slices)
1 medium onion, chopped
1 stalk celery, chopped
1/4 cup fresh parsley
1/4 cup skim milk
2 cloves garlic, chopped fine
2 egg whites, slightly beaten
1/2 teaspoon ground sage
3/4 teaspoon dill
black pepper to taste
vegetable cooking spray

Preheat oven to 350°F. Spray a 9 x 5-inch loaf pan with cooking spray. In a large bowl, mix all ingredients together. Spoon into pan and shape into a loaf. Bake for 50 to 60 minutes. Turn onto serving platter. Serve warm.

Makes: 6 servings

Per serving: Calories: 143   Fat: 5.4 grams   Calcium: 86 mg

✳✳✳✳✳✳✳✳✳✳

Do you have periodontal disease?
It could be a warning of calcium deficiency.

Skinny Fettuccine Alfredo

1 package (12 ounces) fettuccine noodles
1/2 cup Butter Buds®
2/3 cup nonfat yogurt
1/2 cup grated Parmesan cheese
1 egg yolk, slightly beaten
pepper to taste

Cook pasta as directed. Drain. Set aside. Keep warm. In a medium saucepan, melt Butter Buds®. Gradually stir in yogurt, Parmesan cheese, and egg yolk. Pour the sauce over the pasta. Mix well to coat. Serve hot.

Makes: 6 servings

Per serving: Calories: 131   Fat: 3.3 grams   Calcium: 148 mg

****

**A study from Cornell Medical Center and the Bone Disease
Service at the Hospital for Special Surgery in New York
reports that male alcoholics who take calcium
supplements can significantly
increase their bone mass.**

Creamy Chicken

6 chicken breasts, skinned and boned
1 can cream of mushroom soup
1 can plain, nonfat yogurt
1/4 cup chopped parsley
pepper to taste

Preheat oven to 350ºF

Arrange chicken breasts in a nonstick baking pan. Combine soup, yogurt, parsley and pepper in a bowl. Pour over the chicken. Bake uncovered, for one hour. Serve hot.

Makes: 6 servings

Per serving: Calories: 365   Fat: 5.2 grams   Calcium: 176 mg

****
Get to know your bones.

You've got four kinds of bones:

Long bones like the thighbone
Short bones like ankle bones
Flat bones like shoulder blades
Mixed bones like vertebrae

Veal Parmigiana

4 veal cutlets (1 pound), 1/4 inch thick
1/2 cup dry bread crumbs
2 teaspoons grated Parmesan cheese
1 egg
1 tablespoon water
1 1/2 cups spaghetti or marinara sauce
1/2 cup shredded part skim mozzarella cheese
1/4 teaspoon oregano

Preheat oven to 375°F.

Place veal cutlets between two pieces of wax paper and pound down until half as thick as they were. In a shallow dish, or on a piece of waxed paper, mix together bread crumbs and Parmesan cheese. In a dish, beat egg and water slightly. Dip veal into egg mixture and coat with bread crumb mixture. Heat oil in large skillet over medium-high heat. Add veal and brown both sides. Arrange veal cutlets in single layer in shallow baking dish. Pour sauce over veal. Sprinkle with mozzarella cheese and oregano. Bake 20 to 30 minutes or until bubbly. Serve hot.

Makes: 4 servings

Per serving: Calories: 377   Fat: 12.9 grams   Calcium: 206 mg

****
Don't stop working out.
Your fitness level drops dramatically only
a couple of weeks after you turn back
into a couch potato.

Baked Chicken Surprise

6 chicken breasts, split, boned and skinned
1 1/2 cups lowfat Swiss cheese (6 ounces), shredded
1 can (10 3/4 ounces) condensed cream of chicken soup
1/2 cup skim milk
vegetable cooking spray
pepper to taste

Preheat oven to 350°F. Spray large baking dish with vegetable spray. Place chicken breasts in dish. Sprinkle with cheese. In a small bowl combine soup, milk and pepper. Pour mixture over cheese. Bake for 1 hour, or until chicken is tender. Serve hot.

Makes: 6 servings

Per serving: Calories: 385   Fat: 6.2 grams   Calcium: 334 mg

****

If you eat more calories than you burn off,
your body stores them in fat closets
around your waist, stomach,
thighs and upper arms.

Easy Chicken Nuggets

**1 pound boneless, skinless chicken breasts, cut into 1-inch
pieces
1/2 cup low-calorie Italian salad dressing or mustard
4 cups whole grain Total® cereal, crushed (about 1 1/2 cups
crumbs)
vegetable cooking spray**

Preheat oven to 425°F. Spray jelly roll pan (15 1/2 x 10 1/2 x 1-inch) with vegetable cooking spray.

Dip chicken pieces in salad dressing or mustard, then roll in cereal. Place in pan. Bake about 10 minutes or until juices run clear. Serve with prepared mustard, if desired.

Makes: 4 servings

Per serving: Calories: 373   Fat: 6.4 grams   Calcium: 69 mg

® T.M. of General Mills, Inc.

****

**Calcium isn't just in dairy products or veggies.
One serving of many whole grain cereals
with skim milk can give you
a good head start on
your RDA of
calcium.**

Salmon Supper Croquettes

1 medium onion, grated
1/3 cup skim milk
1 can salmon, drained
1/2 cup seasoned bread crumbs
1 egg substitute

In a large bowl combine all ingredients. Mix well. Shape into patties. Fry on both sides in a skillet sprayed with vegetable cooking spray. Serve hot.

Makes: 8 patties   Serving size: 2 patties

Per serving: Calories: 171   Fat: 5.2   Calcium: 161

****

Men are often taller than women
because their tall bones
grow for a longer
period of time.

Baked Sole With Parsley/Yogurt Sauce

4 pounds of sole fillets
2 cups plain, lowfat yogurt
1/2 cup chopped parsley

Preheat oven to 350°F.

Arrange fish fillets in a nonstick baking pan. Cover with yogurt. Sprinkle with 1/2 the parsley. Cover and bake at 350°F for 45 minutes. Remove from oven. Top with remaining parsley. Serve hot.

Makes: 4 servings

Per serving: Calories: 375   Fat: 2.5 grams   Calcium: 513 mg

****

Yogurt tip:
Don't let lowfat yogurt boil–it curdles.
A better way is to heat it slowly before adding it to
hot sauces, soups, etc.

Nachos Casserole

1 cup chunky taco sauce
1 can (4 ounces) green chiles, chopped
1 pound lean ground turkey
1/2 cup chopped onions
1/4 teaspoon cumin
1 cup refried beans
4 ounces plain, nonfat yogurt
1 cup (4 ounces) shredded, reduced-fat cheddar cheese,
    divided
1/4 cup water
4 cups Kellogg's Corn Flakes® cereal
vegetable cooking spray

Optional Garnish:
chopped tomatoes, chopped green onions, sliced olives,
plain, nonfat yogurt/reduced-fat sour cream.

Combine taco sauce and chiles. Set aside. Preheat oven to 350°F.
In a large skillet, cook turkey and onions until meat is browned. Drain off fat. Add cumin, beans, yogurt, 1/2 cup of the cheese, half the taco sauce mixture and water.

Pour 2 cups Kellogg's Corn Flakes® cereal into a 2-quart baking dish coated with cooking spray. Cover with meat mixture. Top with remaining taco sauce mixture. Sprinkle with remaining cereal. Bake about 35 minutes or until thoroughly heated. Sprinkle with remaining cheese. Bake just until cheese melts, about 5 minutes. Garnish with tomatoes, green onions, olives and yogurt
if desired.

Makes: 6 servings   Serving size: 1 cup

Per serving: Calories: 320   Fat: 9.8 grams   Calcium: 213 mg

Pavlova

3 egg whites, room temperature
1/8 teaspoon cream of tartar
1/3 cup sugar
1 teaspoon vanilla extract, divided
1/2 cup nonfat dry milk
1/2 cup ice water
1 1/2 cups fresh or frozen sliced strawberries
1 cup kiwi slices

Preheat oven to 250°F. Line baking sheet with brown paper. Draw an 8-inch circle in the center of the paper. Set it aside.

Beat egg whites and cream of tartar until soft peaks form. Add sugar gradually and 1/2 of the vanilla. Spoon the mixture (meringue) in the center of the circle you drew on the brown paper. Using the back of a spoon or flat edge of knife, spread the mixture to the edges of the circle, and form a 1-inch rim. Bake for 1 1/4 hours or until firm. Turn oven off. Leave meringue in the oven for another 2 hours. Remove.

In a chilled bowl, with chilled beaters, beat nonfat dry milk, water and the rest of the vanilla until stiff peaks form. Spread this mixture over the meringue circle. Arrange fruit on top.

Makes: 8 servings

Per serving: Calories: 93   Fat: 0 grams   Calcium: 107 mg

Peach Yogurt Pie

1 graham cracker prepared crust
1 envelope unflavored gelatin
2/3 cup unsweetened apple juice
1 package (20 ounces/3 cups) frozen peaches, drained,
thawed
1 1/2 cups plain, nonfat yogurt
1/4 cup sugar
1 teaspoon vanilla extract
1/4 cup ground nutmeg

In a small saucepan, sprinkle gelatin over apple juice. Set aside for 5 minutes. When gelatin softens, cook over low heat, stirring constantly until gelatin dissolves, about 5 minutes. Pour mixture into a large bowl.

Place 2 cups of the peaches into a blender or food processor. Process until smooth. Transfer to a bowl. Stir in the gelatin. Add yogurt, sugar, vanilla and nutmeg. Stir until smooth. Cover and chill for 1 hour.

Chop the remaining peaches. Fold into the chilled mixture. Spoon into pie crust and refrigerate until firm.

Makes: 8 servings

Per serving: Calories: 259   Fat: 8.9 grams   Calcium: 100 mg

****

Researchers at Stanford University say that
10 minutes of exercise three times a day
is just as good as 30 minutes
of continuous exercise.
So take an exercise break.

Thick Banana Shake

1 large banana, sliced
1 cup skim milk
1/4 tablespoon vanilla extract
ice

Place all ingredients into blender. Blend at high speed. Serve at once.

Makes: 1 serving

Per serving: Calories: 246   Fat: 1 gram   Calcium: 309 mg

****
Frozen desserts made from skim milk
could be higher in calcium
than regular
ice cream.

Mock Ice Cream Basic Recipe

2 bananas, peeled, sliced, frozen
4 teaspoons skim milk

Put frozen banana slices into blender or food processor. Process, adding skim milk 1 teaspoon at a time, until mixture is thick and creamy. Serve at once.

Variations: Add berries, peaches, or other fresh fruit to your mock ice cream.

Makes: 4 servings

Per serving: Calories: 54   Fat: Trace   Calcium: 10 mg

****
It isn't enough to just take the required amount of calcium.
You have to eat right so that it gets absorbed.

Calcium-Rich Cheese Cake

1 prepared graham cracker crust
2 cups lowfat cottage cheese
2 tablespoons Butter Buds®
4 egg whites
1/2 cup sugar
1/2 cup skim milk
1/4 cup all-purpose flour
1/4 cup lemon juice (optional)
1 tablespoon grated lemon peel (optional)

Preheat oven to 300°F.

Place cottage cheese into blender or food processor. Process until creamy. Add the Butter Buds® and mix well. Add eggs slowly. Add sugar and skim milk beating well after each addition. Add remaining ingredients, processing until smooth.

Pour the mixture into the prepared crust. Bake for 90 minutes or until firm. Cool for several hours before cutting. Serve at room temperature.

Makes: 10 servings

Per serving: Calories: 217   Fat: 6.5 grams   Calcium: 50 mg

****

**Not all cheese is created equal.
Best bet for calcium? Parmesan.**

Rice Pudding

1/2 cup uncooked rice
1 1/2 cups water
1/4 cup raisins
1/4 cup sugar
1 cup skim milk
1/2 teaspoon vanilla extract
dash of nutmeg

Place the water, rice, raisins and nutmeg in the top of a double boiler. Mix thoroughly. Cover. Cook over boiling water for 20 minutes.

Stir in milk and cook, uncovered until the milk is absorbed, about 10 minutes. Stir in sugar and vanilla.

Pour into individual dishes. Chill until ready to serve.

Makes: 6 servings

Per serving: Calories: 92   Fat: Trace   Calcium: 55 mg

****

**Recent studies show that children can build even stronger bones
by taking extra calcium–even if they are already
getting a good amount every day.**

Quick Coffee Cake

1 1/2 cups flour
1 cup granulated sugar
2 teaspoons baking powder
1/2 teaspoon baking soda
1 cup plain, nonfat yogurt
2 egg substitutes

Preheat oven to 350°F.

In a large bowl mix together the flour, sugar, baking powder and baking soda. In a smaller bowl combine yogurt and eggs. Beat thoroughly. Add the dry ingredients to the yogurt and egg mixture. Beat until smooth. Pour into a 9 x 9-inch nonstick baking pan. Bake for 20 minutes

Makes: 6 servings

Per serving: Calories: 251   Fat: 2.4 grams   Calcium: 178 mg

****
Go for evaporated skim milk.
It's just like real milk, but with 60% of the water removed.
Add it straight from the can to sauces, puddings and soups for a great,
rich taste.

Basic Pudding

1 package vanilla pudding mix
2 cups skim milk
1 cup sliced strawberries
1/4 teaspoon vanilla flavoring

Prepare pudding according to package directions adding vanilla. Cool. Before serving fold in sliced strawberries. Heap into tall glasses. Serve.

Makes: 4 servings

Per serving: Calories: 149   Fat: 0.5 grams   Calcium: 160 mg

****

The University of Michigan found that kids under the age of two
who drink only skim milk are
five times more likely to develop
tummy trouble than
kids who drink whole milk.

Yogurt Pudding

1 package strawberry-flavored gelatin
1 cup nonfat strawberry yogurt

Prepare the gelatin according to package directions. Chill until it begins to set. Stir in the yogurt. Mix well. Chill until set. Serve cold.

Makes: 4 servings

Per serving: Calories: 110   Fat: Trace   Calcium: 88 mg

****

There is strong scientific evidence that women who regularly drink
milk at least until they are 20 have protection
against bone loss later in life.
It can't be said often enough . . . take more calcium.

Fruity Yogurt Cup

3 cups mixed fresh fruit
2 cups vanilla, lowfat yogurt

In tall serving glasses, alternate layers of fruits with layers of yogurt. Chill. Garnish with slice of fruit, lemon wedge, or sprinkle with your favorite cereal.

Makes: 6 servings

Per serving: Calories: 187   Fat: 1.2 grams   Calcium: 138 mg

****

High Calcium–Lowfat Topping

Pour a can of evaporated skim milk into a metal pie tin. Place in the freezer until crystals form around the edges. Transfer to a chilled bowl and whip with chilled beaters until fluffy. Add a couple of tablespoons of confectioners sugar. Beat again. Serve on fruit, pie, cake or pudding.

Yogurt Fruit Pops

2 1/2 cups plain, nonfat yogurt
2 bananas
2/3 cup frozen orange juice concentrate

Place all ingredients in blender or food processor. Process until smooth. Divide evenly among popsicle containers. Freeze.

Makes: 8 servings

Per serving: Calories: 103   Fat: less than 1 gram   Calcium: 151 mg

****

Sweet Tooth Fix

Go for a big slice of angel food cake. 69 calories and 0 fat.
Now dunk it into a bowl of fruity nonfat yogurt.
Terrific!

Everyone's Favorite Apple Cobbler

1/2 cup brown sugar
1/2 teaspoon cinnamon
1 tablespoon lemon juice
4 cups sliced, peeled tart apples
1 1/4 cups flour
1 tablespoon baking powder
1/4 cup liquid Butter Buds®
1/4 cup granulated sugar
2 egg whites, slightly beaten
1/2 cup skim milk
1/4 cup lowfat milk powder
1/2 teaspoon vanilla
vegetable cooking spray

Preheat oven to 375°F.

Spray an oven-proof baking dish with nonstick vegetable spray.

In a large mixing bowl combine the brown sugar, cinnamon and lemon juice. Mix well. Add the apples. Mix until apples are well coated. Put mixture into baking dish.

Cream the Butter Buds® and granulated sugar until light. Beat in the egg whites. Mix together the flour, baking powder and lowfat milk powder. Add the dry ingredients to the margarine and sugar mixture alternatively with the skim milk. Mix. Add the vanilla. Mix again. Drop the batter over the apples. Bake for 30 minutes. Serve warm.

Makes: 8 servings

Per serving: Calories: 196   Fat: 0.5 grams   Calcium: 210 mg

Frosty Fruit Yogurt Pie

1 prepared 9-inch pie shell
1 cup (8-oz. container) plain, nonfat yogurt
1 cup fresh strawberries or raspberries
1 tablespoon honey
1 teaspoon vanilla

Place yogurt in freezer section of fridge for 4 hours. Place fruit, honey and vanilla in blender or food processor. Process until smooth. Add the frozen yogurt. Process until smooth. Place the mixture in the freezer compartment for 4 hours. Process until smooth just before spooning it into pie shell to serve.

Makes: 6 servings

Per serving: Calories: 176   Fat: 8.3 grams   Calcium: 96 mg

****

Men who don't drink milk are twice as
likely to develop high blood pressure
as men who drink at least
a quart of milk a day.

No-Guilt Cheesecake

1 prepared graham cracker crust
4 cups DANNON® plain nonfat yogurt
1 cup lowfat cottage cheese
3 egg whites
3/4 cup sugar
2 tablespoons all-purpose flour
1 tablespoon fresh lemon juice
1 teaspoon vanilla

Spoon yogurt into large strainer lined with double thickness of cheesecloth or a coffee filter. Place bowl beneath, but not touching strainer to catch liquid. Chill 24 hours. Discard liquid.

Preheat oven to 325°F.

Place cottage cheese and egg whites into a blender or food processor. Process until smooth. Add drained yogurt, sugar, flour, lemon juice and vanilla. Process again until well blended, about 30 seconds.

Pour into crust. Bake one hour. Cool to room temperature. Cover. Chill overnight. Garnish with fresh fruit.

Makes: 12 servings

Per serving: Calories: 212   Fat: 5.3 grams   Calcium: 167 mg

Apple Cinnamon Tart

1 1/2 cups quick-cooking oats
1 tablespoon + 1/2 teaspoon ground cinnamon
3/4 cup frozen apple juice concentrate, thawed
2 large apples, sliced thin
1 teaspoon lemon juice
1/3 cup cold water
1 envelope unflavored gelatin
2 cups DANNON® plain, nonfat yogurt
1/4 cup honey
1/2 teaspoon almond extract

Preheat oven to 350°F.

In a small bowl combine oats and 1 tablespoon cinnamon. Toss with 1/4 cup apple juice concentrate. Press onto bottom and side of 9-inch pie plate. Bake 5 minutes or until set. Cool on wire rack.

In a medium bowl toss apple slices with lemon juice. Arrange on cooled crust and set aside.

In a small saucepan, combine cold water and remaining 1/2 cup apple juice concentrate. Sprinkle gelatin over water mixture. Let stand 3 minutes to soften. Cook and stir over medium heat until gelatin is completely dissolved. Remove from heat. Add yogurt, honey, remaining 1/2 teaspoon cinnamon and almond extract. Blend well. Pour over apples in crust. Chill several hours or overnight.

Makes: 10 servings

Per serving: Calories: 155   Fat: 1.1 grams   Calcium: 112 mg

Yogurt Cookies

1 1/4 cups all-purpose flour
1/2 teaspoon baking soda
1/2 teaspoon grated orange peel
1/4 cup shortening
1/4 cup liquid Butter Buds®
2/3 cup sugar
1 egg substitute
1/2 cup DANNON® vanilla, lowfat yogurt
1 teaspoon vanilla
vegetable cooking spray

Preheat oven to 350°F. Coat cookie sheets with vegetable cooking spray.

In a medium bowl combine flour, baking soda and orange peel. Set aside. In a large bowl beat shortening and Butter Buds® with electric mixer on medium speed for 30 seconds. Add sugar. Beat on medium speed until fluffy. Beat in egg, yogurt and vanilla. Stir in flour mixture. Drop teaspoonfuls of dough, 2 inches apart onto prepared cookie sheet. Bake 8 minutes or until golden brown. Remove to wire racks to cool.

Makes: 36 cookies   Serving size: 1 cookie

Per serving: Calories: 60   Fat: 1.8 grams   Calcium: 10 mg

****

**Some studies show that children under two should not be
put on skim milk but should have a healthy,
lowfat, balanced diet and plenty
of exercise.**

A Touch Of France

4 cups fresh plums, halved with pits removed
vegetable cooking spray
6 tablespoons granulated sugar
egg substitute for 3 eggs
1 1/3 cups skim milk
2/3 cups flour
1 teaspoon grated lemon rind
1/2 teaspoon cinnamon
2 teaspoons vanilla
1/8 cup confectioners sugar
1/8 cup lowfat powdered milk

Preheat oven to 375°F.

Spray a glass baking dish with nonstick vegetable spray. Sprinkle 1 tablespoon of sugar evenly on the bottom. Arrange the plums, cut side down in the dish. Top with 2 more tablespoons of sugar.

In a blender or food processor combine the rest of the sugar, eggs, milk, flour and spices. Process until well blended and smooth. Pour the mixture over the fruit.

Bake for 1 hour. Remove. Mix together confectioners sugar and lowfat powdered milk and sift over the top of the dessert. Serve warm.

Makes: 8 servings

Per serving: Calories: 231   Fat: 3.8 grams   Calcium: 131 mg

Fruit Trifle

1/2 cup jellied cranberry sauce
3 tablespoons water
1 package (4-serving size) instant vanilla pudding mix
1 cup skim milk
1 cup DANNON® vanilla or lemon lowfat yogurt
1 package (3 ounces) ladyfingers (about 12) split
1 1/2 cups fresh peach slices or frozen peach slices, thawed &
**   drained**
1 1/2 cups fresh strawberry halves

In a small saucepan heat cranberry sauce and water until cranberry sauce is melted. Use a wire whisk to beat until smooth. Cool.

Prepare pudding mixture according to package directions, using skim milk and yogurt in place of milk called for on package.

In a 1 1/2 quart souffle dish or straight-sided serving bowl arrange enough of the ladyfingers to cover bottom and sides of dish. Combine 1 cup peaches and 1 cup strawberries. Spoon half of the fruit mixture over the ladyfingers in the dish. Spread half of the pudding mixture over the fruit. Top with half of cranberry mixture. Arrange remaining ladyfingers on top. Repeat fruit and pudding layers. Spoon remaining cranberry mixture in center. Cover. Chill at least 4 hours.

Makes: 8 servings

Per serving: Calories: 136   Fat: 0.7 grams   Calcium: 95 mg

****

Looking for a change of pace at breakfast?
Try spreading a little nonfat fruit yogurt
on your toast, bagel or English muffin.

Strawberry Bavarian Dessert

1 package (3 ounces) strawberry-flavored gelatin
3/4 cup boiling water
1 container (8 ounces) lowfat strawberry yogurt
2 teaspoons lemon juice
1 package (10 ounces frozen strawberries, thawed, drained)
2 egg whites
1/8 teaspoon cream of tartar
1/4 cup sugar

In a large bowl, dissolve the gelatin in the hot water. Transfer to blender or food processor. Add yogurt and lemon juice and process until blended. Refrigerate until slightly thickened.

Spoon strawberries into individual serving dishes (4).

In a mixing bowl beat egg whites until foamy. Beat in cream of tartar and sugar. Fold the mixture into the chilled yogurt and gelatin. Pour over strawberries. Chill until set.

Makes: 4 servings   Serving size: 1 cup

Per serving: Calories: 250   Fat: 0.8 grams   Calcium: 89 mg

****
Toss a handful of breakfast cereal into some yogurt
for a fast, calcium-rich start to the day.
Look for cereals reinforced with calcium
for some extra bone protection.

Tiramisu

24 vanilla wafers
1/3 cup brandy
1 cup strong black coffee, brewed
4 large eggs, separated
1 cup sugar
3/4 pound Mascarpone cheese
3/4 ounce bittersweet chocolate, grated

Line the bottom and sides of a 2-quart baking dish with the vanilla wafers. Reserve 8 wafers.

Mix together the brandy and coffee. Sprinkle two-thirds of the mixture over the vanilla wafers.

Beat the egg yolks with sugar until they are smooth and creamy. Add the Mascarpone and mix well. In a separate bowl, beat the egg whites and fold into the egg yolk and cheese mixture gently.

Pour half the cheese mixture into the baking dish. Cover with the remaining vanilla wafers. Sprinkle with the rest of the coffee mixture. Top with half the grated chocolate. Add a layer of the cheese mixture. And finish off with the rest of the chocolate. Refrigerate at least 2 hours until chilled through.

Makes: 8 servings

Per serving: Calories: 447   Fat: 26.4 grams   Calcium: 18 mg

****
According to the *Annals of Internal Medicine*
men lose 1% of their bone mass
in their hands and wrists.
The bone loss begins around age 30.

A Cluster of Cream Pies

Basic Cream Pie

1 prepared graham cracker pie crust
1 package instant pudding mix, vanilla
1 cup skim milk
1 cup lowfat, vanilla yogurt

Prepare instant pudding according to package directions. Substitute skim milk and yogurt for the milk called for on the package.

Pour into prepared crust. Chill until set.

Makes: 8 servings

Per serving: Calories: 230   Fat: 7.9 grams   Calcium: 94 mg

Variations:

Instant chocolate pudding
Instant butterscotch pudding
Instant banana pudding

Banana Cream Pie: Add bananas to bottom of pie crust & top with vanilla pudding mixture

Coconut Cream Pie: Sprinkle grated coconut over top of vanilla pudding mixture

Strawberry Cream Pie: Add fresh or frozen strawberries to bottom of pie crust and top with vanilla pudding mixture.

Basic Oatmeal Cookies

1/2 cup liquid Butter Buds®
1/2 cup firmly packed brown sugar
1/2 cup granulated sugar
1 egg substitute
1 teaspoon vanilla
1 tablespoon skim milk
1 cup all-purpose flour
1/2 teaspoon baking soda
1/2 teaspoon baking powder
1 cup uncooked quick rolled oats
1/2 cup raisins

Preheat oven to 350°F.

Put Butter Buds® in a large bowl. Add the two sugars. Cream well. Add the egg, vanilla and milk. Beat together until smooth. Add the flour, baking soda and baking powder. Beat again, until smooth. Add rolled oats and raisins. Combine until well blended.

Drop cookies about 2 inches apart on a nonstick cookie sheet and bake for about 10 minutes or until golden brown. Cool on wire racks.

Makes: 3 dozen cookies   Serving size: 1 cookie

Per serving: Calories: 56   Fat: 0.5 grams   Calcium: 13 mg

****
Studies show that our kids are getting about 300 mg of caffeine a day.
That's about the amount in three cups of coffee.
Too much for small bodies.

Chilly Cheese Cookies

1/2 cup Butter Buds®
1 cup sugar
1 egg subtitute, beaten
1 package (3 ounces) lowfat cream cheese
2 tablespoons plain, lowfat yogurt
1 teaspoon vanilla
2 cups all-purpose flour
1/8 teaspoon baking soda
1/2 teaspoon baking powder

Cream together the Butter Buds®, sugar and egg. Add cheese and yogurt. Blend again until creamy. Add remaining ingredients. Beat until well blended. Form into a ball and chill in refrigerator.

Remove from fridge. Roll out thin and cut into shapes using the bottom of a glass or cookies forms.

Bake at 350°F about 12 minutes or until golden brown.

Makes: 5 dozen cookies   Serving size: 1 cookie

Per serving: Calories: 38   Fat: 0.5 grams   Calcium: 8 mg

✳✳✳✳✳✳✳✳✳✳

**The massive Framingham Heart Study reports that
"our way of life is related to our way of death."**

Biggest health risks? Stress, smoking, alcohol, poor diet, lack of exercise.

Yogurt Cake

1 3/4 cups flour
1/4 teaspoon baking soda
1 3/4 teaspoons baking powder
1/3 cup liquid Butter Buds®
1 cup granulated sugar
2 egg yolks
1 teaspoon vanilla
2/3 cup plain, nonfat yogurt
2 egg whites

Preheat oven to 375°F.

In a large mixing bowl mix together flour, baking soda and baking powder. Put Butter Buds® into a large bowl. Gradually add the sugar to the Butter Buds®, mixing until the color changes to a light yellow and both are well blended. Beat in the 2 egg yolks and the vanilla. Add the dry mixuture. Mix lightly. Add the yogurt. Mix well. Beat the egg whites until stiff. Fold into the mixture. Pour into nonstick round cake pans. Bake for 25 minutes.

Makes: 8 servings
Per serving: Calories: 239   Fat: 1.7 grams   Calcium: 122 mg

****

Studies show that exercise not only prevents bone loss, but actually builds new bone–a double bonus.

Southwestern Snack

3 cups Total® cereal
3 cups hot-air popped popcorn
1 cup small cheese crackers
1 cup pretzel sticks
2 tablespoons vegetable oil
1/2 teaspoon chili powder
1/4 teaspoon ground cumin
1/4 cup garlic powder
2 tablespoons grated Parmesan cheese

Preheat oven to 300°F.

Mix cereal, popcorn, crackers and pretzels in a large plastic bag. Mix oil, chili powder, cumin and garlic powder. Pour over popcorn mixture. Shake well. Immediately sprinkle with cheese. Shake well, again. Pour into ungreased rectangular baking pan, 13 x 9 x 2-inches. Bake 10 minutes without stirring. Cool. Store in a tightly covered container.

Makes: 8 cups   Serving size: 1/2 cup

Per serving: Calories: 154   Fat: 4.6 grams   Calcium: 50 mg

®Reg. T.M. of General Mills, Inc.

****
Recipes made easy

1 ounce = 1/4 cup of grated cheese
1 ounce = 1/8 cup of cottage cheese

Fruit-Cereal Clusters

16 ounces vanilla-flavored candy coating
2 1/2 cups Total® cereal
3/4 cup salted peanuts
1/2 cup chopped dried apricots
1/2 cup chopped pitted dates

Break candy coating into pieces in a 4-quart microwavable casserole or bowl. Microwave uncovered on High, 4 minutes, or until softened. Stir. Microwave uncovered 1 minute longer. Stir until smooth.

Stir in remaining ingredients until evenly coated. Drop by teaspoonfuls onto waxed paper. Refrigerate 30 to 60 minutes or until set.

Makes: About 3 1/2 dozen clusters   Serving size: 1 cluster

Per serving: Calories: 88   Fat: 4.7 grams   Calcium: 40 mg

®Reg. T.M. of General Mills, Inc.

****

Salt is an acquired taste. It takes only six weeks
for your tastebuds to get used to
less salt.

Hawaiian Snack Mix

4 cups Whole Grain Total® cereal
1/4 cup packed brown sugar
1/4 cup liquid Butter Buds®
1 tablespoon grated orange peel
1 cup dried pineapple pieces
1/2 cup banana chips
1/2 cup flaked coconut

Preheat oven to 300°F.

Place cereal in jelly roll pan, 15 1/2 x 10 1/2 x 1-inch.

Heat brown sugar and Butter Buds® in a saucepan over low heat. Stir in orange peel. Pour over cereal. Toss until evenly coated. Bake 20 minutes, stirring twice. Stir in remaining ingredients. Cool. Store in air-tight container.

Makes: 5 1/2 cups   Serving size: 1/2 cup

Per serving: Calories: 186   Fat: 6 grams   Calcium: 105 mg

®Reg. T.M. of General Mills, Inc.

****
Mature women need at least 1500 mg of calcium per day.
Mature men need at least 1000 mg of calcium per day.

Calcium Cocktail I

3 kale leaves
3 collard green leaves
1/4 cup chopped parsley
1 carrot

In a juicer, liquify all ingredients. Serve immediately.

Makes: 1 serving

Per serving: Calories: 95   Fat: less than 1 gram   Calcium: 288 mg

****
What contributes to your osteoporosis risk?
Rheumatoid arthritis
Cystic fibrosis
Diabetes mellitus
Anorexia Nervosa
Fractures
Immobilization

Calcium Cocktail II

4 carrots
2 apples

In a juicer, liquify all ingredients. Serve immediately.

Makes: 1 serving

Per serving: Calories: 287   Fat: less than 1 gram   Calcium: 97 mg

****
Studies show that people with high blood pressure
tend to take in 25% to 40%
less calcium than
people with
normal
blood pressure.

Calcium Cocktail III

1 cup fresh or frozen cranberries, thawed
2 apples
1 small orange or mandarin orange

In a juicer liquify all ingredients. Serve immediately.

Makes: 1 serving

Per serving: Calories: 271   Fat: 1.5 grams   Calcium: 78 mg

****
The best way to get your nutrients and antioxidants
is in raw fruits and vegetables.
The bonus? Low fat.

Calcium Cocktail IV

4 kale leaves
1/2 cup fresh broccoli
1/2 head of cabbage
2 carrots
1/4 cup parsley

In a juicer liquify all ingredients. Serve immediately.

Makes: 1 serving

Per serving: Calories: 246   Fat: 2.1 grams   Calcium: 536 mg

****
What can happen when you take too much calcium?
Although that's not too likely to happen, look
for these symptoms of too much calcium.
Constipation
Acid stomach
Nausea

Romantic No-Fuss Cappuccino

1 teaspoon instant espresso
1/4 cup boiling water
3/4 cup skim milk
dash of cinnamon

Dissolve espresso in the boiling water. Heat milk until very hot, but not boiling. Pour hot milk into blender and blend at high speed. Pour into coffee. Stir lightly. Top with a dash of cinnamon.

Makes: 1 serving

Per serving: Calories: 68   Fat: Trace   Calcium: 230 mg

****

How about a frozen yogurt sandwich?
Put a tablespoon of lowfat frozen yogurt between
two vanilla wafers or graham crackers and freeze.
Great!

The Resources Part

Sample Menus

An Italian Dinner

Pasta With White Clam Sauce	420 mg calcium
Sliced Tomato & Mozzarella Italian	107 mg calcium
Tiramisu	18 mg calcium
Total	**545 mg calcium**

American All The Way

Tomato Corn Chowder	106 mg calcium
Lite Macaroni & Cheese	341 mg calcium
Everyone's Favorite Apple Cobbler	210 mg calcium
Total	**657 mg calcium**

Buffet Bonanza

Easy Chicken Nuggets	69 mg calcium
Mini Salmon Pot Pie	150 mg calcium
Curried Shrimp	278 mg calcium
Stuffed Tomatoes	635 mg calcium
Cheese Squares	44 mg calcium
Fruit Trifle	95 mg calcium
Total	**1270 mg calcium**

Football Nite

Beef & Bean Chili	83 mg calcium
Spinach Pierogi Pizza	204 mg calcium
Pasta Salad Supreme	132 mg calcium
Southwestern Snack	50 mg calcium
No-Guilt Cheesecake	167 mg calcium
Total	**636 mg calcium**

Girls Night Out

Waldorf Plus Salad	64 mg calcium
Salmon Supper Croquettes	161 mg calcium
Tomato-Zucchini Yogurt Surprise	74 mg calcium
Strawberry Bavarian Dessert	89 mg calcium
Total	**388 mg calcium**

Your Personal Calcium Counter

<u>Calcium in mg</u>

Bread

Black, 1 slice	21.8
Cracked wheat, 1 slice	22.9
Egg, chalah, 1 slice	27.6
Garlic, 1 slice	23.8
Italian, 1 slice	16.0
Pita, 1 small	49.2
Pumpernickel, 1 slice	21.8
Raisin, 1 slice	27.3
Rye, 1 slice	19.5
Sourdough, 1 slice	22.5
White, 1 slice	31.2
Whole wheat, 1 slice	25.7
Breadsticks, 1	8.2
Bread stuffing, 1 cup	145.9

Biscuits

From mix, 1	19.8

Muffins

Bran, 1	116.4
Oatmeal, 1	69.5
English, 1	93.8

Bagels

Plain, 1	23.1
Pumpernickel, 1	13.5
Doughnuts	

Cake-type, 1	16.8
Cake-type, choc. covered, 1	23.1
Jelly, 1	21.1
Custard filled, 1	31

Cake

Angel food, 1 slice	41.7
Banana	22.7
Carrot, 1 slice	58.9
Cheesecake, 1 slice	69.3
Chiffon, with icing, 1 slice	69.5
Coffeecake, 1 slice	16.1
Fruitcake, 1 slice	97.9
Gingerbread, 1 slice	55.9
Jelly roll, 1 slice	14.7
Pound cake, 1 slice	55

Pies

Apple, 1 slice	10.8
Banana cream, 1 slice	85.4
Blueberry, 1 slice	38.7
Cherry, 1 slice	12.8
Coconut cream, 1 slice	34.1
Custard, 1 slice	120.9
Lemon meringue, 1 slice	19.7
Mince, 1 slice	38.5
Peach, 1 slice	11.3

Beverages

Apple drink, 1 cup	17.5
Cranberry juice cocktail, 1 cup	7.6
Grapefruit juice drink, 1 cup	8.7
Grape drink, 1 cup	2.5

Cereals

Bran, wheat, unprocessed, 1 cup	69
Cheerios®, 1 cup	48
Corn bran, 1 cup	33
Crispy Wheats & Raisins® 3/4 cup	47
Life®, 2/3 cup	99
Total®, 1 cup	250
Wheaties®, 1 cup	43

Cooked Cereals

Instant Cream of Wheat®, 1 cup, dry	251
Quick Cream of Wheat, 1 cup, dry	247
Instant oats, 1 pkg.	172

Cheese

All servings (except cottage cheese) are one ounce

Blue		149.6
Brick		162
Brie		52.2
Camembert		109.9
Cheddar		204.5
Colby		165
Cottage cheese, regular	(4 oz.)	67.8
Cottage cheese, lowfat	(4 oz.)	77.4
Edam		207.2
Feta		139.6
Monteray		211.6
Mozzarella, part skim		183.1
Parmesan, grated		335.5
Ricotta, part skim		337.3
Swiss		213
American processed		174

Fruit

Apricots, 3 raw	15
Avocado, 1	21
Sour cherries, 1 cup, red, frozen	20
Crabapples, raw, 1 cup slices	20
Black currants, 1/2 cup	62
Dried figs, 10	269
Figs, dried, stewed, 1/2 cup	79
Kiwi fruit, 1 raw	20
Lemon, 1 raw, with peel	66
Cantaloupe, 1/2 raw	28
Orange, 1 raw	52
Prunes, 10 pitted, dried	43
Raisins, seedless, 1 cup	71
Strawberries, raw, 1 cup	21
Watermelon, 1 slice	38

Legumes

Baked beans with tomato sauce, 1/2 cup	77.9
Baked pork and beans, 1/2 cup	80
Boston baked beans, 1/2 cup	71.9
Chickpeas, 1/2 cup	59.9
Pinto, 1/2 cup	39.9
Red kidney beans, 1/2 cup	34.6
White beans, 1/2 cup	45.1

Dairy Products

Cream, half and half, 1 Tbsp.	15.7
Cream, whipped topping, 1 Tbsp.	3
Sour cream, 1 Tbsp.	14
Milk, whole, 1 cup	290.4
Milk, lowfat, 1 cup	296.7
Milk, skim, 1 cup	316.3
Milk, lactaid, 1 cup	300

Buttermilk, 1 cup	285.2
Chocolate milk, 1 cup	280.2
Ice cream, 1 cup	175.7
Ice milk, 1 cup	176.1
Yogurt, plain, whole milk, 4 oz.	136.9
Yogurt, plain, lowfat, 4 oz.	207.1
Yogurt, fruit, lowfat, 4 oz.	172.3

Seafood

Clams, raw, 3 oz.	58.6
Gefilte fish, 1 cup	63.2
Lobster, steamed, 3 oz.	55.2
Mackerel, canned, 3 oz.	263.1
Oysters, raw, 3 oz.	79.9
Salmon, broiled, 3 oz.	132.9
Salmon, canned, 3 oz.	190.7
Sardines, canned in oil, 3 oz.	371.4
Shrimp, canned, 3 oz.	97.7

Vegetables

Beans, lima, green, 1/2 cup	27
Beans, snap, 1/2 cup	21
Beet greens, cooked, 1/2 cup	82
Broccoli, cooked, 1/2 cup	89
Cabbage, bok choy shredded, 1/2 cup	79
Chard, Swiss, chopped, 1/2 cup	51
Collards, raw, 1/2 cup	109
Kale, cooked, 1/2 cup	47
Okra, frozen, cooked, 1/2 cup	88
Spinach, cooked, 1/2 cup	122

Glossary

Additive	A substance added to foods such as coloring agents, flavoring agents, antioxidants, etc.
Aerobic	A physical reaction that requires oxygen to release energy.
Amino acids	Basic building blocks of protein.
Antacid	A medication that neutralizes stomach acid.
Ascorbic acid	Vitamin C, a water-soluble vitamin, one of the antioxidants and a vitamin that has been shown to help in the absorption of calcium.
Beta-carotene	A chemical compound that is changed to vitamin A in the body.
Bone	The part of the body that forms the skeleton. It is made of collagen and calcium phosphate.
Bone Density	The amount of bone mass.
Bone Mass	The actual amount of bone in your bones.
Bone Remodelling	The process in which your body constantly breaks down and rebuilds bone supplies.
Bone resorption	The breaking down and removal of bone tissue.
Calcitonin	A hormone made by the thyroid gland which may decrease the rate of bone loss.
Calcium	The most abundant mineral in your body; necessary for building strong bones and reducing the risk of colon cancer and high blood pressure.

Calorie	A unit that measures food energy.
Cardiovascular disease	A disease that affects the heart or the circulatory system.
Cholesterol

animal | A substance produced in the body that is necessary for many body functions. It also comes from eating products. |
Collagen	A protein that provides the basic structure of bones, cartilage and tissue.
Cortical Bone	The outside layer of bone.
Dietary Guidelines	National guidelines that recommend the amounts of various nutrients that should be taken by different age groups.
Dowager's Hump	Dorsal kyphosis, the hump on the back that is a sign of osteoporosis.
Enzymes	Protein substances produced by cells that cause certain biochemical reactions in the body.
Estrogen	A female sex hormone produced by the ovaries and which plays an important role in the maintenance of bone by helping calcium get absorbed from the intestines.
Fat soluble	Dissolvable in fat.
Femur	The longest bone in the body, going from the hip joint to the knee.
Fluoride	A chemical which is sometimes used to treat osteoporosis. It is also found in the water supply in many communities.

Fortification	When additional nutrients are added to milk, such as vitamin D, the milk is then called, fortified. Most milk in the U.S. is fortified.
Fracture	A break or crack in a bone.
HDL	High-density lipoprotein is a fat/protein that carries fat and cholesterol through the body.
High blood pressure	The medical term is hypertension.
Homogenization	This is the process by which milkfat is broken up and dispersed throughout so that the fat doesn't rise to the top. The result is a smooth, creamy texture.
Hormones	Chemicals produced in glands that regulate certain body functions and activities.
Hypertension	High blood pressure.
Hysterectomy	Surgical removal of the uterus.
Lactose	A sugar in milk that has to be broken down by an enzyme before it can be readily absorbed.
LDL	Low-density lipoprotein is a fat/protein that carries fat and cholesterol through the body. It is sticky and can adhere to the inner walls of blood vessels, blocking them.
Low calorie	Containing 40 calories or less per serving.
Low sodium	Containing 35 mg or less of sodium per serving.
Magnesium	Mineral necessary for the formation of bones.
Menopause	The period when a woman stops menstruating. It usually occurs between the ages of 45 and 55.

Nutrient	Chemical substance obtained from food that is essential for bodily functions.
Obesity	Weighing more than 20% over your desirable weight.
Oil	Fat in liquid form.
Osteoblast	A cell that makes new bone.
Osteoclast	A cell that reabsorbs and removes old bone.
Osteoporosis	A disease, the fourth leading killer of women, that results in bone loss which leads to fractures.
Ovary	A female reproductive gland which produces the female sex hormone and the ovum.
Overweight	Weighing between 10% and 20% more than desirable weight.
Pasteurization	The process of heating milk to destroy bacteria and to extend its shelf life.
Potassium	Vital nutrient needed to regulate body functions.
RDA	Recommended Dietary Allowance is an estimate established by the Food and Nutrition Board of the National Research Council of the amounts of nutrients needed to prevent deficiencies in healthy persons.
Rickets	A disease in youngsters caused by a vitamin D deficiency.
Saturated fat	Refers to the amount of hydrogen in fat.
Trabecular Bone	The inside of bone.

UHT	This stands for ultra high temperature milk and means it is heated to extra high temperatures and packaged in sterilized containers. This process allows milk to be stored, unopened, without refridgeration for up to three months. It should be refrigerated if it is opened.
Ultra-pasteurization	The process of heating milk to extra high temperatures to extend its shelf life.
Unsaturated fat	More liquid at room temperature than saturated fat.
USDA	United States Department of Agriculture.
Vertebra	One of the small bones in the spine.
Vitamin D	A nutrient that helps the body absorb calcium. It is added to most milk and can also be produced in the body by spending as little as 15 minutes a day in the sunshine.
Water soluble	Dissolvable in water.
Weight-bearing exercise	Exercise that causes mechanical stress on the bones and joints.

Resources

American Dietetic Association
216 West Jackson Blvd.
Chicago, IL 60606
312-899-4822

American College of Obstetricians and Gynecologists
Resource Center
409 12th St., SW
Washington, DC 20024

American Academy for the Advancement of Medicine
23121 Verdugo Drive, Suite 204
Laguana Hills, CA 92653

American Cancer Society
Atlanta, GA 30329

American Dental Association
Department of Public Information and Education
211 East Chicago Ave.
Chicago, IL 60611
312-440-2500

American Heart Association
7320 Greenville Avenue
Dallas, TX 75231

American Association of Retired Persons (AARP)
Health Advocacy Services Program Department
601 E. St., NW
Washington, DC 20049
202-434-2640

American Diabetes Association
      1660 Duke St.
      Alexandria, VA 22314
      1-800-232-3472

American Academy of Environmental Medicine
      P.O. Box 16106
      Denver, CO 80216
      303-622-9755

Calcium Information Center
      New York Hospital-Cornell Medical Center
      New York, NY 10021
      212-746-1618

Cancer Information Service
      National Cancer Institute
      9000 Rockville Pike
      Building 31, Room 10A24
      Bethesda, MD 20892

Food and Drug Administration
      5600 Fishers Lane
      Rockville, MD 20857
      301-443-3170

HERS Foundation
      Hysterectomy Educational Resources and Services
      422 Bryn Mawr Ave.
      Bala Cynwyd, PA 19004

International Academy of Nutrition and Preventive Medicine
      P.O. Box 5832
      Lincoln, NE 68505
      402-467-2716

National Osteoporosis Foundation
    1150 17th St., NW
    Suite 500
    Washington, DC 20036

National Health Information Center
    Box 1133
    Washington, DC 20036
    301-565-4167

National Women's Health Network
    224 7th Street, S.E.
    Washington, DC 20003
    202-543-9222

National Institute on Aging (NIA)
    Information Center
    P.O. Box 8057
    Gaithersburg, MD 20898

National Institutes of Health
    Federal Building, Room 6C12
    Bethesda, MD 20892

National Council on the Aging (NCOA)
    600 Maryland Avenue S.W.
    West Wing 100
    Washington, DC 20024

North American Menopause Society
    c/o Department of OB/GYN
    University Hospitals of Cleveland
    2074 Abington Rd.
    Cleveland, OH 44106

Osteoporosis Society of Canada
    P.O. Box 280, Station Q
    Toronto, Ontario M4T 2M1

Calcium-Rich Product List

Here are some products I found on the shelves of my own supermarket. They are a good source of calcium and it would make sense to add these to your own shopping list. Also, become a calcium detective. Read the labels and if you have a choice between a low-calcium product and an enriched-calcium product, pick the calcium. Your bones and your family will thank you.

Look For The Word "Calcium" On The Label

Lactaid® 100 Nonfat Calcium Fortified Milk
Whole Grain Total®
Total® Corn Flakes
Wonder Bread®
Wonder Bread® Lite
Sunny Delight®
Hawaiian Punch®
Tropicana Orange Juice®
Minute Maid Orange Juice®
Merita Bread®
Carnation Instant Breakfast®

Per Serving Nutritional Analysis of Cookbook Recipes

Yogurt Bran Muffins

	Per Serving Nutritional Analysis
Calories	**138**
Total Fat (g)	4.6
% Calories from Fat	**26.6**
Cholesterol (mg)	18
Carbohydrate (g)	24.4
Dietary Fiber (g)	5.2
Protein (g)	4.1
Sodium (mg)	14
Potassium (mg)	184
Calcium (mg)	**32**
Iron (mg)	1.5
Zinc (mg)	1.1

Pineapple Carrot Raisin Muffins

	Per Serving Nutritional Analysis
Calories	**175**
Total Fat (g)	5.1
% Calories from Fat	**23.5**
Cholesterol (mg)	0
Carbohydrate (g)	32.4
Dietary Fiber (g)	5.6
Protein (g)	4.7
Sodium (mg)	226
Potassium (mg)	296
Calcium (mg)	**108**
Iron (mg)	2.8
Zinc (mg)	1.8

Classic Bran Muffins

Per Serving Nutritional Analysis

Calories **178**

Total Fat (g) 6.2
% Calories from Fat **28.4**

Cholesterol (mg) 21.0
Carbohydrate (g) 30.4
Dietary Fiber (g) 5.1
Protein (g) 4.8
Sodium (mg) 271
Potassium (mg) 235
Calcium (mg) **131**
Iron (mg) 3.1
Zinc (mg) 2.1

Classic Lowfat Bran Muffins

Per Serving Nutritional Analysis

Calories **106**

Total Fat (g) 0.5
% Calories from Fat **3.4**

Cholesterol (mg) 1
Carbohydrate (g) 24.3
Dietary Fiber (g) 5.1
Protein (g) 4.9
Sodium (mg) 318
Potassium (mg) 242
Calcium (mg) **130**
Iron (mg) 3.0
Zinc (mg) 2.1

Cheddar Cheese Omelet

Per Serving Nutritional Analysis

Calories	**277**
Total Fat (g)	22.6
% Calories from Fat	**74**
Cholesterol (mg)	348
Carbohydrate (g)	1.3
Dietary Fiber (g)	0
Protein (g)	16.5
Sodium (mg)	338
Potassium (mg)	122
Calcium (mg)	**244**
Iron (mg)	1.3
Zinc (mg)	1.7

Cheese & Vegetable Frittata

Per Serving Nutritional Analysis

Calories	**303**
Total Fat (g)	20.8
% Calories from Fat	**61.9**
Cholesterol (mg)	441
Carbohydrate (g)	6.6
Dietary Fiber (g)	0.9
Protein (g)	22.1
Sodium (mg)	411
Potassium (mg)	345
Calcium (mg)	**314**
Iron (mg)	1.9
Zinc (mg)	2.2

Zesty Cheese Muffins

Per Serving Nutritional Analysis

Calories	**43**
Total Fat (g)	1.1
% Calories from Fat	**23.7**
Cholesterol (mg)	7
Carbohydrate (g)	6.1
Dietary Fiber (g)	0
Protein (g)	1.6
Sodium (mg)	59
Potassium (mg)	24
Calcium (mg)	**56**
Iron (mg)	0.4
Zinc (mg)	0.2

Orange Fig Muffins

Per Serving Nutritional Analysis

Calories	**197**
Total Fat (g)	5.6
% Calories from Fat	**23.2**
Cholesterol (mg)	18
Carbohydrate (g)	37.3
Dietary Fiber (g)	6.4
Protein (g)	4.6
Sodium (mg)	184
Potassium (mg)	390
Calcium (mg)	**118**
Iron (mg)	3.5
Zinc (mg)	2.1

Lowfat Orange Fig Muffins

Per Serving Nutritional Analysis

Calories	**164**
Total Fat (g)	2.9
% Calories from Fat	**14.3**
Cholesterol (mg)	0
Carbohydrate (g)	34.9
Dietary Fiber (g)	6.3
Protein (g)	4.7
Sodium (mg)	188
Potassium (mg)	390
Calcium (mg)	**116**
Iron (mg)	3.4
Zinc (mg)	2.0

Shrimp Creole Eggs

Per Serving Nutritional Analysis

Calories	**238**
Total Fat (g)	15.4
% Calories from Fat	**58.8**
Cholesterol (mg)	380
Carbohydrate (g)	2.6
Dietary Fiber (g)	0.4
Protein (g)	21.6
Sodium (mg)	343
Potassium (mg)	236
Calcium (mg)	**190**
Iron (mg)	2.4
Zinc (mg)	2.0

Leftover Chinese Rice Muffins

	Per Serving Nutritional Analysis
Calories	**59**
Total Fat (g)	0.4
% Calories from Fat	**6.3**
Cholesterol (mg)	0
Carbohydrate (g)	10.8
Dietary Fiber (g)	0.1
Protein (g)	2.7
Sodium (mg)	57
Potassium (mg)	62
Calcium (mg)	**42**
Iron (mg)	0.8
Zinc (mg)	0.3

Homestyle Instant Breakfast I

	Per Serving Nutritional Analysis
Calories	**177**
Total Fat (g)	0.9
% Calories from Fat	**4.3**
Cholesterol (mg)	2
Carbohydrate (g)	40.9
Dietary Fiber (g)	4.4
Protein (g)	5.9
Sodium (mg)	65
Potassium (mg)	702
Calcium (mg)	**161**
Iron (mg)	0.8
Zinc (mg)	1.0

Homestyle Instant Breakfast II

	Per Serving Nutritional Analysis
Calories	**230**
Total Fat (g)	1.0
% Calories from Fat	**3.9**
Cholesterol (mg)	2
Carbohydrate (g)	50.2
Dietary Fiber (g)	2.8
Protein (g)	8.5
Sodium (mg)	90
Potassium (mg)	740
Calcium (mg)	**244**
Iron (mg)	0.8
Zinc (mg)	1.7

Mixed Fruit Muesli

	Per Serving Nutritional Analysis
Calories	**216**
Total Fat (g)	1.7
% Calories from Fat	**6.8**
Cholesterol (mg)	2
Carbohydrate (g)	42.0
Dietary Fiber (g)	3.6
Protein (g)	10.4
Sodium (mg)	91
Potassium (mg)	530
Calcium (mg)	**247**
Iron (mg)	1.4
Zinc (mg)	1.8

A Taste Of The Tropics

Per Serving Nutritional Analysis

Calories	**89**
Total Fat (g)	0.7
% Calories from Fat	**7.0**
Cholesterol (mg)	1
Carbohydrate (g)	17.3
Dietary Fiber (g)	1.7
Protein (g)	4.6
Sodium (mg)	46
Potassium (mg)	351
Calcium (mg)	**126**
Iron (mg)	0.5
Zinc (mg)	1.0

Blueberry Lemon Muffins

Per Serving Nutritional Analysis

Calories	**165**
Total Fat (g)	6.8
% Calories from Fat	**37.1**
Cholesterol (mg)	18
Carbohydrate (g)	22.4
Dietary Fiber (g)	0.3
Protein (g)	3.6
Sodium (mg)	67
Potassium (mg)	82
Calcium (mg)	**89**
Iron (mg)	1.0
Zinc (mg)	0.4

Lowfat Blueberry Lemon Muffins

Per Serving Nutritional Analysis

Calories	**96**
Total Fat (g)	0.3
% Calories from Fat	**2.6**
Cholesterol (mg)	1
Carbohydrate (g)	17.7
Dietary Fiber (g)	0.3
Protein (g)	4.7
Sodium (mg)	132
Potassium (mg)	67
Calcium (mg)	**51**
Iron (mg)	0.9
Zinc (mg)	0.1

Creamy Cheese Breakfast Sandwich

Per Serving Nutritional Analysis

Calories	**272**
Total Fat (g)	4.4
% Calories from Fat	**14**
Cholesterol (mg)	3
Carbohydrate (g)	43.4
Dietary Fiber (g)	6.7
Protein (g)	17.7
Sodium (mg)	749
Potassium (mg)	338
Calcium (mg)	**112**
Iron (mg)	3.0
Zinc (mg)	2.0

Oatmeal Plus

Per Serving Nutritional Analysis

Calories | **190**

Total Fat (g)	3.0
% Calories from Fat	**14.4**

Cholesterol (mg)	2
Carbohydrate (g)	27.5
Dietary Fiber (g)	4.4
Protein (g)	13.3
Sodium (mg)	646
Potassium (mg)	192
Calcium (mg)	**272**
Iron (mg)	9.1
Zinc (mg)	1.5

Simply Surprising Yogurt Omelet

Per Serving Nutritional Information

Calories | **332**

Total Fat (g)	12.5
% Calories from Fat	**35.4**

Cholesterol (mg)	4
Carbohydrate (g)	4.6
Dietary Fiber (g)	0
Protein (g)	46.8
Sodium (mg)	688
Potassium (mg)	1315
Calcium (mg)	**256**
Iron (mg)	7.9
Zinc (mg)	5.2

Elegant Eggs

Per Serving Nutritional Analysis

Calories	**194**
Total Fat (g)	6.6
% Calories from Fat	**31.1**
Cholesterol (mg)	220
Carbohydrate (g)	18.3
Dietary Fiber (g)	0
Protein (g)	14.4
Sodium (mg)	422
Potassium (mg)	289
Calcium (mg)	**189**
Iron (mg)	1.6
Zinc (mg)	1.5

Cheesy Cinnamon Toast

Per Serving Nutritional Analysis

Calories	**384**
Total Fat (g)	3.6
% Calories from Fat	**8.0**
Cholesterol (mg)	1
Carbohydrate (g)	48.4
Dietary Fiber (g)	6.5
Protein (g)	45.3
Sodium (mg)	499
Potassium (mg)	337
Calcium (mg)	**389**
Iron (mg)	3.8
Zinc (mg)	3.6

Buttermilk Pancakes

Per Serving Nutritional Analysis

Calories	**160**
Total Fat (g)	2.4
% Calories from Fat	**13.9**
Cholesterol (mg)	3
Carbohydrate (g)	22.7
Dietary Fiber (g)	0
Protein (g)	10.2
Sodium (mg)	372
Potassium (mg)	267
Calcium (mg)	**138**
Iron (mg)	2.3
Zinc (mg)	1.0

Country Breakfast For A Crowd

Per Serving Nutritional Analysis

Calories	**173**
Total Fat (g)	4.4
% Calories from Fat	**25.0**
Cholesterol (mg)	4
Carbohydrate (g)	17.8
Dietary Fiber (g)	1.4
Protein (g)	12.1
Sodium (mg)	259
Potassium (mg)	653
Calcium (mg)	**176**
Iron (mg)	1.8
Zinc (mg)	1.5

Chinese Breakfast In A Hurry

Per Serving Nutritional Analysis

Calories	**691**
Total Fat (g)	1.2
% Calories from Fat	**1.6**
Cholesterol (mg)	1
Carbohydrate (g)	157.7
Dietary Fiber (g)	3.0
Protein (g)	12.7
Sodium (mg)	56
Potassium (mg)	630
Calcium (mg)	**179**
Iron (mg)	6.6
Zinc (mg)	3.4

"Nuked" Eggs

Per Serving Nutritional Analysis

Calories	**230**
Total Fat (g)	8.6
% Calories from Fat	**35.5**
Cholesterol (mg)	3
Carbohydrate (g)	3.6
Dietary Fiber (g)	0.6
Protein (g)	31.6
Sodium (mg)	473
Potassium (mg)	902
Calcium (mg)	**176**
Iron (mg)	5.5
Zinc (mg)	3.5

Skinny Spicy Muffins

Per Serving Nutritional Analysis

Calories	**103**
Total Fat (g)	0.3
% Calories from Fat	**2.8**
Cholesterol (mg)	2
Carbohydrate (g)	20.3
Dietary Fiber (g)	0.2
Protein (g)	3.2
Sodium (mg)	101
Potassium (mg)	63
Calcium (mg)	**32**
Iron (mg)	1.1
Zinc (mg)	0.2

Apple Cinnamon Oatmeal

Per Serving Nutritional Analysis

Calories	**187**
Total Fat (g)	2.2
% Calories from Fat	**10.2**
Cholesterol (mg)	2
Carbohydrate (g)	34.6
Dietary Fiber (g)	4.7
Protein (g)	8.6
Sodium (mg)	64
Potassium (mg)	377
Calcium (mg)	**170**
Iron (mg)	1.3
Zinc (mg)	1.4

Slim Crêpes

Per Serving Nutritional Analysis

Calories	**20**
Total Fat (g)	0
% Calories from Fat	**1.9**
Cholesterol (mg)	1
Carbohydrate (g)	1.9
Dietary Fiber (g)	0
Protein (g)	3.0
Sodium (mg)	45
Potassium (mg)	83
Calcium (mg)	**43**
Iron (mg)	0
Zinc (mg)	0.1

Basic Omelet

Per Serving Nutritional Analysis

Calories	**391**
Total Fat (g)	12.9
% Calories from Fat	**30.8**
Cholesterol (mg)	8
Carbohydrate (g)	11
Dietary Fiber (g)	0
Protein (g)	54.1
Sodium (mg)	861
Potassium (mg)	1536
Calcium (mg)	**405**
Iron (mg)	8.0
Zinc (mg)	5.6

Yogurt Cheese

Per Serving Nutritional Analysis

Calories	**16**
Total Fat (g)	0.1
% Calories from Fat	**2.9**
Cholesterol (mg)	1
Carbohydrate (g)	2.2
Dietary Fiber (g)	0
Protein (g)	1.6
Sodium (mg)	22
Potassium (mg)	72
Calcium (mg)	**56**
Iron (mg)	0
Zinc (mg)	0.3

Party Canapé Spread

Per Serving Nutritional Analysis

Calories	**88**
Total Fat (g)	2.4
% Calories from Fat	**23.8**
Cholesterol (mg)	5
Carbohydrate (g)	11.2
Dietary Fiber (g)	1.5
Protein (g)	6.0
Sodium (mg)	236
Potassium (mg)	102
Calcium (mg)	**152**
Iron (mg)	0.8
Zinc (mg)	0.9

Cheese Squares

Per Serving Nutritional Analysis

Calories	**45**
Total Fat (g)	0.7
% Calories from Fat	**19.1**
Cholesterol (mg)	3
Carbohydrate (g)	4.8
Dietary Fiber (g)	0.2
Protein (g)	2.1
Sodium (mg)	167
Potassium (mg)	21
Calcium (mg)	**44**
Iron (mg)	0.3
Zinc (mg)	0.2

Splendid Spinach Dip

Per Serving Nutritional Analysis

Calories	**21**
Total Fat (g)	0.6
% Calories from Fat	**23.7**
Cholesterol (mg)	0
Carbohydrate (g)	2.6
Dietary Fiber (g)	0.4
Protein (g)	1.5
Sodium (mg)	75
Potassium (mg)	98
Calcium (mg)	**53**
Iron (mg)	0.3
Zinc (mg)	0.3

Chunky Chili Dip

Per Serving Nutritional Analysis

Calories	**32**
Total Fat (g)	2.4
% Calories from Fat	**68.6**
Cholesterol (mg)	1
Carbohydrate (g)	1.8
Dietary Fiber (g)	0.1
Protein (g)	0.7
Sodium (mg)	60
Potassium (mg)	54
Calcium (mg)	**25**
Iron (mg)	0.1
Zinc (mg	0.1

Cheese Lovers' Curry Dip

Per Serving Nutritional Analysis

Calories	**8**
Total Fat (g)	0.1
% Calories from Fat	**12.8**
Cholesterol (mg)	0
Carbohydrate (g)	0.4
Dietary Fiber (g)	0
Protein (g)	1.2
Sodium (mg)	39
Potassium (mg)	12
Calcium (mg)	**7**
Iron (mg)	0
Zinc (mg)	0

Yogurt Lovers' Curry Dip

Per Serving Nutritional Analysis

Calories	**16**
Total Fat (g)	1.0
% Calories from Fat	**57.6**
Cholesterol (mg)	0
Carbohydrate (g)	1.1
Dietary Fiber (g)	0.1
Protein (g)	0.6
Sodium (mg)	28
Potassium (mg)	30
Calcium (mg)	**20**
Iron (mg)	0.1
Zinc (mg)	0.1

Cucumber Yogurt Dip

Per Serving Nutritional Analysis

Calories	**10**
Total Fat (g)	0
% Calories from Fat	**4.2**
Cholesterol (mg)	0
Carbohydrate (g)	1.6
Dietary Fiber (g)	0.2
Protein (g)	0.9
Sodium (mg)	11
Potassium (mg)	63
Calcium (mg)	**31**
Iron (mg)	0.1
Zinc (mg)	0.2

Artichoke Dip

Per Serving Nutritional Analysis

Calories **33**

Total Fat (g)	2.0
% Calories from Fat	**53.7**

Cholesterol (mg)	2
Carbohydrate (g)	2.2
Dietary Fiber (g)	0.8
Protein (g)	1.7
Sodium (mg)	90
Potassium (mg)	64
Calcium (mg)	**48**
Iron (mg)	0.2
Zinc (mg)	0.2

South-of-the-Border Bean Dip

Per Serving Nutritional Analysis

Calories **84**

Total Fat (g)	0.4
% Calories from Fat	**4.4**

Cholesterol (mg)	0
Carbohydrate (g)	15
Dietary Fiber (g)	5.8
Protein (g)	5.6
Sodium (mg)	22
Potassium (mg)	346
Calcium (mg)	**39**
Iron (mg)	1.9
Zinc (mg)	0.7

Antipasto

Per Serving Nutritional Analysis

Calories	**374**
Total Fat (g)	25.8
% Calories from Fat	**61**
Cholesterol (mg)	77
Carbohydrate (g)	8.1
Dietary Fiber (g)	1.5
Protein (g)	29.1
Sodium (mg)	624
Potassium (mg)	490
Calcium (mg)	**645**
Iron (mg)	4.1
Zinc (mg)	3.0

Zippy Cheese

Per Serving Nutritional Analysis

Calories	**8**
Total Fat (g)	0.1
% Calories from Fat	**11.8**
Cholesterol (mg)	0
Carbohydrate (g)	0.5
Dietary Fiber (g)	0
Protein (g)	1.3
Sodium (mg)	40
Potassium (mg)	19
Calcium (mg)	**12**
Iron (mg)	0.2
Zinc (mg)	0.1

Veggie Bites

	Per Serving Nutritional Analysis
Calories	**164**
Total Fat (g)	8.1
% Calories from Fat	**44.4**
Cholesterol (mg)	5
Carbohydrate (g)	10.4
Dietary Fiber (g)	1.5
Protein (g)	12.4
Sodium (mg)	518
Potassium (mg)	444
Calcium (mg)	**148**
Iron (mg)	2.0
Zinc (mg)	1.3

Sliced Tomato & Mozzarella Italian

	Per Serving Nutritional Analysis
Calories	**53**
Total Fat (g)	2.6
% Calories from Fat	**43.4**
Cholesterol (mg)	8
Carbohydrate (g)	3.3
Dietary Fiber (g)	0.7
Protein (g)	4.4
Sodium (mg)	80
Potassium (mg)	150
Calcium (mg)	**107**
Iron (mg)	0.3
Zinc (mg)	0.5

Savory Marinated Veggies

Per Serving Nutritional Analysis

Calories	**181**
Total Fat (g)	5.8
% Calories from Fat	**24.6**
Cholesterol (mg)	2
Carbohydrate (g)	31.4
Dietary Fiber (g)	10.1
Protein (g)	8.4
Sodium (mg)	413
Potassium (mg)	1563
Calcium (mg)	**95**
Iron (mg)	3.3
Zinc (mg)	1.2

Mushroom Blues

Per Serving Nutritional Analysis

Calories	**43**
Total Fat (g)	2.9
% Calories from Fat	**58.2**
Cholesterol (mg)	2
Carbohydrate (g)	3.3
Dietary Fiber (g)	0.4
Protein (g)	1.3
Sodium (mg)	82
Potassium (mg)	86
Calcium (mg)	**18**
Iron (mg)	0.4
Zinc (mg)	0.2

Tomato Soup

Per Serving Nutritional Analysis

Calories	**55**
Total Fat (g)	0.7
% Calories from Fat	**11.4**
Cholesterol (mg)	1
Carbohydrate (g)	9.7
Dietary Fiber (g)	1.2
Protein (g)	3.2
Sodium (mg)	257
Potassium (mg)	300
Calcium (mg)	**94**
Iron (mg)	0.8
Zinc (mg)	0.4

Cheese Soup

Per Serving Nutritional Analysis

Calories	**75**
Total Fat (g)	1.7
% Calories from Fat	**23.6**
Cholesterol (mg)	4
Carbohydrate (g)	5.4
Dietary Fiber (g)	0.1
Protein (g)	6.9
Sodium (mg)	574
Potassium (mg)	221
Calcium (mg)	**148**
Iron (mg)	0.4
Zinc (mg)	0.7

Creamy Potato Soup

	Per Serving Nutritional Analysis
Calories	**100**
Total Fat (g)	3.2
% Calories from Fat	**26.0**
Cholesterol (mg)	2
Carbohydrate (g)	13.1
Dietary Fiber (g)	1.2
Protein (g)	7.6
Sodium (mg)	310
Potassium (mg)	530
Calcium (mg)	**189**
Iron (mg)	4.3
Zinc (mg)	0.9

Satin Salmon Chowder

	Per Serving Nutritional Analysis
Calories	**269**
Total Fat (g)	6.8
% Calories from Fat	**21.6**
Cholesterol (mg)	31
Carbohydrate (g)	32.3
Dietary Fiber (g)	2.2
Protein (g)	23.7
Sodium (mg)	654
Potassium (mg)	786
Calcium (mg)	**363**
Iron (mg)	1.7
Zinc (mg)	2.2

Corny Chowder

Per Serving Nutritional Analysis

Calories **114**

Total Fat (g) 0.8
% Calories from Fat **6.2**

Cholesterol (mg) 4
Carbohydrate (g) 20.4
Dietary Fiber (g) 1.7
Protein (g) 6.3
Sodium (mg) 230
Potassium (mg) 357
Calcium (mg) **161**
Iron (mg) 0.5
Zinc (mg) 0.8

Cream of Asparagus Soup

Per Serving Nutritional Analysis

Calories **41**

Total Fat (g) 0.5
% Calories from Fat **8.6**

Cholesterol (mg) 1
Carbohydrate (g) 5.8
Dietary Fiber (g) 0
Protein (g) 5.6
Sodium (mg) 324
Potassium (mg) 185
Calcium (mg) **99**
Iron (mg) 0.4
Zinc (mg) 0.6

Tomato Corn Chowder

Per Serving Nutritional Analysis

Calories	**88**
Total Fat (g)	1.0
% Calories from Fat	**9.2**
Cholesterol (mg)	1
Carbohydrate (g)	17.2
Dietary Fiber (g)	0.7
Protein (g)	4.2
Sodium (mg)	454
Potassium (mg)	280
Calcium (mg)	**106**
Iron (mg)	0.8
Zinc (mg)	0.6

Cream of Broccoli Soup

Per Serving Nutritional Analysis

Calories	**68**
Total Fat (g)	0.3
% Calories from Fat	**3.4**
Cholesterol (mg)	1
Carbohydrate (g)	12.1
Dietary Fiber (g)	1.7
Protein (g)	7.9
Sodium (mg)	312
Potassium (mg)	340
Calcium (mg)	**112**
Iron (mg)	1.0
Zinc (mg)	0.7

Russian Summer Beet Soup

	Per Serving Nutritional Analysis
Calories	**118**
Total Fat (g)	2.8
% Calories from Fat	**20.8**
Cholesterol (mg)	58
Carbohydrate (g)	14.1
Dietary Fiber (g)	1.8
Protein (g)	9.9
Sodium (mg)	263
Potassium (mg)	565
Calcium (mg)	**252**
Iron (mg)	4.3
Zinc (mg)	1.2

No-Dairy Clam Chowder

	Per Serving Nutritional Analysis
Calories	**310**
Total Fat (g)	2.1
% Calories from Fat	**5.5**
Cholesterol (mg)	62
Carbohydrate (g)	39.3
Dietary Fiber (g)	2.7
Protein (g)	40.8
Sodium (mg)	631
Potassium (mg)	1640
Calcium (mg)	**112**
Iron (mg)	28.1
Zinc (mg)	3.7

Mock Cream-of-Chicken Soup

	Per Serving Nutritional Analysis
Calories	**30**
Total Fat (g)	0.1
% Calories from Fat	**3.7**
Cholesterol (mg)	0
Carbohydrate (g)	6.6
Dietary Fiber (g)	0.8
Protein (g)	1.0
Sodium (mg)	394
Potassium (mg)	205
Calcium (mg)	**10**
Iron (mg)	0.3
Zinc (mg)	0.1

Dilly Vichissoise

	Per Serving Nutritional Analysis
Calories	**139**
Total Fat (g)	0.5
% Calories from Fat	**3.1**
Cholesterol (mg)	2
Carbohydrate (g)	29.1
Dietary Fiber (g)	2.7
Protein (g)	4.9
Sodium (mg)	114
Potassium (mg)	712
Calcium (mg)	**133**
Iron (mg)	2.7
Zinc	0.7

Chilled Casbah Soup

	Per Serving Nutritional Analysis
Calories	**82**
Total Fat (g)	0.5
% Calories from Fat	**4.9**
Cholesterol (mg)	1
Carbohydrate (g)	16.6
Dietary Fiber (g)	1.1
Protein (g)	4.5
Sodium (mg)	56
Potassium (mg)	573
Calcium (mg)	**129**
Iron (mg)	0.3
Zinc (mg)	0.8

Chilly Cucumber "Soop"

	Per Serving Nutritional Analysis
Calories	**58**
Total Fat (g)	0.2
% Calories from Fat	**2.8**
Cholesterol (mg)	1
Carbohydrate (g)	9.9
Dietary Fiber (g)	0.3
Protein (g)	4.6
Sodium (mg)	60
Potassium (mg)	247
Calcium (mg)	**158**
Iron (mg)	0.2
Zinc (mg)	0.8

Turkey Vegetable Soup

	Per Serving Nutritional Analysis
Calories	**187**
Total Fat (g)	5.3
% Calories from Fat	**24.8**
Cholesterol (mg)	45
Carbohydrate (g)	22.2
Dietary Fiber (g)	4.8
Protein (g)	13.7
Sodium (mg)	314
Potassium (mg)	802
Calcium (mg)	**119**
Iron (mg)	5.4
Zinc (mg)	2.0

Hearty Minestrone

	Per Serving Nutritional Analysis
Calories	**114**
Total Fat (g)	2.2
% Calories from Fat	**16**
Cholesterol (mg)	0
Carbohydrate (g)	20.5
Dietary Fiber (g)	3.6
Protein (g)	6.0
Sodium (mg)	248
Potassium (mg)	670
Calcium (mg)	**95**
Iron (mg)	2.8
Zinc (mg)	0.8

Bouillabaisse

Per Serving Nutritional Analysis

Calories **223**

Total Fat (g) 2.3
% Calories from Fat **10.2**

Cholesterol (mg) 140
Carbohydrate (g) 10.2
Dietary Fiber (g) 1.6
Protein (g) 34.5
Sodium (mg) 517
Potassium (mg) 767
Calcium (mg) **141**
Iron (mg) 6.1
Zinc (mg) 3.7

Stuffed Tomatoes

Per Serving Nutritional Analysis

Calories **335**

Total Fat (g) 21.5
% Calories from Fat **56.1**

Cholesterol (mg) 75
Carbohydrate (g) 13.6
Dietary Fiber (g) 3.3
Protein (g) 24.3
Sodium (mg) 681
Potassium (mg) 710
Calcium (mg) **635**
Iron (mg) 6.8
Zinc (mg) 3.1

Broccoli Lovers' Salad

Per Serving Nutritional Analysis

Calories	**90**
Total Fat (g)	3.1
% Calories from Fat	**28.8**
Cholesterol (mg)	57
Carbohydrate (g)	10.7
Dietary Fiber (g)	2.0
Protein (g)	6.5
Sodium (mg)	327
Potassium (mg)	281
Calcium (mg)	**139**
Iron (mg)	0.9
Zinc (mg)	0.8

Traditional Greek Salad

Per Serving Nutritional Analysis

Calories	**235**
Total Fat (g)	15.9
% Calories from Fat	**54.9**
Cholesterol (mg)	17
Carbohydrate (g)	21.7
Dietary Fiber (g)	6.7
Protein (g)	7.6
Sodium (mg)	358
Potassium (mg)	886
Calcium (mg)	**441**
Iron (mg)	9.8
Zinc (mg)	1.9

Tasty Tofu Salad

Per Serving Nutritional Analysis

Calories	**147**
Total Fat (g)	11.4
% Calories from Fat	**64.8**
Cholesterol (mg)	0
Carbohydrate (g)	8.6
Dietary Fiber (g)	2.3
Protein (g)	5.4
Sodium (mg)	127
Potassium (mg)	483
Calcium (mg)	**134**
Iron (mg)	7.6
Zinc (mg)	0.8

Waldorf Plus Salad

Per Serving Nutritional Analysis

Calories	**211**
Total Fat (g)	8.7
% Calories from Fat	**33.9**
Cholesterol (mg)	0
Carbohydrate (g)	33.6
Dietary Fiber (g)	6.2
Protein (g)	4.4
Sodium (mg)	63
Potassium (mg)	574
Calcium (mg)	**64**
Iron (mg)	1.2
Zinc (mg)	0.8

Yogurty Slaw

	Per Serving Nutritional Analysis
Calories	**59**
Total Fat (g)	2.7
% Calories from Fat	**39.1**
Cholesterol (mg)	0
Carbohydrate (g)	7.9
Dietary Fiber (g)	1.4
Protein (g)	1.5
Sodium (mg)	215
Potassium (mg)	249
Calcium (mg)	**56**
Iron (mg)	0.4
Zinc (mg)	0.3

Pasta Salad Supreme

	Per Serving Nutritional Analysis
Calories	**575**
Total Fat (g)	12.4
% Calories from Fat	**20.0**
Cholesterol (mg)	215
Carbohydrate (g)	87.9
Dietary Fiber (g)	2.7
Protein (g)	23.5
Sodium (mg)	240
Potassium (mg)	313
Calcium (mg)	**132**
Iron (mg)	5.2
Zinc (mg)	2.3

Hearty Chicken Salad

	Per Serving Nutritional Analysis
Calories	**172**
Total Fat (g)	5.8
% Calories from Fat	**31.1**
Cholesterol (mg)	60
Carbohydrate (g)	5.6
Dietary Fiber (g)	1.1
Protein (g)	23.3
Sodium (mg)	149
Potassium (mg)	358
Calcium (mg)	**59**
Iron (mg)	1.3
Zinc (mg)	1.2

Super Duper Spinach Salad

	Per Serving Nutritional Analysis
Calories	**291**
Total Fat (g)	11.5
% Calories from Fat	**33.6**
Cholesterol (mg)	33
Carbohydrate (g)	30.8
Dietary Fiber (g)	8.7
Protein (g)	20.5
Sodium (mg)	1153
Potassium (mg)	1871
Calcium (mg)	**646**
Iron (mg)	6.3
Zinc (mg)	3.8

Quicky Potato Salad

	Per Serving Nutritional Analysis
Calories	**133**
Total Fat (g)	0.2
% Calories from Fat	**1.5**
Cholesterol (mg)	1
Carbohydrate (g)	28
Dietary Fiber (g)	2.3
Protein (g)	5.5
Sodium (mg)	44
Potassium (mg)	859
Calcium (mg)	**103**
Iron (mg)	1.1
Zinc (mg)	1.0

Russian Potato Salad

	Per Serving Nutritional Analysis
Calories	**244**
Total Fat (g)	0.6
% Calories from Fat	**2.5**
Cholesterol (mg)	5
Carbohydrate (g)	48.1
Dietary Fiber (g)	4.5
Protein (g)	8.9
Sodium (mg)	450
Potassium (mg)	1534
Calcium (mg)	**149**
Iron (mg)	2.2
Zinc (mg)	1.8

Thousand Island Dressing

Per Serving Nutritional Analysis

Calories	**27**
Total Fat (g)	1.3
% Calories from Fat	**42.8**
Cholesterol (mg)	0
Carbohydrate (g)	2.8
Dietary Fiber (g)	0
Protein (g)	1.2
Sodium (mg)	66
Potassium (mg)	56
Calcium (mg)	**40**
Iron (mg)	0
Zinc (mg)	0.2

Tofu Dressing

Per Serving Nutritional Analysis

Calories	**119**
Total Fat (g)	11.7
% Calories from Fat	**85.0**
Cholesterol (mg)	0
Carbohydrate (g)	1.8
Dietary Fiber (g)	0.5
Protein (g)	2.8
Sodium (mg)	83
Potassium (mg)	59
Calcium (mg)	**36**
Iron (mg)	1.9
Zinc (mg)	0.3

Basic Buttermilk Dressing

	Per Serving Nutritional Analysis
Calories	**9**
Total Fat (g)	0.2
% Calories from Fat	**18.4**
Cholesterol (mg)	1
Carbohydrate	1.3
Dietary Fiber (g)	0.2
Protein (g)	0.7
Sodium (mg)	63
Potassium (mg)	41
Calcium (mg)	**25**
Iron (mg)	0.2
Zinc (mg)	0.1

Basic Yogurt Dressing

	Per Serving Nutritional Analysis
Calories	**71**
Total Fat (g)	0.2
% Calories from Fat	**2.5**
Cholesterol (mg)	2
Carbohydrate (g)	11.3
Dietary Fiber (g)	0.1
Protein (g)	6.6
Sodium (mg)	87
Potassium (mg)	327
Calcium (mg)	**228**
Iron (mg)	0.1
Zinc (mg)	1.1

Blue Cheese Dressing

Per Serving Nutritional Analysis

Calories **14**

Total Fat (g)	0.7
% Calories from Fat	**45.5**
Cholesterol (mg)	2
Carbohydrate (g)	0.8
Dietary Fiber (g)	0
Protein (g)	1.1
Sodium (mg)	40
Potassium (mg)	31
Calcium (mg)	**32**
Iron (mg)	0
Zinc (mg)	0.2

Parsley Herb Dressing

Per Serving Nutritional Analysis

Calories **16**

Total Fat (g)	0.2
% Calories from Fat	**13.1**
Cholesterol (mg)	1
Carbohydrate (g)	1.4
Dietary Fiber (g)	0.2
Protein (g)	2.2
Sodium (mg)	70
Potassium (mg)	84
Calcium (mg)	**36**
Iron (mg)	1.9
Zinc (mg)	0.1

The "Other" Hollandaise

	Per Serving Nutritional Analysis
Calories	**19**
Total Fat (g)	1.0
% Calories from Fat	**46.6**
Cholesterol (mg)	40
Carbohydrate (g)	1.2
Dietary Fiber (g)	0
Protein (g)	1.3
Sodium (mg)	14
Potassium (mg)	40
Calcium (mg)	**33**
Iron (mg)	0.1
Zinc (mg)	0.2

Sinless Sour Cream

	Per Serving Nutritional Analysis
Calories	**11**
Total Fat (g)	0.1
% Calories from Fat	**12.3**
Cholesterol (mg)	1
Carbohydrate (g)	0.6
Dietary Fiber (g)	0
Protein (g)	1.8
Sodium (mg)	58
Potassium (mg)	16
Calcium (mg)	**11**
Iron (mg)	0
Zinc (mg)	0.1

Tartar Sauce

Per Serving Nutritional Analysis

Calories	**11**
Total Fat (g)	0.1
% Calories from Fat	**12.6**
Cholesterol (mg)	1
Carbohydrate (g)	0.5
Dietary Fiber (g)	0
Protein (g)	1.8
Sodium (mg)	61
Potassium (mg)	13
Calcium (mg)	**9**
Iron (mg)	0
Zinc (mg)	0.1

Mock Mayo

Per Serving Nutritional Analysis

Calories	**13**
Total Fat (g)	0.3
% Calories from Fat	**19.5**
Cholesterol (mg)	1
Carbohydrate (g)	0.7
Dietary Fiber (g)	0
Protein (g)	2
Sodium (mg)	61
Potassium (mg)	16
Calcium (mg)	**10**
Iron (mg)	0
Zinc (mg)	0.1

Fake Cream Cheese

Per Serving Nutritional Analysis

Calories	**61**
Total Fat (g)	5.8
% Calories from Fat	**85.3**
Cholesterol (mg)	1
Carbohydrate (g)	0.4
Dietary Fiber (g)	0
Protein (g)	1.8
Sodium (mg)	124
Potassium (mg)	15
Calcium (mg)	**11**
Iron (mg)	0
Zinc (mg)	0.1

Creamy Cauliflower

Per Serving Nutritional Analysis

Calories	**63**
Total Fat (g)	3.4
% Calories from Fat	**46.3**
Cholesterol (mg)	2
Carbohydrate (g)	6
Dietary Fiber (g)	1.3
Protein (g)	2.9
Sodium (mg)	97
Potassium (mg)	213
Calcium (mg)	**70**
Iron (mg)	0.4
Zinc (mg)	0.3

Creamed Peas

Per Serving Nutritional Analysis

Calories	**98**
Total Fat (g)	0.6
% Calories from Fat	**5**
Cholesterol (mg)	1
Carbohydrate (g)	16.2
Dietary Fiber (g)	2.8
Protein (g)	7.4
Sodium (mg)	123
Potassium (mg)	353
Calcium (mg)	**156**
Iron (mg)	1.8
Zinc (mg)	1.3

Texas Potato Topper

Per Serving Nutritional Analysis

Calories	**22**
Total Fat (g)	0.9
% Calories from Fat	**35.5**
Cholesterol (mg)	0
Carbohydrate (g)	2.2
Dietary Fiber (g)	0
Protein (g)	1.4
Sodium (mg)	66
Potassium (mg)	64
Calcium (mg)	**50**
Iron (mg)	0.2
Zinc (mg)	0.2

Two-Cheese Spaghetti Squash

Per Serving Nutritional Analysis

Calories	**87**
Total Fat (g)	4.0
% Calories from Fat	**40.5**
Cholesterol (mg)	11
Carbohydrate (g)	8.1
Dietary Fiber (g)	0.1
Protein (g)	5.2
Sodium (mg)	200
Potassium (mg)	168
Calcium (mg)	**185**
Iron (mg)	1.6
Zinc (mg)	0.6

Lean Creamed Spinach

Per Serving Nutritional Analysis

Calories	**44**
Total Fat (g)	0.6
% Calories from Fat	**11.2**
Cholesterol (mg)	1
Carbohydrate (g)	6.6
Dietary Fiber (g)	2.9
Protein (g)	4.4
Sodium (mg)	103
Potassium (mg)	363
Calcium (mg)	**156**
Iron (mg)	2.0
Zinc (mg)	0.6

Baked Leeks With Cheese

Per Serving Nutritional Analysis

Calories	**168**
Total Fat (g)	6.8
% Calories from Fat	**38.3**
Cholesterol (mg)	22
Carbohydrate (g)	17.8
Dietary Fiber (g)	2.2
Protein (g)	6.8
Sodium (mg)	286
Potassium (mg)	260
Calcium (mg)	**226**
Iron (mg)	2.7
Zinc (mg)	0.8

Summer Vegetable Casserole

Per Serving Nutritional Analysis

Calories	**200**
Total Fat (g)	11.9
% Calories from Fat	**51.1**
Cholesterol (mg)	19
Carbohydrate (g)	17.7
Dietary Fiber (g)	5.7
Protein (g)	8
Sodium (mg)	250
Potassium (mg)	438
Calcium (mg)	**166**
Iron (mg)	2.4
Zinc (mg)	1.6

Savory Mashed Potatoes

Per Serving Nutritional Analysis

Calories	**107**
Total Fat (g)	2.4
% Calories from Fat	**20**
Cholesterol (mg)	1
Carbohydrate (g)	17.6
Dietary Fiber (g)	1.3
Protein (g)	4.2
Sodium (mg)	44
Potassium (mg)	536
Calcium (mg)	**102**
Iron (mg)	0.7
Zinc (mg)	0.8

Tomato-Zucchini Yogurt Surprise

Per Serving Nutritional Analysis

Calories	**34**
Total Fat (g)	0.3
% Calories from Fat	**7.2**
Cholesterol (mg)	1
Carbohydrate (g)	5.8
Dietary Fiber (g)	1.4
Protein (g)	2.4
Sodium (mg)	156
Potassium (mg)	318
Calcium (mg)	**74**
Iron (mg)	1.3
Zinc (mg)	0.4

Cheese-Filled Potato Shells

	Per Serving Nutritional Analysis
Calories	**75**
Total Fat (g)	0.4
% Calories from Fat	**4.9**
Cholesterol (mg)	2
Carbohydrate (g)	12.6
Dietary Fiber (g)	1.2
Protein (g)	5.4
Sodium (mg)	197
Potassium (mg)	392
Calcium (mg)	**55**
Iron (mg)	1.0
Zinc (mg)	0.5

Eggplant Parmesan

	Per Serving Nutritional Analysis
Calories	**271**
Total Fat (g)	17.3
% Calories from Fat	**56.4**
Cholesterol (mg)	56
Carbohydrate (g)	16.2
Dietary Fiber (g)	3.1
Protein (g)	13.9
Sodium (mg)	283
Potassium (mg)	403
Calcium (mg)	**299**
Iron (mg)	1.2
Zinc (mg)	1.6

Spinach Cheese Casserole

Per Serving Nutritional Analysis

Calories	**95**
Total Fat (g)	2.4
% Calories from Fat	**22**
Cholesterol (mg)	7
Carbohydrate (g)	6.3
Dietary Fiber (g)	1.6
Protein (g)	12.6
Sodium (mg)	504
Potassium (mg)	278
Calcium (mg)	**154**
Iron (mg)	1.0
Zinc (mg)	0.7

Carrots and Raisins Revisited

Per Serving Nutritional Analysis

Calories	**129**
Total Fat (g)	2.7
% Calories from Fat	**17.7**
Cholesterol (mg)	1
Carbohydrate (g)	21.7
Dietary Fiber (g)	3.2
Protein (g)	6.3
Sodium (mg)	88
Potassium (mg)	545
Calcium (mg)	**189**
Iron (mg)	0.8
Zinc (mg)	1.0

Cheese & Tomato Rice

	Per Serving Nutritional Analysis
Calories	**152**
Total Fat (g)	1.2
% Calories from Fat	**7.6**
Cholesterol (mg)	2
Carbohydrate (g)	27.6
Dietary Fiber (g)	0.5
Protein (g)	4.8
Sodium (mg)	204
Potassium (mg)	90
Calcium (mg)	**77**
Iron (mg)	1.7
Zinc (mg)	0.7

Baked Macaroni & Cheese

	Per Serving Nutritional Analysis
Calories	**241**
Total Fat (g)	4.5
% Calories from Fat	**19.7**
Cholesterol (mg)	7
Carbohydrate (g)	22.6
Dietary Fiber (g)	0.7
Protein (g)	19.2
Sodium (mg)	316
Potassium (mg)	352
Calcium (mg)	**288**
Iron (mg)	2.6
Zinc (mg)	2.2

Scalloped Potatoes In A Hurry

	Per Serving Nutritional Analysis
Calories	**107**
Total Fat (g)	2.1
% Calories from Fat	**18.2**
Cholesterol (mg)	6
Carbohydrate (g)	15.4
Dietary Fiber (g)	1.1
Protein (g)	5.4
Sodium (mg)	315
Potassium (mg)	446
Calcium (mg)	**139**
Iron (mg)	0.7
Zinc (mg)	0.7

Veggie Pizza

	Per Serving Nutritional Analysis
Calories	**364**
Total Fat (g)	6.1
% Calories from Fat	**14.1**
Cholesterol (mg)	8
Carbohydrate (g)	66.1
Dietary Fiber (g)	11.8
Protein (g)	17
Sodium (mg)	341
Potassium (mg)	612
Calcium (mg)	**167**
Iron (mg)	4.0
Zinc (mg)	3.2

Meatless Lasagne

	Per Serving Nutritional Analysis
Calories	**209**
Total Fat (g)	8.9
% Calories from Fat	**37.5**
Cholesterol (mg)	18
Carbohydrate (g)	21.8
Dietary Fiber (g)	3.7
Protein (g)	11.8
Sodium (mg)	364
Potassium (mg)	545
Calcium (mg)	**230**
Iron (mg)	1.7
Zinc (mg)	1.6

Spinach Pierogi Pizza

	Per Serving Nutritional Analysis
Calories	**195**
Total Fat (g)	9.9
% Calories from Fat	**47.6**
Cholesterol (mg)	9
Carbohydrate (g)	15.6
Dietary Fiber (g)	1.6
Protein (g)	9.0
Sodium (mg)	389
Potassium (mg)	234
Calcium (mg)	**204**
Iron (mg)	0.9
Zinc (mg)	0.9

Beef & Bean Chili

Per Serving Nutritional Analysis

Calories	**358**
Total Fat (g)	13.2
% Calories from Fat	**31.9**
Cholesterol (mg)	43
Carbohydrate (g)	41.2
Dietary Fiber (g)	9.8
Protein (g)	22.4
Sodium (mg)	393
Potassium (mg)	1532
Calcium (mg)	**83**
Iron (mg)	6.8
Zinc (mg)	4.1

Broccoli Cauliflower Tetrazzini

Per Serving Nutritional Analysis

Calories	**314**
Total Fat (g)	8.3
% Calories from Fat	**23.4**
Cholesterol (mg)	10
Carbohydrate (g)	46.6
Dietary Fiber (g)	5.2
Protein (g)	14.4
Sodium (mg)	280
Potassium (mg)	442
Calcium (mg)	**243**
Iron (mg)	2.7
Zinc (mg)	1.6

Light Chicken Cordon Bleu

Per Serving Nutritional Analysis

Calories	**235**
Total Fat (g)	4.9
% Calories from Fat	**19.7**
Cholesterol (mg)	81
Carbohydrate (g)	8.0
Dietary Fiber (g)	0.5
Protein (g)	37.3
Sodium (mg)	506
Potassium (mg)	397
Calcium (mg)	**308**
Iron (mg)	2.1
Zinc (mg)	2.8

Curried Chicken

Per Serving Nutritional Analysis

Calories	**945**
Total Fat (g)	31.7
% Calories from Fat	**31.2**
Cholesterol (mg)	32.2
Carbohydrate (g)	43.7
Dietary Fiber (g)	1.1
Protein (g)	113.5
Sodium (mg)	399
Potassium (mg)	1223
Calcium (mg)	**300**
Iron (mg)	5.2
Zinc (mg)	9.2

Baked Chicken With Yogurt

	Per Serving Nutritional Analysis
Calories	**411**
Total Fat (g)	4.0
% Calories from Fat	**9.8**
Cholesterol (mg)	166
Carbohydrate (g)	12.6
Dietary Fiber (g)	0.1
Protein (g)	69.7
Sodium (mg)	452
Potassium (mg)	953
Calcium (mg)	**150**
Iron (mg)	2.8
Zinc (mg)	3.0

One-Step Oven Fish

	Per Serving Nutritional Analysis
Calories	**223**
Total Fat (g)	1.7
% Calories from Fat	**7.2**
Cholesterol (mg)	99
Carbohydrate (g)	5.3
Dietary Fiber (g)	0.2
Protein (g)	44.1
Sodium (mg)	174
Potassium (mg)	1154
Calcium (mg)	**177**
Iron (mg)	2.7
Zinc (mg)	1.7

Lite Macaroni & Cheese

	Per Serving Nutritional Analysis
Calories	**260**
Total Fat (g)	3.3
% Calories from Fat	**13.5**
Cholesterol (mg)	9
Carbohydrate (g)	31.6
Dietary Fiber (g)	0.9
Protein (g)	15.8
Sodium (mg)	261
Potassium (mg)	182
Calcium (mg)	**341**
Iron (mg)	1.8
Zinc (mg)	1.8

Lite Tuna Casserole

	Per Serving Nutritional Analysis
Calories	**157**
Total Fat (g)	2.0
% Calories from Fat	**12.2**
Cholesterol (mg)	23
Carbohydrate (g)	11
Dietary Fiber (g)	2.3
Protein (g)	22.1
Sodium (mg)	513
Potassium (mg)	340
Calcium (mg)	**99**
Iron (mg)	1.9
Zinc (mg)	1.4

Italian Tuna Casserole

	Per Serving Nutritional Analysis
Calories	**349**
Total Fat (g)	4
% Calories from Fat	**10.4**
Cholesterol (mg)	18
Carbohydrate (g)	42.2
Dietary Fiber (g)	3.3
Protein (g)	34.7
Sodium (mg)	992
Potassium (mg)	744
Calcium (mg)	**114**
Iron (mg)	4.6
Zinc (mg)	2.4

Sole Florentine

	Per Serving Nutritional Analysis
Calories	**135**
Total Fat (g)	1.3
% Calories from Fat	**8.7**
Cholesterol (mg)	2
Carbohydrate (g)	8.8
Dietary Fiber (g)	2.1
Protein (g)	22
Sodium (mg)	171
Potassium (mg)	751
Calcium (mg)	**241**
Iron (mg)	2.6
Zinc (mg)	0.6

Baked Salmon Loaf

Per Serving Nutritional Analysis

Calories	**146**
Total Fat (g)	3.9
% Calories from Fat	**24.2**
Cholesterol (mg)	30
Carbohydrate (g)	13.4
Dietary Fiber (g)	1.1
Protein (g)	13.9
Sodium (mg)	447
Potassium (mg)	265
Calcium (mg)	**147**
Iron (mg)	0.9
Zinc (mg)	0.9

Salmon Burgers To Go

Per Serving Nutritional Analysis

Calories	**335**
Total Fat (g)	12.1
% Calories from Fat	**36.6**
Cholesterol (mg)	64
Carbohydrate (g)	14.1
Dietary Fiber (g)	1.1
Protein (g)	39.8
Sodium (mg)	1094
Potassium (mg)	845
Calcium (mg)	**357**
Iron (mg)	5.7
Zinc (mg)	4.2

Curried Shrimp

Per Serving Nutritional Analysis

Calories	**256**
Total Fat (g)	2.8
% Calories from Fat	**10.1**
Cholesterol (mg)	334
Carbohydrate (g)	14.9
Dietary Fiber (g)	1.5
Protein (g)	41.6
Sodium (mg)	810
Potassium (mg)	684
Calcium (mg)	**278**
Iron (mg)	6.5
Zinc (mg)	3.4

Mini Salmon Pot Pie

Per Serving Nutritional Analysis

Calories	**214**
Total Fat (g)	11.5
% Calories from Fat	**48.6**
Cholesterol (mg)	24
Carbohydrate (g)	16.5
Dietary Fiber (g)	0.3
Protein (g)	10.8
Sodium (mg)	587
Potassium (mg)	247
Calcium (mg)	**150**
Iron (mg)	2.2
Zinc (mg)	0.6

Italian Manicotti With Spinach

Per Serving Nutritional Analysis

Calories	**250**
Total Fat (g)	6.6
% Calories from Fat	**23.8**
Cholesterol (mg)	15
Carbohydrate (g)	24.2
Dietary Fiber (g)	2.9
Protein (g)	23.6
Sodium (mg)	743
Potassium (mg)	643
Calcium (mg)	**300**
Iron (mg)	3.7
Zinc (mg)	2.2

Quick Broccoli Quiche

Per Serving Nutritional Analysis

Calories	**353**
Total Fat (g)	14.6
% Calories from Fat	**37.7**
Cholesterol (mg)	5
Carbohydrate (g)	20.9
Dietary Fiber (g)	1.8
Protein (g)	33.5
Sodium (mg)	911
Potassium (mg)	797
Calcium (mg)	**214**
Iron (mg)	4.6
Zinc (mg)	2.9

Pasta With White Clam Sauce

Per Serving Nutritional Analysis

Calories	**427**
Total Fat (g)	4.9
% Calories from Fat	**10.4**
Cholesterol (mg)	66
Carbohydrate (g)	58.5
Dietary Fiber (g)	3.9
Protein (g)	37.0
Sodium (mg)	543
Potassium (mg)	1335
Calcium (mg)	**420**
Iron (mg)	42.8
Zinc (mg)	4.3

Chicken Divine

Per Serving Nutritional Analysis

Calories	**405**
Total Fat (g)	4.7
% Calories from Fat	**10.8**
Cholesterol (mg)	166
Carbohydrate (g)	15.4
Dietary Fiber (g)	2.6
Protein (g)	71.9
Sodium (mg)	430
Potassium (mg)	1069
Calcium (mg)	**236**
Iron (mg)	3.1
Zinc (mg)	3.2

Chicken Mushroom Casserole

Per Serving Nutritional Analysis

Calories	**357**
Total Fat (g)	4.2
% Calories from Fat	**10.9**
Cholesterol (mg)	164
Carbohydrate (g)	7.9
Dietary Fiber (g)	1.2
Protein (g)	69.7
Sodium (mg)	428
Potassium (mg)	1058
Calcium (mg)	**105**
Iron (mg)	3.0
Zinc (mg)	3.1

Turkey Meatloaf

Per Serving Nutritional Analysis

Calories	**143**
Total Fat (g)	5.4
% Calories from Fat	**34.1**
Cholesterol (mg)	45
Carbohydrate (g)	10
Dietary Fiber (g)	1.7
Protein (g)	13.7
Sodium (mg)	260
Potassium (mg)	351
Calcium (mg)	**86**
Iron (mg)	3.8
Zinc (mg)	1.6

Skinny Fettuccine Alfredo

Per Serving Nutritional Analysis

Calories	**131**
Total Fat (g)	3.3
% Calories from Fat	**27.9**
Cholesterol (mg)	47
Carbohydrate (g)	12.8
Dietary Fiber (g)	0.3
Protein (g)	6.5
Sodium (mg)	486
Potassium (mg)	103
Calcium (mg)	**148**
Iron (mg)	0.7
Zinc (mg)	0.7

Creamy Chicken

Per Serving Nutritional Analysis

Calories	**365**
Total Fat (g)	5.2
% Calories from Fat	**13.4**
Cholesterol (mg)	164
Carbohydrate (g)	6.7
Dietary Fiber (g)	0.3
Protein (g)	68.5
Sodium (mg)	404
Potassium (mg)	955
Calcium (mg)	**176**
Iron (mg)	4.6
Zinc (mg)	2.9

Veal Parmigiana

Per Serving Nutritional Analysis

Calories	**377**
Total Fat (g)	12.9
% Calories from Fat	**31.3**
Cholesterol (mg)	104
Carbohydrate (g)	25.7
Dietary Fiber (g)	3.9
Protein (g)	38.1
Sodium (mg)	853
Potassium (mg)	974
Calcium (mg)	**206**
Iron (mg)	3.6
Zinc (mg)	5.6

Baked Chicken Surprise

Per Serving Nutritional Analysis

Calories	**385**
Total Fat (g)	6.2
% Calories from Fat	**15.2**
Cholesterol (mg)	174
Carbohydrate (g)	3.5
Dietary Fiber (g)	0
Protein (g)	74
Sodium (mg)	431
Potassium (mg)	794
Calcium (mg)	**334**
Iron (mg)	2.2
Zinc (mg)	3.5

Easy Chicken Nuggets

Per Serving Nutritional Analysis

Calories	**256**
Total Fat (g)	5.3
% Calories from Fat	**18.6**
Cholesterol (mg)	68
Carbohydrate (g)	23.5
Dietary Fiber (g)	30
Protein (g)	29.2
Sodium (mg)	450
Potassium (mg)	294
Calcium (mg)	**263**
Iron (mg)	18.9
Zinc (mg)	15.9

Salmon Supper Croquettes

Per Serving Nutritional Analysis

Calories	**171**
Total Fat (g)	5.2
% Calories from Fat	**28**
Cholesterol (mg)	20
Carbohydrate (g)	12.8
Dietary Fiber (g)	1.2
Protein (g)	17.1
Sodium (mg)	549
Potassium (mg)	414
Calcium (mg)	**161**
Iron (mg)	2.2
Zinc (mg)	1.4

Baked Sole With Parsley/Yogurt Sauce

	Per Serving Nutritional Analysis
Calories	**375**
Total Fat (g)	2.5
% Calories from Fat	**6.4**
Cholesterol (g)	2
Carbohydrate (g)	9.2
Dietary Fiber (g)	0.2
Protein (g)	74.4
Sodium (mg)	345
Potassium (mg)	1992
Calcium (mg)	**513**
Iron (mg)	4.2
Zinc (mg)	1.2

Nachos Casserole

	Per Serving Nutritional Analysis
Calories	**320**
Total Fat (g)	9.8
% Calories from Fat	**29.5**
Cholesterol (mg)	64
Carbohydrate (g)	28.9
Dietary Fiber (g)	3.4
Protein (g)	23.7
Sodium (mg)	655
Potassium (mg)	536
Calcium (mg)	**213**
Iron (mg)	3.4
Zinc (mg)	3.0

Pavlova

Per Serving Nutritional Analysis

Calories	**93**
Total Fat (g)	0.3
% Calories from Fat	**2.7**
Cholesterol (mg)	1
Carbohydrate (g)	18.8
Dietary Fiber (g)	1.6
Protein (g)	4.5
Sodium (mg)	63
Potassium (mg)	305
Calcium (mg)	**107**
Iron (mg)	0.3
Zinc (mg)	0.3

Peach Yogurt Pie

Per Serving Nutritional Analysis

Calories	**259**
Total Fat (g)	8.9
% Calories from Fat	**30.2**
Cholesterol (mg)	1
Carbohydrate (g)	41.5
Dietary Fiber (g)	1.2
Protein (g)	4.6
Sodium (mg)	209
Potassium (mg)	213
Calcium (mg)	**100**
Iron (mg)	1
Zinc (mg)	0.7

Thick Banana Shake

Per Serving Nutritional Analysis

Calories	**246**
Total Fat (g)	1.0
% Calories from Fat	**4.0**
Cholesterol (mg)	4
Carbohydrate (g)	44.2
Dietary Fiber (g)	2.7
Protein (g)	9.5
Sodium (mg)	127
Potassium (mg)	857
Calcium (mg)	**309**
Iron (mg)	0.4
Zinc (mg)	1.2

Mock Ice Cream Basic Recipe

Per Serving Nutritional Analysis

Calories	**54**
Total Fat (g)	0.3
% Calories from Fat	**4.3**
Cholesterol (mg)	0
Carbohydrate (g)	13.6
Dietary Fiber (g)	1.4
Protein (g)	0.8
Sodium (mg)	3
Potassium (mg)	234
Calcium (mg)	**10**
Iron (mg)	0.2
Zinc (mg)	0.1

Calcium-Rich Cheese Cake

	Per Serving Nutritional Analysis
Calories	**217**
Total Fat (g)	6.5
% Calories from Fat	**27.1**
Cholesterol (mg)	3
Carbohydrate (g)	30.5
Dietary Fiber (g)	0.1
Protein (g)	8.8
Sodium (mg)	399
Potassium (mg)	112
Calcium (mg)	**50**
Iron (mg)	0.7
Zinc (mg)	0.4

Rice Pudding

	Per Serving Nutritional Analysis
Calories	**92**
Total Fat (g)	0.2
% Calories from Fat	**1.8**
Cholesterol (mg)	1
Carbohydrate (g)	20
Dietary Fiber (g)	0.7
Protein (g)	2.7
Sodium (mg)	24
Potassium (mg)	126
Calcium (mg)	**55**
Iron (mg)	0.9
Zinc (mg)	0.4

Quick Coffee Cake

Per Serving Nutritional Analysis

Calories	**251**
Total Fat (g)	2.4
% Calories from Fat	**8.5**
Cholesterol (mg)	1
Carbohydrate (g)	45.7
Dietary Fiber (g)	0
Protein (g)	11.6
Sodium (mg)	303
Potassium (mg)	305
Calcium (mg)	**178**
Iron (mg)	2.6
Zinc (mg)	1.3

Basic Pudding

Per Serving Nutritional Analysis

Calories	**149**
Total Fat (g)	0.5
% Calories from Fat	**2.7**
Cholesterol (mg)	2
Carbohydrate (g)	32.6
Dietary Fiber (g)	0.9
Protein (g)	4.5
Sodium (mg)	257
Potassium (mg)	270
Calcium (mg)	**160**
Iron (mg)	0.2
Zinc (mg)	0.6

Yogurt Pudding

	Per Serving Nutritional Analysis
Calories	**110**
Total Fat (g)	0.1
% Calories from Fat	**0.7**
Cholesterol (mg)	1
Carbohydrate (g)	23.8
Dietary Fiber (g)	0.3
Protein (g)	4.2
Sodium (mg)	87
Potassium (mg)	131
Calcium (mg)	**88**
Iron (mg)	0.2
Zinc (mg)	0.4

Fruity Yogurt Cup

	Per Serving Nutritional Analysis
Calories	**187**
Total Fat (g)	1.2
% Calories from Fat	**5.4**
Cholesterol (mg)	4
Carbohydrate (g)	40.7
Dietary Fiber (g)	2.4
Protein (g)	5.5
Sodium (mg)	54
Potassium (mg)	330
Calcium (mg)	**138**
Iron (mg)	0.4
Zinc (mg)	0.7

Yogurt Fruit Pops

	Per Serving Nutritional Analysis
Calories	**103**
Total Fat (g)	0.3
% Calories from Fat	**2.7**
Cholesterol (mg)	1
Carbohydrate (g)	21.2
Dietary Fiber (g)	0.9
Protein (g)	4.9
Sodium (mg)	55
Potassium (mg)	453
Calcium (mg)	**151**
Iron (mg)	0.2
Zinc (mg)	0.8

Everyone's Favorite Apple Cobbler

	Per Serving Nutritional Analysis
Calories	**196**
Total Fat (g)	0.5
% Calories from Fat	**2.5**
Cholesterol (mg)	3
Carbohydrate (g)	41.9
Dietary Fiber (g)	1.6
Protein (g)	4.9
Sodium (mg)	309
Potassium (mg)	226
Calcium (mg)	**210**
Iron (mg)	1.5
Zinc (mg)	0.4

Frosty Fruit Yogurt Pie

Per Serving Nutritional Analysis

Calories	**176**
Total Fat (g)	8.3
% Calories from Fat	**41.9**
Cholesterol (mg)	1
Carbohydrate (g)	21.7
Dietary Fiber (g)	1.4
Protein (g)	4.2
Sodium (mg)	223
Potassium (mg)	146
Calcium (mg)	**96**
Iron (mg)	0.7
Zinc (mg)	0.6

No-Guilt Cheesecake

Per Serving Nutritional Analysis

Calories	**212**
Total Fat (g)	5.3
% Calories from Fat	**22.3**
Cholesterol (mg)	2
Carbohydrate (g)	33
Dietary Fiber (g)	0
Protein (g)	8.5
Sodium (mg)	262
Potassium (mg)	242
Calcium (mg)	**167**
Iron (mg)	0.6
Zinc (mg)	0.9

Apple Cinnamon Tart

Per Serving Nutritional Analysis

Calories	**155**
Total Fat (g)	1.1
% Calories from Fat	**5.9**
Cholesterol (mg)	1
Carbohydrate (g)	32.7
Dietary Fiber (g)	2.5
Protein (g)	5.1
Sodium (mg)	43
Potassium (mg)	293
Calcium (mg)	**112**
Iron (mg)	1.1
Zinc (mg)	0.9

Yogurt Cookies

Per Serving Nutritional Analysis

Calories	**53**
Total Fat (g)	1.8
% Calories from Fat	**30.6**
Cholesterol (mg)	1
Carbohydrate (g)	7.5
Dietary Fiber (g)	0
Protein (g)	1.4
Sodium (mg)	60
Potassium (mg)	35
Calcium (mg)	**10**
Iron (mg)	0.4
Zinc (mg)	0.1

A Touch Of France

Per Serving Nutritional Analysis

Calories **231**

Total Fat (g)	3.8
% Calories from Fat	**15**
Cholesterol (mg)	3
Carbohydrate (g)	33.7
Dietary Fiber (g)	1.3
Protein (g)	15.1
Sodium (mg)	230
Potassium (mg)	567
Calcium (mg)	**131**
Iron (mg)	2.6
Zinc (mg)	1.6

Fruit Trifle

Per Serving Nutritional Analysis

Calories **136**

Total Fat (g)	0.7
% Calories from Fat	**4.8**
Cholesterol (mg)	7
Carbohydrate (g)	30.5
Dietary Fiber (g)	1.5
Protein (g)	3.1
Sodium (mg)	139
Potassium (mg)	231
Calcium (mg)	**95**
Iron (mg)	0.3
Zinc (mg)	0.5

Я не

Strawberry Bavarian Dessert

Per Serving Nutritional Analysis

Calories	**250**
Total Fat (g)	0.8
% Calories from Fat	**2.6**
Cholesterol (mg)	3
Carbohydrate (g)	57.6
Dietary Fiber (g)	1.4
Protein (g)	6.0
Sodium (mg)	114
Potassium (mg)	214
Calcium (mg)	**89**
Iron (mg)	0.4
Zinc (mg)	0.4

Tiramisu

Per Serving Nutritional Analysis

Calories	**447**
Total Fat (g)	26.4
% Calories from Fat	**55.3**
Cholesterol (mg)	165
Carbohydrate (g)	41.7
Dietary Fiber (g)	0.2
Protein (g)	6.3
Sodium (mg)	113
Potassium (mg)	76
Calcium (mg)	**18**
Iron (mg)	0.9
Zinc (mg)	0.4

Basic Cream Pie

Per Serving Nutritional Analysis

Calories	**230**
Total Fat (g)	7.9
% Calories from Fat	**30.6**
Cholesterol (mg)	2
Carbohydrate (g)	36.8
Dietary Fiber (g)	0
Protein (g)	3.7
Sodium (mg)	390
Potassium (mg)	141
Calcium (mg)	**94**
Iron (mg)	0.7
Zinc (mg)	0.5

Basic Oatmeal Cookies

Per Serving Nutritional Analysis

Calories	**56**
Total Fat (g)	0.5
% Calories from Fat	**7.7**
Cholesterol (mg)	1
Carbohydrate (g)	10.6
Dietary Fiber (g)	0.3
Protein (g)	1.6
Sodium (mg)	93
Potassium (mg)	58
Calcium (mg)	**13**
Iron (mg)	0.5
Zinc (mg)	0.2

Chilly Cheese Cookies

Per Serving Nutritional Analysis

Calories	**38**
Total Fat (g)	0.5
% Calories from Fat	**11.6**
Cholesterol (mg)	1
Carbohydrate (g)	6.7
Dietary Fiber (g)	0
Protein (g)	1.1
Sodium (mg)	52
Potassium (mg)	22
Calcium (mg)	**8**
Iron (mg)	0.3
Zinc (mg)	0.1

Yogurt Cake

Per Serving Nutritional Analysis

Calories	**239**
Total Fat (g)	1.7
% Calories from Fat	**6.6**
Cholesterol (mg)	56
Carbohydrate (g)	47.8
Dietary Fiber (g)	0
Protein (g)	5.5
Sodium (mg)	320
Potassium (mg)	97
Calcium (mg)	**122**
Iron (mg)	1.6
Zinc (mg)	0.5

Southwestern Snack

	Per Serving Nutritional Analysis
Calories	**154**
Total Fat (g)	4.6
% Calories from Fat	**26.9**
Cholesterol (mg)	3
Carbohydrate (g)	24.1
Dietary Fiber (g)	1.2
Protein (g)	3.8
Sodium (mg)	452
Potassium (mg)	74
Calcium (mg)	**50**
Iron (mg)	2.4
Zinc (mg)	1.1

Fruit-Cereal Clusters

	Per Serving Nutritional Analysis
Calories	**88**
Total Fat (g)	4.7
% Calories from Fat	**45.5**
Cholesterol (mg)	2
Carbohydrate (g)	11
Dietary Fiber (g)	7
Protein (g)	1.6
Sodium (mg)	39
Potassium (mg)	85
Calcium (mg)	**40**
Iron (mg)	1.2
Zinc (mg)	1.1

Hawaiian Snack Mix

Per Serving Nutritional Analysis

Calories	**186**
Total Fat (g)	6
% Calories from Fat	**27.8**
Cholesterol (mg)	2
Carbohydrate (g)	33.2
Dietary Fiber (g)	3.4
Protein (g)	1.9
Sodium (mg)	158
Potassium (mg)	210
Calcium (mg)	**105**
Iron (mg)	7.2
Zinc (mg)	5.7

Calcium Cocktail I

Per Serving Nutritional Analysis

Calories	**99**
Total Fat (g)	1.1
% Calories from Fat	**8.4**
Cholesterol (mg)	0
Carbohydrate (g)	20.7
Dietary Fiber (g)	5.6
Protein (g)	5.6
Sodium (mg)	114
Potassium (mg)	1004
Calcium (mg)	**288**
Iron (mg)	15.6
Zinc (mg)	1.0

Calcium Cocktail II

Per Serving Nutritional Analysis

Calories	**287**
Total Fat (g)	1.6
% Calories from Fat	**4.5**
Cholesterol (mg)	0
Carbohydrate (g)	71.3
Dietary Fiber (g)	16.1
Protein (g)	3.5
Sodium (mg)	101
Potassium (mg)	1248
Calcium (mg)	**97**
Iron (mg)	1.9
Zinc (mg)	0.7

Calcium Cocktail III

Per Serving Nutritional Analysis

Calories	**271**
Total Fat (g)	1.4
% Calories from Fat	**4.1**
Cholesterol (mg)	0
Carbohydrate (g)	69.5
Dietary Fiber (g)	14.6
Protein (g)	2.1
Sodium (mg)	1
Potassium (mg)	622
Calcium (mg)	**78**
Iron (mg)	0.8
Zinc (mg)	0.3

Calcium Cocktail IV

Per Serving Nutritional Analysis

Calories	**246**
Total Fat (g)	2.1
% Calories from Fat	**6.8**
Cholesterol (mg)	0
Carbohydrate (g)	53.5
Dietary Fiber (g)	8.2
Protein (g)	12.7
Sodium (mg)	230
Potassium (mg)	2474
Calcium (mg)	**536**
Iron (mg)	18.9
Zinc (mg)	2.1

Romantic No-Fuss Cappuccino

Per Serving Nutritional Analysis

Calories	**68**
Total Fat (g)	0.3
% Calories from Fat	**4.5**
Cholesterol (mg)	3
Carbohydrate (g)	9.6
Dietary Fiber (g)	0
Protein (g)	6.5
Sodium (mg)	97
Potassium (mg)	368
Calcium (mg)	**230**
Iron (mg)	0.2
Zinc (mg)	0.8